INDIAN EDUCATION IN CANADA: THE LEGACY

NAKODA INSTITUTE OCCASIONAL PAPERS

INDIAN EDUCATION IN CANADA

Volume 1: The Legacy

Edited by
Jean Barman, Yvonne Hébert,
and Don McCaskill

Nakoda Institute Occasional Paper No. 2

UNIVERSITY OF BRITISH COLUMBIA PRESS
Vancouver
1986

INDIAN EDUCATION IN CANADA: VOLUME 1: THE LEGACY

© University of British Columbia Press 1986
All rights reserved
Reprinted 1989

This book has been published with the help of a grant from the Nakoda Institute.

Canadian Cataloguing in Publication Data
(Nakoda Institute occasional paper; no. 2)
Includes bibliographic index.
Contents: v. 1. The legacy
ISBN 0-7748-0243-X (v. 1)

1. Indians of North America - Canada - Education - History - Addresses, essays, lectures.
I. Barman, Jean, 1939- II. Hébert, Yvonne M., 1942- III. McCaskill, Don N. IV. Nakoda
Institute. V. Series.
E96.2.I53 1986   371.97'97071   C85-091572-4

International Standard Book Number 0-7748-0243-X

Printed in Canada

CONTENTS

FOREWORD

The Nakoda Institute Occasional Papers series is sponsored under the auspices of the Stoney Indian Tribe at Morley, Alberta.

The Nakoda Institute is a Learning Centre incorporated as a registered non-profit company which provides adult and advanced educational opportunities for the local and off-reserve communities. The Institute recognizes the importance of encouraging Indian people to achieve self-determination and to enhance their economic, social, and cultural development. Its philosophy represents an Indian way of life and thinking, and it provides a tangible educational facility for people to use in their learning and spiritual development. The Institute is open to all who share a sincere interest in the advancement of Indian culture and quality of life in Canada.

The Institute will, from time to time, publish materials which reflect its goals and aspirations.

Recognizing the cultural heritage and historical role of native people in Canada, the Institute is proud to undertake the publishing of this volume focusing upon Indian education in Canada. A central focus in these papers is a theme formally advanced in the 1972 position paper of the National Indian Brotherhood entitled "Indian Control of Indian Education." Another positive development in the 1970's was the establishment of the Cultural/ Educational Centres programme funded by the Department of Indian Affairs. There are now sixty-five centres across Canada serving the Indian communities by working on Native languages, developing curriculum materials, providing resource centres (libraries, archives and museums), and printing Native publications. Community-based cultural education centres such as the Stoney Cultural Education Program continue to be leaders in promoting true Indian control of Indian education for the First Indian Nations of Canada.

Further information regarding the Nakoda Learning Centre and its publications programme may be obtained from the Stoney Tribe, Box 120, Morley, Alberta, T0L 1N0.

Chief John Snow
Stoney Indian Tribe
Morley, Alberta

PREFACE

Indian education is undergoing rapid change in Canada. Control over education has become a principal concern of Indian communities and is increasingly seen as a critical vehicle for the advancement and empowerment of aboriginal peoples. Native Indian teacher programmes have been established in every region of Canada, as have Native studies programmes in many postsecondary institutions.

Indian Education in Canada is designed to facilitate discussion of these crucial developments among teachers and students, educational planners and the general public. Volume 1: *The Legacy* analyzes the history of Indian education in Canada, while Volume 2: *The Challenge* focuses on recent developments. The essays in the two volumes, written by both scholars and practitioners, are a combination of analyses, case studies and position statements. Each essay is self-contained and so can be read either by itself or in conjunction with the introductory overview which sets the contributions in each volume within the overall field of Indian education. Almost all of the essays are original, appearing in print for the first time; and as a group, they take an activist stance favouring Indian control of Indian education. The two volumes deal solely with Indian schooling of children in its broader context, and thus do not include Métis or Inuit education or pre-contact and adult education, all subjects that demand separate consideration.

Our greatest debt is to the individual authors for their co-operation and enthusiasm. The support of the Nakoda Institute has been critical for publication. University of Regina's Faculty of Education, its Educational Studies group, and the Policy, Planning and Research Branch of the Saskatchewan Department of Education funded a meeting by the three editors in October 1984. The manuscript was typed by Louise Pelletier at the University of Regina with technical skill and endless patience. University of British Columbia Press, and especially Brian Scrivener, gave constant encouragement. Our colleagues, students, friends and families have provided valuable insights together with unstinting support. To all these groups and individuals, we are very grateful.

Jean Barman, Yvonne Hébert and Don McCaskill
Vancouver, Calgary and Peterborough
September 1985

1

The Legacy of the Past: An Overview

Jean Barman, Yvonne Hébert and Don McCaskill

Throughout the world, aboriginal people are taking control of their own lives. After centuries of subjugation, they are reaffirming the validity of their cultures and redefining their identities within the context of contemporary society. Underlying this revitalization is a shift of power from external entities, including colonial administrations, to the aboriginal peoples themselves. Political self-determination is growing, economic priorities are being reordered, and territorial bases are being re-established.

Central to this process is control over education. The key to the future of any society lies in the transmission of its culture and worldview to succeeding generations. The socialization of children, through education, shapes all aspects of identity, instilling knowledge of the group's language, history, traditions, behaviour, and spiritual beliefs. It is for this reason that aboriginal peoples have placed such a high priority on regaining control over the education of their children.

Canada's Indians have made control over education a central component of a more general campaign for political self-determination and cultural revitalization. The actual process is in its early stages, most of the changes having occurred only within the past decade. Given this relatively short time span, the accomplishments are considerable. Many Indian communities now operate their own schools. Most of Canada's 577 Indian bands administer all or part of the educational activity of the Department of Indian Affairs. Two Indian-controlled provincial school districts exist, one in Quebec, the other in British Columbia. Most provinces and several major cities have Indian education programmes. At the same time, control is less than complete, subject to priorities, guidelines, and funding set by external agencies.[1]

Why should this be the case? Why is it only now in the late twentieth century that Canada's aboriginal peoples are beginning to regain control over the education of their children? What is there about the legacy of the past which makes it so challenging to overcome?

THE BEGINNINGS OF CULTURAL INTERACTION

To understand why Canada's aboriginal peoples have only very recently regained some measure of control over their children's education, it is necessary to comprehend the historical relationship which has existed over the past four centuries between the Indians and their European colonizers. The legacy of the past is formidable and pervasive, as the seven essays in this volume make abundantly clear. Cultural interaction has been characterized by co-operation and conflict but, more importantly, by misconceptions and contradictions. For the most part, the aboriginal population accepted the new arrivals at face value, while Europeans assumed the superiority of their culture over that of any aboriginal peoples. Out of that misconception grew the European conviction that in order for the Indians to survive, they would have to be assimilated into the European social order. Aboriginal cultures were dismissed as irrelevant, while in reality they were vital and coherent, so much so that they have survived centuries of European domination.

The first chapter in this volume, by Marie Battiste, evokes the traditional environment of one Indian culture, the Micmac of eastern Canada. Focusing on the Micmac system of literacy prior to European contact, Battiste demonstrates the existence of a coherent, sophisticated system of written symbolic communication. Its consequence was a shared cognitive experience creating a common ideal of how the world worked and what constituted proper action. Thus all aspects of tribal life were bound together.

Traditional Indian cultures acquired much of their strength from a close reciprocal relationship with the physical environment. The geographical area known as Canada contained over fifty Indian nations divided into tribes and bands with institutions, customs, and languages of considerable distinctiveness. For instance, the society of the Six Nations living in the fertile area around Lake Ontario and along the St. Lawrence River was characterized by agriculture, permanent villages, a well-established system of laws and individual legal rights, formal religion, and rich traditions expressed in music, dances, and festivals. Three levels of government existed: the village, the nation, and the League of Six Nations Confederacy, consisting of fifty chiefs proportionately representing each nation and meeting several times a year in council. In contrast, the Indians of the Great Plains were nomadic, a lifestyle necessitated by their reliance on the buffalo for most everyday needs. The different tribes followed the wanderings of buffalo herds, dispersing into small bands during the winter when the buffalo were scattered and reuniting each spring to discuss the affairs of the nation and celebrate such ceremonies as the sun dance. Along the Pacific northwest coast, an area with abundant food supplies, tribes and bands lived in permanent populous villages and possessed intricate social organization, well-defined mechanisms for the accumulation and distribution of wealth, highly developed art forms and elaborate religious traditions.[2]

Whatever their ecological base and specific lifestyle, Canada's aboriginal peoples shared certain cultural attributes, including a belief in the unity of all aspects of life and consequent lack of distinction between the "secular" and the "sacred." The responsibilities of family life were valued highly, particularly the obligation to educate children in a holistic fashion. As Jacqueline Gresko documents in her chapter about the Plains Cree and the Coast Salish, the process of education encompassed all aspects of the child's life. Children were raised to assume adult roles in an atmosphere of warmth and affection. Learning emphasized such values as respect for all living things, sharing, self-reliance, individual responsibility, and proper conduct. Children also had to learn how to utilize the environment most effectively for economic survival. Integral to all aspects of the education of the young was the spiritual, and events in the lifecycle from birth to death were marked with ceremonies stressing the individual's link to the spiritual and the sacred. Cultural continuity was thus ensured.

The arrival of Europeans in Canada in the early sixteenth century almost immediately impinged upon the aboriginal population. Battiste and Cornelius Jaenen analyse early cultural interactions. The newcomers' ethnocentricity predetermined an attitude of superiority, reflected in such assumptions as the Micmacs being incapable of writing and aboriginal children benefitting from European-style schooling.

Four principal groups among the newcomers interacted with the Indians. The fur traders who early spread out across the continent relied upon the aboriginal population not only for pelts but, in many instances, also for their physical and emotional survival in an unfamiliar environment. Interaction was characterized by economic interdependence and in some cases also by mutual respect. Both societies were modified through contact, many traders acquiring Indian spouses and families, the Indians a new basis of wealth.[3]

Throughout North America, permanent European settlement soon followed on the fur trade. The reciprocal basis which marked interaction between fur traders and Indians was almost nonexistent with the settlers, who perceived the aboriginal population either as a threat or as a nuisance which persisted in claiming the best lands without utilizing them efficiently from a European perspective. The settlers' principal object was to remove the Indians onto reserves of less desirable land.[4]

The third principal agent of interaction was the Christian missionaries, who were an integral component of the growing European dominance. While concerned with the spiritual well-being of the White population, most missionaries soon perceived Indian conversion as equally important. The missionary impulse dated back as far as Christianity itself, emanating from the belief in one God come to save all mankind. The effort to convert Canada's aboriginal population was not unique but rather one small part of a wordwide effort with extraordinary similarity between locales.[5]

Settlers and missionaries looked to the fourth major agent of interaction, the state, to implement their desired relationship with the aboriginal population. For a time, colonial and Indian interests coincided. Into the nineteenth century, British interaction was nation-to-nation to the benefit of both cultures: the British acquired valuable military allies as well as needed land through treaty negotiations, and the Indians obtained the finance from annual payments for land to undertake agricultural and resource development. The Indians themselves determined the pace and direction of cultural change, and, according to the historian John Milloy, most tribal governments sought to use the benefits of civilization selectively in order to revitalize their culture.[6]

Gradually, however, the state moved closer to the basis of interaction sought by missionaries and settlers. Across the Western world, the missionary imperative to convert aboriginal peoples was increasingly interpreted as the necessity to "civilize" them. The goal became their assimilation as individuals into the dominant culture, which was premised on European values and patterns of behaviour. As early as the seventeenth century, as Jaenen demonstrates, efforts were being made to "francize" selected aboriginal youths, that is, to educate them and incorporate them into European New World society at its lowest rungs. Over time these ideas with which the French had experimented took firmer hold. The shift and its implications are well illustrated by Battiste in the case of the Micmac.

Part of the reason for this change in attitude lay, as J. Donald Wilson points out in this volume, in the Indians' diminishing utility as Indians. As the nineteenth century progressed, Indians were becoming less valued for their original cultural attributes, whether as partners in the fur trade or as military allies. Settlement assumed priority. This new paternalistic, one-sided relationship received its legal justification in the British North America Act, which in Section 91 took away Indians' independent status by making them wards of the federal government. As consolidated in the Indian Acts of 1876 and 1880, Indian self-government was abolished, and finance and all social services, including education, were placed under federal control. Lands reserved for Indians' use were to be managed on their behalf until such time as individual Indians enfranchized themselves or became sufficiently "civilized" to be allowed a measure of self-government.[7]

EDUCATION FOR ASSIMILATION

For the dominant society in Canada, the need for paternalism toward the aboriginal population was confirmed in the years immediately following Confederation. The new Dominion rapidly expanded, first through the acquisition of Rupert's Land and the North West Territories and then through the entry into Confederation of Manitoba and British Columbia. As a consequence, the Indian population residing within the boundaries of Canada increased in just four years from about 23,000 to over 100,000, or from 0.7 to 2.5 per cent of the population.[8] Government treatment of Indians living west of Ontario was characterized by imposition, treaty negotiations rapidly forcing the surrender of Indian lands for future White settlement. The disappearance of the buffalo as a principal source of livelihood in the late 1870's made inevitable the exchange of a nomadic culture based on hunting for a settled agricultural existence considered more acceptable by Europeans.[9] In this volume, Gresko describes the transition among the Plains Cree. As non-Indian settlement became a reality following the completion of the transcontinental railroad, so demands grew that the aboriginal population be assimilated, with education being perceived as "the primary vehicle in the civilization and advancement of the Indian race."[10]

The schooling of Indian children according to the precepts and practices of the dominant society was not a new phenomenon in Canada going back to the largely unsuccessful efforts of Catholic religious orders who accompanied the first French settlers to North America. Early Protestant missionaries focused, as Wilson details in the case of Ontario, on the provision of day schools similar in form and curriculum to those available to the poor of Britain. In other cases, up to about 1850, young Indians attended the local White schools. While some Indians looked upon formal education with suspicion, other families felt there were practical advantages to be acquired through their offsprings' acquaintance with the dominant society, particularly where schooling could be acquired alongside a traditional education.[11] As Penny Petrone makes clear in her historical collection of Indian writings, not only did various individuals and bands request the establishment of schools, but many young Indians became educated in the schools of the dominant society without losing contact with their own culture.[12]

The Indian education policy initiated by the federal government after Confederation was fundamentally different from earlier efforts. Part of the reason went beyond resolution of the "Indian problem," to use the common terminology of the federal Department of Indian Affairs, created in 1880 to implement policy.[13] Treaty agreements had frequently included clauses promising schools as soon as bands settled permanently on their reserved land, a transition which was now occurring. As well, up to the mid-nineteenth century, formal schooling even for White children had been largely voluntary; thereafter, provincial governments took an increasing role in the provision of facilities to ensure that all children, whatever their socioeconomic status, received a basic education.[14] That Indian children should do likewise was not publicly questioned. The most effective means by which to educate them became the issue.

In 1879, the federal government commissioned a report evaluating the American policy favouring separate Indian residential schools. The Americans believed that Indian children were best prepared for assimilation into the dominant society if they were removed from the influences of home, family, and community. Up to this time, as Wilson shows, only a handful of relatively unsuccessful experiments in boarding education had been attempted. The Davin Report approved American practice with the proviso that schools be operated so far as possible by missionaries, who had already demonstrated their commitment to "civilizing" Canada's Indians.[15] The Department of Indian Affairs accepted the proposal, offering some financing to upgrade and maintain existing schools while also encouraging the various denominations to construct new institutions. Preference was given to the creation of large industrial residential schools located away from reserves and, a few years later, to boarding schools nearer reserves for younger children. There, attendance would be ensured, and all aspects of life, from dress to use of English language to behaviour, would be carefully regulated. Curriculum was to be limited to basic education combined with half-day practical training in agriculture, the crafts, or household duties in order to prepare pupils for their expected future existence on the lower fringes of the dominant society. Although day schools were considered to be less satisfactory agents of cultural assimilation, as Ken Coates mentions in his chapter, they also continued to exist and to be created, especially in long-settled areas of Canada.

The implementation of this new policy is analysed from several perspectives in this volume.[16] Wilson describes two Anglican institutions, the Shingwauk Industrial School for boys and the Wawanosh Home for girls in the Lake Superior region of Ontario. Gresko contrasts the origins of two Catholic residential schools, Qu'Appelle in Saskatchewan and St. Mary's in British Columbia, while Jean Barman details the formation of Anglican All Hallows, a British Columbia boarding school unique for its admission of both Indian and White girls. Taken together, these case studies suggest that, despite increasingly onerous federal regulations demanding uniformity among schools, early institutions possessed distinctive characteristics deriving from the personalities and commitment of their leaders. In some schools, so Gresko and Barman argue, a certain degree of sensitivity and even understanding was displayed toward the cultures from which pupils came.

INDIANS IN SCHOOL

While both the number of schools and total enrolment grew over the last two decades of the nineteenth century, it soon became evident that young Indians were not so willingly dispossessed of their cultures as the dominant society had expected. By 1900, out of a total Indian population of about 20,000 aged between six and fifteen, 3,285 Indian children were enrolled in 22 industrial and 39 boarding schools and another 6,349 in 226 day schools.[17] However, young Indians who became "civilized" were not necessarily abandoning their culture. Many had been sent, as was one residential pupil of 1880's, specifically in order to learn "the whiteman's magic art of writing, 'the talking paper,' as we called it then." The schooling received was often somewhat primitive. To quote a day pupil of the 1890's: "I do not remember any book learning acquired there. A bell was rung each morning to announce that school was opened. We all usually showed up with painted faces, breech cloths, and a blanket. To insure his attendance the next day, each child was given a biscuit of hardtack before leaving."[18]

Having acquired basic literacy and some familiarity with the dominant society, many young Indians returned home to become knowledgeable about their own culture. According to one former pupil, Indians were using "the best that the white man had to teach" and "endeavouring to work out their own plans and their own self-determination." And "given the right kind of encouragement at that time, the majority of my people would today [1958] be taking an active and useful part in our national life."[19] Such a course of events was not viewed favourably by the dominant society. One leading official of the Department of Indian Affairs claimed that the "most promising pupils are found to have retrograded and to have become leaders in the pagan life of their reserves."[20] In other words, despite extended separation from family and community, educated Indians continued to take pride in their past. Others attempted to move between the two cultures and enter the paid labour market, in some cases apparently doing so rather too well to suit the dominant society. In the words of a future federal minister for Indian Affairs in 1897, "we are educating these Indians to compete industrially with our own peoples, which seems to me a very undesirable use of public money."[21]

POLICY REASSESSMENT

From the turn of the century, a number of factors coalesced to alter the dominant society's attitude toward Canada's aboriginal population. Large-scale immigration was expanding the labour force, reducing the need to rely on Indian workers. For example, a British Columbia Indian agent reported in 1911 that employers were no longer forced to hire former pupils: "when applying for work outside of the reserve he is often refused because white men are as a rule unwilling to work alongside of Indians."[22] Indians were becoming irrelevant. Their proportion of the total population dropped to just 1.5 per cent by 1911, and most were safely tucked away on reserves, no longer a threat to White settlement.[23]

The Indian education policy put in place during the 1880's came increasingly to be perceived as too generous, as well as misdirected in its emphasis on immediate assimilation. As Gresko, Barman, and Coates emphasize in their chapters, frugality had always been the rule in schools' expenditures on food, accommodation, clothing, and equipment. Indeed, part of the reason for the original reliance on missionaries to operate schools related to the savings that thereby ensued to the public purse. Schools were allotted a per-pupil grant which assumed that labour would be voluntary or supported out of church funds. Now, federal officials began to begrudge the costs of maintaining existing institutions and were even less inclined to pay to expand the residential system to encompass all Indian youth. Originally, the attitude had been that while residential education was expensive, it must be regarded, "when viewed with relationship to the future interest of the country, as an excellent investment." By the turn of the century that attitude had changed, and "only the certainty of some practical results can justify the large expense entailed upon the country by the maintenance of these schools."[24]

Authorities found much to criticize. The health of children kept for years on end in plain or even primitive boarding conditions was inevitably put at risk. One estimate considered "that fifty per cent of the children who passed through these schools did not live to benefit from the education which they had received therein."[25] Those who survived were a disappointment, either "retrograding" or persisting in "competing economically." Wilson documents the growing discouragement of one headmaster and his consequent change in policy from pupils' "amalgamation" into White society to their "autonomy" separate from it. As the annual reports of the Department of Indian Affairs summed up, perhaps too much was being done for the

Indians: "It has to be carefully considered how far the country can be properly burdened with the cost of giving them superior advantages."[26]

The revised education policy announced in 1910 had as its goal "to fit the Indian for civilized life in his own environment." "To this end, the curriculum in residential schools has been simplified, and the practical instruction given is such as may be immediately of use to the pupil when he returns to the reserve after leaving school."[27] As Barman demonstrates, even the limited educational opportunities previously available were cut back. While raising the per-pupil subsidy in existing schools, enrolment was effectively curtailed through new health regulations requiring more space per child and physical improvements whose cost had to be borne principally by the religious group operating a school. Emphasis in the provision of new facilities was to be on fairly simple day schools offering a little education to more children at far less cost to the federal government.

The revised policy, which held until mid-century, ensured that the formal education of Indian children would remain minimal, even as that being accorded the White children was becoming more extensive. The anthropologist Diamond Jenness has described the situation based on considerable personal observation during the 1920's:

> In many parts of Canada the Indians had no schools at all; in others only elementary mission schools in which the standard of teaching was exceedingly low. A few mission boarding-schools, subsidized by the government, accepted Indian children when they were very young, raised them to the age of sixteen, then sent them back to their people, well indoctrinated in the Christian faith, but totally unfitted for life in an Indian community and, of course, not acceptable in any white one.

Jenness was concerned that the missionaries should not be blamed, since "they lacked the resources and the staffs to provide a proper education....It was not the missions that shirked their responsibility, but the federal government, and behind that government the people of Canada."[28] Not surprisingly, the proportion of Indian day-school pupils enrolled in grade 1 remained at half or more of all those in school, and the proportion of residential-school pupils in grade 1 at a third or more. In 1930, as indicated by Figure 1, three-quarters of Indian pupils across Canada were in grades 1 to 3, receiving only a very basic literacy education. Only three in every hundred went past grade 6. By comparison, well over half the children in provincial public schools in 1930 were, as indicated by Figure 2, past grade 3; almost a third were beyond grade 6.[29] The formal education being offered young Indians was not only separate from but unequal to that provided their non-Indian contemporaries.

The last chapter essays in this volume focus on Indian education during the twentieth century. Dianne Persson's case study of Blue Quills in Alberta utilizes the oral recollections of former pupils to recreate the frequently harsh and uncaring texture of school life. Coates describes the almost negligible level of day schooling which the Department of Indian Affairs considered suitable for the Yukon.

THE INDIAN RESPONSE

Indian reaction to compulsory education varied. Although school attendance was mandatory from 1920, some families successfully resisted. As a consequence, as late as 1951, eight out of every twenty Indians in Canada over age five reported in the federal census that they possessed no formal schooling.[30] Other families acquiesced. The Cree leader John Tootoosis, born in 1899, has recalled that, although his father was "very troubled by the idea of sending his sons to residential school," he nonetheless "wanted them to learn to read, write and count and be able to speak the language of the white man....He did not have these skills himself, had often needed them and knew that Indian people would have a better chance in the future if they had them."[31] The Huron chief Max Gros-Louis, born three decades later, said "my father, although he was illiterate, wanted his children to have a better education."[32]

Young Indians in school soon became aware of their situation. Some, like Gros-Louis, became discriminatory in their receptivity to what was being taught: "Indians and Eskimos, like any other people, want to learn, but when it comes to the inventory of white knowledge they are selective."[33] In cases where children entered school ignorant of its "civilizing" function, they were soon made aware through such standard practices as physical punishment for speaking their own language even when they knew no English, systematic denigration of their culture as "barbaric," and personal characterization as "goddamn savages."[34] The quality of teaching was frequently problematic, not suprising given that almost all schools were staffed by individuals whose commitment was primarily religious.[35] While children in day schools maintained some contact with a familiar environment, those in residential institutions were away for months and years on end, obeying externally imposed rules and often not developing the necessary self-confidence to cope with an independent existence in adulthood. On the basis of his generation's experience in residential school during the first two decades of the century, John Tootoosis explained:

When an Indian comes out of these places it is like being put between two walls in a room and left hanging in the middle. On one side are all the things he learned from his people and their way of life that was being wiped out, and on the other are the white man's ways which he could never fully understand since he never had the right amount of education and could not be part of it. There he is, hanging in the middle of the two cultures and he is not a white man and he is not an Indian. They washed away practically everything an Indian needed to help himself, to think the way a human person should in order to survive.[36]

Pupils who were nonetheless determined to learn experienced special frustration. By the time they had acquired basic literacy, most were old enough to be put in the standard half-day programme, where each afternoon was given over to occupational training consisting of the domestic and outdoor physical labour necessary to a school's economic survival. Thus, a fatherless boy sent to school at age seven only reached grade 5 by the time "I had to leave there when I was eighteen."[37] Children who began their formal education at a later age were at an even greater disadvantage: a Vancouver Island boy who started grade 1 in 1920 at age twelve "coming into my manhood and growing up sexually" found himself expelled two years later charged with getting a classmate pregnant.[38]

For the minority who progressed academically and then wanted to continue their education past the mandatory leaving age of sixteen or eighteen, the situation was almost always hopeless. One young woman who turned sixteen about 1920 reported, "I could have gone to high school or finished school anywhere but I wan't allowed to because that's as high as I was going to go, that's as high as *Indian* girls went."[39] The situation persisted through the Second World War: one frustrated father described how when young people "were fifteen or sixteen they would just tell the Indians: 'That's that. You go now. You're finished.' That was the ruling of the white man over the Indian. No matter how hard you tried to keep them in school, when they reached that age they just told the Indians to go home."[40]

During these years both educated and uneducated Indians repeatedly brought the discriminatory and inherently contradictory conditions of schooling to the attention of the Department of Indian Affairs. Examples from the Prairies reveal both the high value which was assessed quality education and Indian willingness to interact positively with Whites to achieve that goal. A 1911 Saskatchewan delegation to the Superintendent of Indian Affairs requested more emphasis be given to classwork, and less to farming.[41] About the same time, an elderly Cree chief wrote to the Governor General requesting that residential schools be replaced by local day schools as promised by treaty in order to keep children from being "torn from their mother's arms or homes."[42] Half a dozen years later the Rev. Edward Ahenakew, a Cree graduate of the

University of Saskatchewan, urged the federal government to put more money into education in order to "give the Indian self-respect....Surely the government is not thinking of being hampered by a race of ignorant and non-self-supporting people for all time to come....Conditions as they are are neither fair to the Indians nor to the white people who have to live in the same country with them."[43] Ahenakew's unpublished notes written in 1923 make clear his comprehension of the issues. He described the residential school, much as Tootoosis did, as taking away "all the initiative there may be in an Indian."

> For those who do live [through the experience], who survive and who graduate from the school at the age of eighteen, during every day of their training they have acted under orders. They never needed to use their own minds and wills....when suddenly given their freedom they do not know how to use it. Their initiative is lost....[They] sit on the fence between the whites and the Indians, belonging to neither, fitting into neither world....You cannot make a white man out of an Indian. It is much better to make our children into good Indians, for we *are* Indians in our person and in our thinking.

Ahenakew continued: "The world around us is too far advanced for any such playing at education." Given that "people who have come as immigrants to this land" are "supplied with the best of teachers, is it justice that the weak Indian nation, which gave of its blood to prove its loyalty [by active military service during the First World War], should have to be satisfied with teachers who seldom have any qualifications to teach?" He urged "placing the education of our children where responsibility for the education of white children now rests: with the provincial governments—the Dominion Government subsidizing each province in proportion to its Indian population." Given good local day schools with qualified teachers, "regular school attendance would be generally accepted."[44]

Edward Ahenakew helped formulate the resolution passed in 1931 by the League of Indians of Western Canada requesting that the Department of Indian Affairs establish local reserve schools, since children in residential institutions were making such slow progress.[45] A year later the league was urging that residential pupils be allowed to spend more time in the classroom and that teachers be properly qualified. Emendations on these unanswered petitions in departmental files suggest that their veracity was accepted: "The question of giving more attention to class room work has been commented on before by visiting school inspectors and others," and teaching positions were sometimes "merely posts provided for persons for whom billets had to be found."[46]

Little changed, however. At mid-century, only one-third of Indian pupils went beyond grade 3, compared with over 60 per cent of the children in provincial public schools across Canada. Ten per cent were now beyond grade 6, but so were three times as many of their White contemporaries. Attitudes toward individual pupils remained similar to what they had been a generation before, as evidenced by the experience of Jane Willis in residential school on her local island off James Bay in Quebec between 1948 and 1956. The culture from which she came was characterized as "a lot of useless garbage....I was made to feel untrustworthy, inferior, incapable, and immoral....I was brainwashed into believing that 'Indian' was synonymous with 'sub-human,' 'savage,' 'idiot,' and 'worthless.'" To the extent that attitudes were altering, it was emanating from the students themselves. In Willis' case, despite "years of having the Indian educated out of us" and a half-day programme from age twelve which "made it necessary for some students to spend two, or even three years in one grade," a few individuals, like Willis, persisted in continuing formal education beyond the mandatory leaving age. Even then, Willis' request to be allowed to go on to high school was at first denied on traditional paternalistic grounds: "If we let you out, the next thing we know, the whole island will be as evil and as corrupt as the white people and other Indians outside."[47]

FEDERAL RECOGNITION OF FAILURE

As Coates and Persson make clear in this volume, recognition that the treatment of Canada's Natives was contradictory as well as grossly discriminatory developed slowly in the years after the Second World War. Across the world, segregation based on race was being called into question. Indians in Canada had again contributed to the war effort but were not, as many church and veterans' groups now discovered, even citizens, since very few had chosen to be enfranchised. The dominant society's ignorance of and disinterest in Canada's Indians began to be breeched. Calls grew for an end to unequal treatment in all areas, including education.

A Joint Committee of the Senate and House of Commons was appointed in 1946 to revise the Indian Act; among other recommendations, it proposed that wherever possible young Indians be schooled together with non-Indian children. The federal goal became immediate Indian integration—to its critics, cultural assimilation in a new guise—into the dominant society through education.[48] The Indian Act was revised in 1951, permitting the federal government to make financial agreements with provincial and other authorities for Indian children to attend public and private schools educating non-Indians. By 1960, almost a quarter of the 38,000 young Indians in school were attending provincially-controlled institutions, and the total proportion of Indian pupils beyond grade 6 doubled over the decade to almost 20 per cent. These shifts toward integration coincided, however, with other changes in the relationship between Indians and Whites with more significant longterm consequences for education.

INDIAN SELF-DETERMINATION AND INDIAN EDUCATION

For almost a century, since Confederation, the initiative in interaction between Canada's aboriginal population and the dominant society had rested with the dominant society. The official goal had been assimilation, the eradication of Indian cultures in favour of their European counterpart. That policy had failed, owing both to Indian unwillingness to abandon their cultures and to federal parsimony in the provision of educational facilities, especially after 1910. During the postwar years the balance in the relationship slowly shifted, at first as a result of a changing attitude in the dominant society but increasingly as a consequence of Indian self-determination. Colonialism was being resisted in many areas of the world. The American civil rights movement set an example for all racial minorities, and the grassroots activism which characterized the 1960's in the United States soon spread across the border. Community development programmes initiated by the Department of Indian Affairs to make Indians more self-reliant were a logical extension of this movement. Such activity, which also included leadership training courses and encouragement of local school committees, gave Indians new self-confidence in their potential to effect change.[49] As well, the Christian churches, led by the Anglicans, began to reassess their historical basis of interaction with Indians and to move toward greater equality in the relationship, to become facilitators of Indian aspirations rather than agents of assimilation.[50] While Indian rights organizations had existed sporadically in the past, their role had been minimized by geographical isolation, linguistic diversity, legal restrictions against political acitivity, prohibitions on travel outside of a reserve, and lack of explicit common objectives. The appearance of Indian political organizations, such as the Federation of Saskatchewan Indians in 1961, gave impetus to self-determination. The culmination came in 1968 with the formation of the National Indian Brotherhood as an organization committed to resolving the problems facing Indian people within the context of Indian culture.[51]

The federal government sought to placate the growing criticism by initiating the Hawthorn survey of Indian conditions, which in 1966-67 recommended continued integration in education along with increased attention by the Department of Indian Affairs to Indian interests.[52] However, the next year, a new Liberal government led by Pierre Trudeau came to power on the promise of a "just society." Its approach to Indians, enunciated in a White Paper of June 1969, was premised on the achievement of individual Indian equality at the expense of cultural survival. All legislative and constitutional bases of discrimination were to be removed; Indians would receive the same services, including education, available to members of the dominant society. The Department of Indian Affairs would be abolished and the reserve system dismantled. Indians as individuals would become equal participants in the "just society."[53]

Indian reaction to the White Paper was overwhelmingly negative. Indian groups coalesced in opposition, the proposal being seen as a mechanism for the federal government to escape from its historical responsibility for Indian affairs, including the obligation to right past injustices in such areas as land claims and treaties. To the young Indian leader Harold Cardinal, the proposal was only a "thinly disguised program of extermination through assimilation."[54] Indians became convinced as never before of the necessity to take control of their destiny.

So far as education was concerned, the conviction grew that the only solution lay in Indian control. As documented by the anthropologists A. Richard King and Harry Wolcott in their vivid portraits of a Yukon residential school and a British Columbia day school during the early 1960's, the qualitative changes in Indian education had often been minimal at the level of the locality.[55] The schools and their teachers remained alien, the representatives of an external culture being imposed upon Native peoples. But growing Indian self-determination meant that very soon action followed words. Indians in northeastern Alberta became so incensed that in 1971 they took over their local federal school to prevent its closure, making Blue Quills the first school in Canada to be controlled by an Indian band. Their success, documented in this volume by Persson, encouraged other bands to consider direct action in education and elsewhere. The White Paper's formal retraction soon followed. After more than a century, cultural assimilation was finally abandoned as the official goal of the government of Canada.[56]

Shortly after, in 1972, the National Indian Brotherhood issued a position paper calling for Indian control of Indian education. This was almost immediately accepted in principle by the federal government. The paper had at its heart "two educational principles recognized in Canadian society: Parental Responsibility and Local Control of Education," rights denied to the Indians of Canada since Confederation. The document reaffirmed the federal government's historical commitment to provide schooling, but asserted that "only Indian people can develop a suitable philosophy of education based on Indian values adapted to modern living." Indian children must be given "a strong sense of identity, with confidence in their own personal worth and

ability," a process best undertaken when Indian bands exercise "full responsibility in providing the best possible education for our children."[57]

INDIAN CONTROL OF INDIAN EDUCATION

While control over education remains at the heart of self-determination,
actual transfer of control has been hindered by the lack of a direct legal basis
for transfer in the agreement reached in 1973 between the federal government and the National Indian Brotherhood.[58] Despite repeated Indian initiatives,
the federal government has been unwilling to resolve the impasse, as acknowledged in a 1982 position paper, that "the failure to establish guiding principles and develop operational guidelines has impeded the development of
Indian education and restricted implementation of the Department's policy."[59]

The principal area of contention centres on control over finance and
thereby on the boundaries of Indian decision-making authority. In its funding of the development of Indian control, the Department of Indian Affairs
has focused on having Indians make the decisions regarding content and
participants, as well as overseeing the process of procuring and allocating
funds. Indians have had far less control over the passage of funds from the
Department to provincial and local departments of education through tuition
agreements for the 50 per cent of Indian children who continue to attend
provincial schools.[60] Indian groups have also become frustrated at the federal expectation that transfer of facilities to local control should entail no
additional cost, particularly when the department has apparently spent
more per pupil to educate a child provincially than federally or in a band-
operated school. In 1981-82, $3,675 was spent provincially as compared with
$3,215 federally and $3,360 in a band-operated school.[61] Through its continued refusal to allow funding, the federal Department of Indian Affairs is
perceived as preventing the development of full responsibility and account-
ability for Indian education by Indians themselves. The boundaries of
decision-making authority remain limited.

Progress in the direction of Indian control has nonetheless occurred, as
Battiste and Persson document. Individual bands have been encouraged to
take over full or partial administration of reserve schools operated by the
Department of Indian Affairs. By the early 1980's, 450 of the 577 Indian
bands in Canada had done so. As well, by 1984, 187 bands were operating
their own schools, almost half of them located in British Columbia, the
others primarily on the Prairies.[62] In 1983-84, just a fifth of the Indian
children in school were attending band-operated schools.[63] Most of the
remaining federal residential schools have been closed, to be replaced either
by local schools or by the provision of boarding facilities at nearby inte-

grated institutions. Parents of children at provincial and private integrated institutions have been encouraged to become involved with local school boards. Two school districts have become Indian controlled, the Nishga in British Columbia and the Cree in Quebec, both emanating indirectly out of legal cases acknowledging aboriginal rights.[64] In another similarly isolated area, northern Alberta, the largely Native Northland school district established in 1960 remains externally administered.[65] In several provinces and major cities as well as in many individual schools, special programmes have been initiated to encourage Indian cultural and language content, particularly where institutions enrol a considerable number of Indian pupils.

Change has gone beyond the elementary and secondary levels. Adult education programmes have been established in many communities. As of 1985, sixty-five cultural education centres offered programmes in Indian languages and cultures. At the post-secondary level, special programmes for Indian students have come into existence, most of them directed toward training teachers or lawyers. Indian and Native studies programmes now exist at a number of universities to educate both Indians and non-Indians. The Saskatchewan Indian Federated College was created in 1976 as an administratively and economically independent institution academically integrated with the University of Regina.

CONCLUSION

The cultural interaction of the past four centuries between Canada's aboriginal peoples and their European colonizers has had as a principal objective control over education, but the concerted effort by the dominant society to assimilate Canada's Indians through education has failed. Control over the education of Indian children is now passing back to Indians themselves. Just as control has historically been a means to an end, so today it is the critical means making possible the revitalization and resurgence of Indian culture in Canada into the twenty-first century.

FIGURE 1
GRADE DISTRIBUTION OF INDIAN CHILDREN IN SCHOOL IN CANADA, 1890-1984

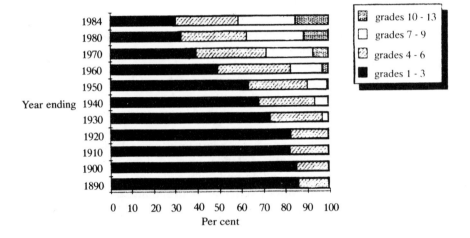

FIGURE 2
GRADE DISTRIBUTION OF CHILDREN IN PROVINCIAL SCHOOLS IN CANADA, 1920-84

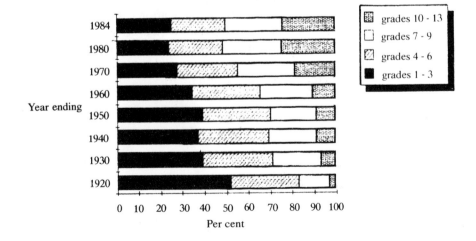

NOTES TO CHAPTER ONE

1. See *Recent Developments in Native Education* (Toronto: Canadian Education Association, 1984), and *Indian Education Paper: Phase 1* (Ottawa: Department of Indian Affairs and Northern Development [DIA], 1982). A third Native school district, the Inuit in Quebec, is beyond the scope of this volume.
2. This and the following paragraph are adapted from Don McCaskill, "When Cultures Meet: Indians in Canada," *Bridges* (June 1984): 10-20.
3. See Arthur J. Ray, *Indians in the Fur Trade: Their Role as Hunters, Trappers and Middlemen in the Lands Southwest of Hudson Bay, 1660-1870* (Toronto: University of Toronto Press, 1974); A.J. Ray and Donald B. Freeman, *"Give Us Good Measure": An Economic Analysis of Relations Between the Indians and the Hudson's Bay Company Since 1763* (Toronto: University of Toronto Press, 1978); and Robin Fisher, *Contact and Conflict: Indian-European Relations in British Columbia, 1774-1890* (Vancouver: University of British Columbia Press, 1977).
4. See, for instance, Leslie Upton, "Colonists and Micmacs," *Journal of Canadian Studies* 10 (1975): 44-56.
5. The history of missionary activity is recounted in John Webster Grant, *Moon of Wintertime: Missionaries and the Indians of Canada in Encounter since 1534* (Toronto: University of Toronto Press, 1984). See also Jean Usher, "Duncan of Metlakatla: The Victorian Origins of a Model Indian Community," in *The Shield of Achilles: Aspects of Canada in the Victorian Age*, ed. W.L. Morton (Toronto: McClelland and Stewart, 1968), 286-310, and her "Apostles and Aborigines: The Social Theory of the Church Missionary Society," *Social History* 7 (1971): 28-52. On similarities between the treatment of indigenous peoples around the world, see E. Palmer Patterson II, *The Canadian Indian: A History Since 1500* (Don Mills: Collier Macmillan, 1972), 3-24; James S. Frideres, ed., *Native People in Canada*, 2d ed. (Scarborough: Prentice-Hall, 1983), 294-323; Philip O. Altback and Gail P. Kelly, eds., *Education and Colonialism* (New York: Longman, 1978), esp. 1-49; Robert J. Hind, "The Internal Colonial Concept," *Comparative Studies in Society and History* 26 (1984): 543-67; and Josiane Hamers and Michel Blane, *Bilinguisme et bilingualité* (Brussels: Pierre Mardaga, 1983).
6. John S. Milloy, "The Early Indian Acts: Developmental Strategy and Constitutional Change," in *As Long as the Sun Shines and Water Flows: A Reader in Canadian Native Studies*, ed. Ian A.L. Getty and Antoine S. Lussier, Nakoda Institute Occasional Paper No. 1 (Vancouver: University of British Columbia Press, 1983), 60.
7. For details, see John L. Tobias, "Protection, Civilization, Assimilation: An Outline History of Canada's Indian Policy," *Western Canadian Journal of Anthropology* 6 (1976), reprinted in Getty and Lussier, *As Long as the Sun Shines*, 30-55.
8. *Census of Canada*, 1871, vol. 1, 332-33; 1881, vol. 1, 300-301; and 1941, 684-91. Estimates of Indian population over time can be found both in the decennial federal census, as part of the tables breaking down population by racial or ethnic origin, and in the annual reports of DIA.
9. See John L. Tobias, "Canada's Subjugation of the Plains Cree, 1879-1885," *Canadian Historical Review* 64 (1983): 519-48. For the history of Indians on the Prairies, see Gerald Friesen, *The Canadian Prairies: A History* (Toronto: University of Toronto Press, 1984), esp. 10-44 and 129-61.
10. DIA, *Annual Report [AR]*, 1876, 6.
11. See Helen Ralston, "Religion, Public Policy, and the Education of Micmac Indians of Nova Scotia, 1605-1872," *Canadian Review of Sociology and Anthropology* 18, no. 4 (1981): 470-98.
12. Penny Petrone, *First People, First Voices* (Toronto: University of Toronto Press, 1983).
13. See, for instance, DIA, *AR*, 1872, 2, and 1895, xxiii.
14. See J. Donald Wilson, Robert M. Stamp and Louis-Philippe Audet, ed., *Canadian Education: A History* (Scarborough: Prentice-Hall, 1970).
15. Nicholas Flood Davin, *Report on Industrial Schools for Indians and Half-breeds* (Ottawa, 1879). On the development of American Indian education policy, see Francis Paul Prucha,

The Great Father: The United States Government and the American Indians (Lincoln: University of Nebraska Press, 1984), vol. 1, 135-58, and vol. 2, 687-715, 814-40, and 1060-68; and Frederick E. Hoxie, *A Final Promise: The Campaign to Assimilate the Indians, 1880-1920* (Lincoln: University of Nebraska Press, 1984), 189-210.

16. Also useful is E. Brian Titley, "The Industrial Schools: An Experiment in Canadian Indian Education," in *Schools in the West: Essays in Canadian Educational History*, ed. Nancy M. Sheehan, J. Donald Wilson and David C. Jones (Calgary: Detselig, 1986).

17. DIA, *AR*, 1900, 26-45, and *Census of Canada*, 1941, vol. 1, 684-91. Statistical details on each school under DIA control were regularly included in a "School Statement" in the annual report.

18. Dan Kennedy (Ochankugahe), *Recollections of an Assiniboine Chief*, ed. James R. Stevens (Toronto: McClelland and Stewart, 1972), 48, 54-55; and Mike Mountain Horse, *My People the Bloods*, ed. Hugh A. Dempsey (Calgary: Glenbow-Alberta Institute and Blood Tribal Council, 1979), 15.

19. Joseph F. Dion, *My Tribe the Crees*, ed. Hugh A. Dempsey (Calgary: Glenbow Museum, 1979), 157.

20. Duncan Campbell Scott, "Indian Affairs, 1867-1912," in *Canada and Its Provinces*, ed. Adam Shortt, (Toronto: Edinburgh University Press, 1913), vol. 7, 615. For a case study, see Clellan S. Ford, *Smoke from Their Fires: The Life of a Kwakiutl Chief* (New Haven: Yale University Press for the Institute of Human Relations, 1941), 86-96, 100-109.

21. Canada, House of Commons, Debates, 1897, col. 4076, 14 June 1897, quoted in D.J. Hall, "Clifford Sifton and Canadian Indian Administration, 1896-1905," *Prairie Forum* 2 (1977), reprinted in Getty and Lussier, *As Long as the Sun Shines*, 134. Also see Rolf Knight, *Indians at Work: An Informal History of Native Indian Labour in British Columbia, 1858-1930* (Vancouver: New Star, 1978). For an example of educated young Indians entering the paid labour force, see Tom Boulanger, *An Indian Remembers: My Life as a Trapper in Northern Manitoba* (Winnipeg: Peguis Publishers, 1971), 8-9.

22. DIA, *AR*, 1911, 385.

23. *Census of Canada*, 1941, vol. 1, 686-92. On federal Indian policy, see Hall, "Clifford Sifton"; his *Clifford Sifton, Volume 1: The Young Napoleon* (Vancouver: University of British Columbia Press, 1981), 127-28, 269-71; Titley, "Industrial Schools"; and his "Duncan Campbell Scott and Indian Educational Policy," in *An Imperfect Past: Education and Society in Canadian History*, ed. J. Donald Wilson (Vancouver: Centre for the Study of Curriculum and Instruction, University of British Columbia, 1984), 141-53.

24. DIA, *AR*, 1894, xxi, and 1897, xxvii. Grant, *Moon of Wintertime*, discusses the problem of finance from the missionary perspective; see 181-82, 191-96. The effect of federal financial frugality on individual schools is examined in John S. Long, "Education in the James Bay region during the Horden Years," *Ontario History* 70 (1978): 75-89.

25. Scott, "Indian Affairs," 615. Also see 1902 memorandum from Martin Benson quoted in Titley, "Industrial Schools."

26. DIA, *AR*, 1898, xxvii.

27. Scott, "Indian Affairs," 616; and DIA, *AR*, 1909, xxxiv, 1910, 273-75, and 1911, 337. For a defence of this position, written by a Montreal school inspector in 1939, see A.E. Wescott, "Curricula for Indian Schools," in *The North American Indian Today*, ed. C.T. Loram and T.F. MacIlwraith (Toronto: University of Toronto Press, 1943), 283-93.

28. Diamond Jenness, "Canada's Indians Yesterday. What of Today?" *Canadian Journal of Economics and Political Science* 20, no. 1 (February 1954), reprinted in Getty and Lussier, *As Long as the Sun Shines*, 162.

29. Grade distribution of Indian pupils is taken from "School Statements" in DIA, *AR*, 1890, 1900, 1910, 1920, 1930, 1940, 1950 and 1960; *The Canadian Indian: Statistics* (Ottawa: DIA, 1973); and 1980 and 1984 data kindly supplied by DIA. Grade distribution of children in provincial schools is taken from *Annual Survey of Education* (Ottawa: Dominion Bureau of Statistics), for 1921 and 1930; *Elementary and Secondary Education in Canada* (Ottawa: Dominion Bureau of Statistics), for 1938/40 and 1948/50; *Survey of Elementary and Secondary Education* (Ottawa: Dominion Bureau of Statistics), for 1960 and 1970; *Elementary-Secondary School Enrolment* (Ottawa: Statistics Canada), for 1980; and 1984 data kindly

supplied by Statistics Canada. Data for 1920, some of which comes from 1921, was based only on the six provinces then dividing pupils into grades. Pupils in kindergarten and in special classes were excluded from all calculations.

30. *Census of Canada*, 1951, vol. 2, Table 51. Also see James Redford, "Attendance at Indian Residential Schools in British Columbia, 1890-1920," *BC Studies* 44 (Winter 1979-80): 41-56. For an example of one young Indian deliberately kept out of school, see George Barker, *Forty Years a Chief* (Winnipeg: Peguis Publishers, 1979), 16-17.

31. Norma Sluman and Jean Goodwill, *John Tootoosis: A Biography of a Cree Leader* (Ottawa: Golden Dog Press, 1982), 95, 97.

32. Max Gros-Louis, *First among the Hurons* (Montreal: Harvest House, 1973), 27-28.

33. Ibid., 36.

34. For examples from Indian recollections, see Sluman and Goodwill, *John Tootoosis*, 106; Gros-Louis, *First among the Hurons*, 25, 31; Dorothy Haegert, *Children of the First People* (Vancouver: Tillicum Library, 1983), 67, 78, 116; Jean E. Speare, ed., *The Days of Augusta* (Vancouver: J.J. Douglas, 1973), 7, 17-18; Peter Webster, *As Far as I Know: Reminiscences of an Ahousat Elder* (Campbell River, BC: Campbell River Museum and Archives, 1983), 41; and Margaret Whitehead, *Now You Are My Brother: Missionaries in British Columbia*, *Sound Heritage* series no. 34 (Victoria: Provincial Archives of British Columbia, 1981), 50, 61, 64.

35. This issue is elaborated by Grant, *Moon of Wintertime*, 162-66, 176-96.

36. Sluman and Goodwill, *John Tootoosis*, 107, 109. Also see Speare, *The Days of Augusta*, 7, 15; D. Bruce Sealey, *The Education of Native Peoples in Manitoba*, Monographs in Education 3 (Winnipeg: University of Manitoba, 1980), 34; and Ken Coates, " 'Betwixt and Between': The Anglican Church and the Children of the Carcross (Chooutla) Residential School, 1911-1954," *BC Studies* 64 (Winter 1984-85): 27-47.

37. Petrone, *First People, First Voices*, 47. Also see Haegert, *Children of the First People*, 20, and Speare, *The Days of Augusta*, 18.

38. Webster, *As Far as I Know*, 41-42.

39. Whitehead, *Now You Are My Brother*, 67. Tootoosis's experience was similar; see Sluman and Goodwill, *John Tootoosis*, 107.

40. James P. Spradley, *Guests Never Leave Hungry: The Autobiography of James Sewid, a Kwakiutl Indian* (New Haven: Yale University Press, 1969), 191.

41. Delia Opekokew, *The First Nations: Indian Government and the Canadian Confederation* (Saskatoon: Federation of Saskatchewan Indians, 1980), 32-33.

42. DIA, RG 10, Black Series, no. 422752, quoted in Sluman and Goodwill, *John Tootoosis*, 101-2.

43. Article by Edward Ahenakew in *Saskatchewan Daily Star*, 1 June 1918, in DIA, School Files, vol. 6001, on microfilm from originals in Public Archives of Canada.

44. Edward Ahenakew, *Voices of the Plains Cree*, ed. Ruth M. Buck (Toronto: McClelland and Stewart, 1973), 127-35.

45. Sluman and Goodwill, *John Tootoosis*, 151. On the educational initiatives taken by Indians on the Prairies, see Stan Cuthand, "The Native Peoples of the Prairie Provinces in the 1920's and 1930's," in *One Century Later: Western Canadian Reserve Indians Since Treaty 7*, ed. Ian A.L. Getty and Donald B. Smith (Vancouver: University of British Columbia Press, 1978), 31-42.

46. Sluman and Goodwill, *John Tootoosis*, 157-58. On an educational initiative taken locally by British Columbia Indians, see Spradley, *Guests Never Leave Hungry*, 126.

47. Jane Willis, *Geniesh: An Indian Girlhood* (Toronto: New Press, 1973), 59, 82, 86, 102-3, 105, 121, 199.

48. See, for instance, Tobias, "Canada's Subjugation of the Plains Cree." 52.

49. Sally M. Weaver, *Making Canadian Indian Policy: The Hidden Agenda 1968-70* (Toronto: University of Toronto Press, 1981), 13-31.

50. See, for instance, Charles E. Hendry, *Beyond Traplines: Toward an Assessment of the Work of the Anglican Church of Canada with Canada's Native Peoples* (Toronto: Anglican Church, 1969).

51. See Frideres, *Native People in Canada*, 233-66; Paul Tennant, "Native Indian Political

Organization in British Columbia, 1900-1969: A Response to Internal Colonialism," *BC Studies* 55 (1981): 3-49; and E. Palmer Patterson II, "Andrew Paul (1892-1959): Finding a Voice for the 'New Indian,' " *Western Canadian Journal of Anthropology* 6 (1976): 63-82. On the formation of the National Indian Brotherhood, see Harold Cardinal, *The Rebirth of Canada's Indians* (Edmonton: Hurtig, 1977), 107-16; J. Rick Ponting and Roger Gibbons, eds., *Out of Irrelevance: A Socio-Political Introduction to Indian Affairs in Canada* (Toronto: Butterworth, 1980), 195-218. The group's name was later changed to the Assembly of First Nations.

52. A.B. Hawthorn, ed., *A Survey of the Contemporary Indians of Canada: Economic, Political, Educational Needs and Policies,* 2 vols. (Ottawa: DIA, 1966-67).

53. The White Paper's official title was *Statement of the Government of Canada on Indian Policy, 1969* (Ottawa: Queen's Printer, 1969). For analysis of this period, see Weaver, *Making Canadian Indian Policy.*

54. Cardinal, *The Rebirth of Canada's Indians,* 1.

55. A. Richard King, *The School at Mopass: A Problem of Identity* (New York: Holt, Rinehart and Winston, 1967); and Harry F. Wolcott, *A Kwatkiutl Village and School* (New York: Holt, Rinehart and Winston, 1967).

56. The federal shift is analyzed in Cardinal, *The Rebirth of Canada's Indians,* 57-88, and Weaver, *Making Canadian Indian Policy,* 171-89.

57. *Indian Control of Indian Education* (Ottawa: National Indian Brotherhood, 1972), reprinted in abridged form in *Indian Education Paper,* Appendix A.

58. Ibid.

59. Ibid., 15.

60. Data supplied by DIA. In the school year ending in 1984, 36,053 (49.8 per cent) of the 72,403 registered Indian children in school in Canada were in provincial schools, compared with 20, 916 (28.9 per cent) in federal schools and 15,434 (21.3 per cent) in band-operated schools.

61. *Recent Developments in Native Education,* 20.

62. Ibid., 14. See also Syd Pauls, "The Case for Band Controlled Schools," *Canadian Journal of Native Education* 12, no. 1 (1984): 31-36, which includes an analysis of the problems facing band-controlled schools.

63. The proportion has risen steadily since 1980, the first year that band-operated schools were separated out for statistical purposes by DIA. In 1980, 7.7 per cent of registered Indian pupils were in band-operated schools. Thereafter the proportion rose annually to 9.6, 16.3, 20.5 and, in 1984, to 21.3 per cent.

64. On the Nishga, see Daniel Raunet, *Without Surrender without Consent: A History of the Nishga Land Claims* (Vancouver: Douglas & McIntyre, 1984).

65. *The Canadian Journal of Native Education* contains numerous articles on the Northland school district; see esp. John W. Chalmers, "Northland: The Founding of a Wilderness System," 12, no. 2 (1985): 2-45; "Editors' Response," 12, no. 2 (1985): 46-49; and Derek J. Allison, "The Promise of Northland," 11, no. 1 (1983): 27-36.

2

Micmac Literacy and Cognitive Assimilation

Marie Battiste

Literacy is an ambivalent process of modern consciousness. When people refer to the processes of becoming literate in terms of the youth of their own culture, literacy is called cultural transmission. But when a certain literacy is forced upon youths outside that culture, it becomes cultural and cognitive assimilation. The functions of literacy, as a shield in cultural transmission and as a sword of cognitive imperialism, have been hidden by the interactions of the myths and modern conceptions of literacy.

Certain myths have disguised the functions and value of literacy in society.[1] Viewed as the benign liberator of the mind, literacy is perceived to be the modernizing agent of society and an economic commodity necessary for national development.[2] Thus guided by mistaken assumptions about the desirability and economic effects of literacy, tribal states and underdeveloped nations have instituted policies which have imposed modern values on tribal, preindustrial societies without regard for their language and culture in the hopes of being able to overcome their social, economic, racial, and political impotence.

Modern conceptions of literacy have further disguised its processes because they are fragmented and limited: fragmented by the search among western scholars for normative standards which can be universally applied; and limited by the bias toward instrumental objectives of modern liberal social theory and Western school practices. Literacy, however, is not an all or nothing proposition; its elements cannot be universally applied.[3] Rather, literacy is a relative social concept more reflective of culture and context than of the levels of formal instruction by which it is usually measured.

Little is known about the role and functions of literacy within various cultural contexts and how these different contexts affect attitudes and values. Still less is known of children's preschool literacy experiences in their homes and communities. Recent studies have shown, however, that literacy has not been used in the same way in all cultures, nor have its results been the same.[4] Yet modern studies have not inquired about how literacy functions outside of Western institutions of learning, and, more importantly, what factors govern its acceptance, rejection, and diffusion. In the last two decades, the consistent failure of the schools to achieve societal literacy suggests that much more is involved than the formal processes taught in schools.[5]

Recent historical comparative and ethnographic studies in different communities reveal that the acquisition and diffusion of literacy are related to a society's perception of literacy's value and function.[6] Thus, any attempt to define literacy must include a specification of context and an examination of that society's experiences.[7] The social and cultural environment is crucial to understanding any society's literacy, for the context is an integral and active part of the acquisition of literacy. Contextual analysis in literacy studies has begun to unravel the bias of the myths and concepts of literacy, since most members of societies are unaware of the fundamental rules of their cultural or environmental systems.[8]

The hidden bias of the myths and concepts of literacy became apparent to me in 1975 when my people, the Micmac communities of eastern Canada, had to choose an orthography for use in reserve schools. A practical and efficient writing system, purported to reflect the phonemic system of the Micmac language, was introduced, but it was met with initial resistance. Reasons for community resistance to the new script lay in the sociocultural and historical factors associated with earlier scripts.

The Micmac Indians are an Algonkian-speaking tribe of northeastern America who for over three hundred years have had several different kinds of literacies which have served the social, cultural, and spiritual needs of tribal society. Pictographs, petroglyphs, notched sticks, and wampum were the primary Native texts of Algonkian ideographic literacy. These provide the context for all other kinds of literacies for the Micmac, who have remained faithful to the deep structure of the Micmac literacy and consciousness in the Algonkian traditions. Europeans adapted aboriginal symbols and designs found on earlier Native texts and developed hieroglyphic characters which were used for teaching prayers. These modified Algonkian hieroglyphics remain the essence of Micmac literacy, even though four roman scripts have also been developed to serve different purposes of European missionaries, Canadian governments, and Native groups over the last 250 years. The forceful attempt to create English literacy in Micmac society has created transitional problems of cognitive incoherence and cultural ambiguity. These problems raise important questions concerning the doctrine and actual functions of modern literacy in tribal society.

THE CONTEXT OF ABORIGINAL LITERACY

Through the use of pictographs, petroglyphs, notched sticks, and wampum, early North American Indians achieved a form of written communication and recording which served the social, political, cultural, and spiritual needs of the early period, fully describing the ideal and material world. Aboriginal literacy embodied tribal epistemology in Native texts, which interacted with and depended upon the oral tradition. Ancient oral Indian tradition was and is dependent upon the highly prized oral skills of its tribal men and women. Using ideographic symbolization of concepts and ideas, Algonkian Indians supplemented the oral tradition with ideological catalogues which helped to record and store valuable knowledge, information, and records on available natural materials such as birchbark, rocks, and shells.

The various Native texts in tribal North America represented the worldview of tribal people, particularly their ideas and beliefs about knowledge, power, and medicine. These Native texts represented another form of knowledge that has since been eradicated from western thought. A fundamental element in tribal epistemology lay in two traditional knowledge sources:

1) from the immediate world of personal and tribal experiences, that is, one's perceptions, thoughts, and memories which included one's shared experiences with others; and
2) from the spiritual world evidenced through dreams, visions, and signs which were often interpreted with the aid of medicine men or elders.

Native texts thus documented knowledge of the two worlds in holistic, meaningful ideographs. These ideographs were interactive, invoking the memory, creativity, and logic of the people and were transmitted to succeeding generations through the oral tradition and appropriate rituals. In effect, religious traditions and rituals provided access to the storehouse of knowledge and, through the medium of analogy, provided harmony for all life, including plants and animals.

Native texts appear to have served both a public and private function. Wampum was the public record, maintained by a wampum keeper or tribal historian. The wampum—strings and belts of tubular shells—was regularly brought forward at ceremonial gatherings. Political records of treaties and presents, represented through conventional symbols, were woven with shells into strings or belts. The arrangement of shells in relation to colour conveyed knowledge and an attitude: for example, white shells represented peace and friendship, and purple shells represented war and death. Because of the utility and value of the shells, they were also used as international, intertribal, and colonial currency by the woodland tribes and the immigrants, often rated against sterling and later the dollar.

Pictographs, petroglyphs, and notched sticks served more diversified, principally personal, uses. The Algonkian Indians used them to communicate information and messages to friends and relatives about their whereabouts or of routes and directions taken, to relate stories, to enlist warriors into battle, or to tell of herbal cures.[9] Algonkian petroglyphs and pictography also communicated historical and practical information and history. One of the best examples of this form is the *Walam Olum* or Red Score of the Lenape nation of the Algonkian, which presents a cosmogony and national history. The symbols were derived from the pictographic legacy of the Algonkian, Iroquian, and Siouxan nations and are directly related to the *Midewiwin* texts. The 184 symbols of the *Walam Olum* record aboriginal histories and describe the arrival of the Europeans through stories about the chiefs and their activities. The number of the symbols also represents the number of days between the spring equinox and autumn equinox of the northern hemisphere summer.[10]

Algonkian Indians were known to have also used pictographs and petroglyphs for communicating with the spirit world or for conveying individual visions and experiences with the spirit world.[11] The petroglyphs incised on birchbark scrolls of the *Midewiwin* or Grand Medicine society are an example of the written spiritual literacy among the Algonkian nations.[12] Other texts represented a Native theory of knowledge which is predicated on the existence of spirits, power, or medicine. Plants, animals, humans, and spirits of the universe communicated in the spirit world as one. Thus, many Micmac petroglyphs illustrate the journeys of Micmacs to the world beyond.

Through the use of symbolic literacy, the Algonkian nations, including the Micmac, achieved a form of written communication and recording which served their social, political, cultural, and spiritual needs. It created a deep and lasting communal bond which affected all aspects of tribal spiritual and secular life. This symbolic epistemology wove together the natural fact of being born into a certain family, a certain language, a spiritual world, and a material world. It created a shared belief of how the world works and what constitutes proper action. The sharing of these common ideals created a collective cognitive experience for tribal societies and tolerance for other societies.

This common cognitive experience was, and remains, the core of tribalism.[13] The tightly bound community of sentiments united by symbolic literacy identified "what ought to be" with "what is," thus denying the experience of moral doubt. All aspects of Micmac life, such as law, religion, and art, expressed the view that the ideal and the reality were at root inseparable. Consistency between past and present was favoured over criticism—the articulation of inconsistency—as Natives sought to discover the universal lessons behind the ideals of a changing world.

A unity of consciousness created by symbolic literacy and dialogue dominated tribal cognitive and spiritual knowledge and extended itself to humans and the material environment. It bonded the people together with a strong worldview and an ideal of the Good in which others participated. This worldview created an extensive, coherent, concrete, and intense moral communion that was perceived as natural instinct among the people and that was able to make the most of the better aspects of human nature while effectively suppressing man's evil side.

In symbolic literacy, reason was the awareness of a highly concrete ideal implicit in the reality of nature. It knew no distinction between *is* and *ought* or between theory and practice. Individual consciousness tended faithfully to reflect the collective culture, and obedience to the spiritual soul was obedience to the tribal society.

Micmacs had no need for authoritative or recorded human opinion since each person determined what was wisdom. Likewise, Micmac society had no need for elite scholars or experts; the most principled and persuasive speakers became leaders of the tribe because they expressed and lived Micmac ideals of the Good.

THE MYTH OF THE ILLITERATE SAVAGE

Most of the aboriginal literacies of America were destroyed or transformed or neglected by Euro-Christian travellers and missionaries. Some of the neglect stemmed from ethnocentrism and from the mistaken belief that Indians were not capable of writing. In 1580, Montaigne spoke of the Tupi-Guarani of Brazil as "so new and infantile, that he is yet to learn his A.B.C."[14] But when Europeans did encounter undeniable evidence of writing, of literacy equivalent to their own, they did their best to eradicate it as if it posed a threat to the Scripture or literacies they brought with them, as for example, in the situation of the Toltec and Mayan parchment or paper books.

The lack of Western knowledge of the continent and its people, the nature of American Indian literacies, and the lack of European understanding of symbolic literacy were also threats to Native culture. The interaction of these factors created the myth that the Natives were illiterate savages who possessed only an oral tradition. This myth justified the need to teach them

European literacy and knowledge. In the creation of the myth, symbolic epistemology, which interacted with and depended upon the oral tradition, was subordinated to the oral traditions. Fragmented from the context of symbolic literacy, the oral traditions lost much of their coherence. The metaphorical language of the travellers' reports emphasized the "bestial" nature of primitive life. Micmac experience with the Christian immigrants slowly fragmented the unity of consciousness of their symbolic system.

The tradition of aboriginal epistemology and symbolic literacy of the Natives were barely noted in the written observations of the Europeans. In 1497, John Cabot's exploration uncovered "fallen trees bearing marks" which caught his attention.[15] In 1652, Father Gabriel Druilletes reported the Algonkian Indians using coal for pen, bark for paper, and writing with peculiar characters. He noted: "They use certain marks, according to their ideas as a local memory to recollect the points, articles, and maxims which they heard."[16] In 1653, Father Bressani reported Indians of New France using "little sticks instead of books, which they sometimes mark with certain signs....By the aid of these they can repeat the names of a hundred or more presents, the decisions adopted in councils and a thousand other particulars."[17] Few of the early travellers understood the significance of the symbolic literacy or its legacy because of the myth of the illiterate savage. However, the operating contradictions of the myth in Micmac society were illustrated in memoirs of Father Pierre Biard, who noted in 1616 that the Micmacs

> have rather a happy disposition, and a fair capacity for judging and valuing material and common things, deducing their reasons with great nicety, and always seasoning them with some pretty comparison. They have a very good memory for material things, such as having seen you before, or the peculiarities of a place where they may have been, or what took place in their presence twenty or thirty years before, etc.; but to learn anything by heart—there's the rock: there is no way of getting a consecutive arrangement of words into their pates. [Y]ou will see these poor barbarians, notwithstanding their great lack of government, power, letters, art and riches, yet holding their head so high they greatly underrate us, regarding themselves as our superior.[18]

The sequential literacies of European aristocratic society, which relied upon a sequential phonetic script of written letters, were alien to the Micmac, who moved in a holistic and implicit world of symbolic literacy and collective dialogue. It has always been difficult for Micmacs to accept the romantic humanitarian image of the righteous immigrant who laboured selflessly for mankind to spread Christianity and culture to the nonliterate Natives. The historical disclosure of the economic and political motives of colonial undertakings, together with recent research by this author, show that the educational and literacy efforts of the colonists among the Micmac sought to justify the removal of the rightful power, wealth, and glory of the Micmac peoples as well as to deprive the Micmacs of their great achievements in knowledge and literacy.[19] Both religious and governmental authorities have manipulated the nature of Micmac society and literacy to the Natives' psychological and economic detriment. The development of the myth of the illiterate savage was instrumental in denying them human dignity, respect, or entitlement to their wealth.

However, neither the myth of the illiterate savage nor the image of the Christian as a moral hero deceived Micmac leaders. Europeans boasted about their homeland and culture and condemned those of the Micmac, but Micmacs rejected their pretence since the conflict between European pretences and conduct was apparent.[20] Critical reflection on secular European thought followed the same wisdom. Micmac society was an affluent and literate society comparable to European society. Micmac life was not "nasty, brutish or short" as it was stereotyped; instead it was comfortable and ecologically stable, with great diversity of food and a steadier balance between humans and the natural environment. Micmac education was a vital part of ecological life; it was not an imagined preparation for the utility of aristocratic society. Everything Micmac youths learned extended their knowledge of the world and guided their ability to fit harmoniously into it. Micmacs had little need for the imported secular thought of aristocratic Europe in their educational system.

Spiritual thought was treated differently by Micmacs since it addressed the paradoxes of the symbolic system. Each family synthesized Catholic teaching into Micmac educational systems. As Micmacs witnessed the puzzling dichotomy between Christian theology and conduct, they attempted to reconcile why the actions of the Christians revealed that which its teaching sought to prevent. As a consequence, the force of theology diminished in tribal society. But the best of the teachings became synthesized into broader aboriginal ideals. At the same time, the myth of the illiterate savage predominated in European thought. It dramatized the world vision and historical sense of colonialization, while ignoring centuries of aboriginal civilization. It justified the transformation of wealth and power through violence and oppression. It became the mythogenesis of Canada.

LITERACY AS COGNITIVE ASSIMILATION

In 1610, Chief Membertou and 140 Micmacs voluntarily entered into a spiritual and political alliance with France in a ceremony which included baptism and a gift of wampum.[21] From that time to the French and English uprising in 1744, French Catholic missionaries lived and worked among Micmacs of eastern Canada, converting them to Catholicism and to a faith which blended well with the Micmacs' tribal spiritual rituals. The missionaries' continued presence among Micmacs also assured the King of France of the Micmacs' continued political and economic alliance. Missionaries learned the Native language, preaching to them about the road to salvation and teaching them the prayers which were to pave that road. The first use of ideographic symbolization for literary purposes is attributed to Father Christian Le Clerq, who in 1677 incorporated the Biblical ideals into the existing symbolic literacy of the Micmac which he called a "formulary." He wrote in his journal:

> Our Lord inspired me with the idea of [characters] the second year of my mission, when being much embarassed as to the method by which I should teach the Micmac Indians to pray to God, I noticed some children were making marks with charcoal upon birchbark, and were counting these with the fingers very accurately at each word of prayers which they pronounced. This made me believe that by giving them some formulary, which would aid their memory by definite characters, I should advance much more quickly than by teaching them through the method of making them repeat a number of times that which I said to them.[22]

Le Clerq reported being very surprised with Micmac facility with the system. He wrote that Micmacs have

> much readiness in understanding this kind of writing that they learn in a single day what they would never have been able to grasp in an entire week without the aid of these leaflets.[23]

By incorporating the Catholic rituals into the existing symbolic literacy and the oral traditions, the Micmac families rapidly diffused this system throughout the nation within the traditional social and cultural contexts. Father taught son, mother taught daughter, and children taught each other. The system involved a design for each word or word phrase and was recorded with charcoal on birchbark leaflets which each family preserved in birchbark boxes bedecked with wampum and porcupine quills.[24] Although Le Clerq reported success in using the characters for the remaining ten years of his mission, little survives of his characters. The scholar William Ganong concluded, however, in his search for the origin of the characters that Le

Clerq used all the aboriginal designs he found and developed new character designs for the new words of prayers.[25]

In 1735, Father Pierre Antoine Maillard began a twenty-seven year mission among Micmacs of Cape Breton Island, during which he expanded hieroglyphic literacy and contributed to the transformation of ideographic literacy to roman script. In the second year of his mission, Maillard reported having discovered an innovative method of using hieroglyphics to teach Micmacs how to pray.[26] Subsequent scholars investigating the origin of Maillard's hieroglyphics have concluded that Maillard was the beneficiary of Le Clerq's work, although the new prayers, chants, and instructions which he composed required almost all new characters.[27]

Unlike Le Clerq, who frequently characterized Micmacs as savages and barbarians incapable of advancing to letter literacy, Maillard perceived them as curious and intelligent people, capable of learning anything they wanted to learn. He was frequently challenged by their enquiring minds. He astutely realized that if Micmacs learned to write French, they would have access to sensitive political and religious literature. Maillard, a political activist in the French and English war, feared that if Micmacs knew how to read and write letters, they would be better able to incite each other through their correspondence, to the detriment of French Catholic interests. Despite the fact that Maillard had developed a roman script for the Micmac language, which he used for his own language and grammar improvement, he chose to teach them only the hieroglyphics. He thus closed letter literacy to Micmacs; he prepared his hieroglyphic literature of prayers, chants and instructions and then appointed catechists among the tribal hierarchy and elders "to see to the religious instruction of children, preside at public prayers on Sundays, administer baptism, receive matrimonial promises, and officiate at funerals."[28]

The similarity of spiritual function between Catholic priests and medicine people ensured the success of collective dialogues among the families. Medicine people had specialized knowledge of reading and writing the sacred symbols on birchbark which for centuries catalogued the proper rituals and chants for various spiritual functions. The priest and his reliance on the Bible was analogous to the Micmac traditions. The apprenticing of young men to the medicine society was a long and rigorous training involving the learning of symbols, chants, and rituals, and the nature of the interaction with the spirit world. As spiritual intermediaries, the medicine people aided tribal members in achieving a personal and direct interaction and communion with the spirits. From these quests came wisdom, knowledge, guidance, and a special place in the world. The Micmacs applied the same process to the priest; they had to learn the tribal language and epistemology from the medicine societies in the traditional manner.

The spiritual foundation of Micmac literacy was also similar to Catholic doctrines. Both systems addressed universal concepts. Catholic teachings of a universal God and his lesson to man affirmed the aboriginal ideals; thus Micmac spiritual culture and sacred view of nature were broadened, not altered, by the Catholic theology. Vision quests were analogous to individual prayer. The Catholic teaching that man was destined to eternal damnation in hell unless he practised a Christian life of faith, ritual, and sacrifice was analogous to tribal beliefs in the need to live up to the great ideals of the Micmacs' symbolic literacy, rituals, and legends and their concept of self-control. Catholic doctrines of love of God and one's fellow man, its prayers for the dead to help him enter the spiritual world, and sacred symbols were all analogous to tribal beliefs and symbols. Micmac society embraced the two spiritual worlds as one, enlarging the rituals but not changing the ideological foundation.

European theology and languages, which were familiar to the tribal worlds of the Micmacs, gave no hint of their latent use as instruments of domination and empire in European thought. The foundations of the idea of language as an instrument of imperialism were inherent and epitomized in the initial contact between Europeans and Micmacs. The justification for the first European grammar, the Spanish *Gramatica* in 1492, was that "language is the *perfect* instrument of Empire."[29] The negative mythical depiction of Micmac society, knowledge and values became the justification for civilizing the Micmac and confiscating their wealth. While operating in the same manner described in other colonial situations, it took several centuries for the English grammar and literacy to become instruments of domination of the Micmac mind.[30]

Despite Maillard's and earlier missionaries' attempts to restrict Micmacs to hieroglyphic literacy, Micmac ingenuity prevailed, and soon the Indians acquainted themselves with yet another mode of communicating with one another: alphabetic scripts. Micmacs had many opportunities to witness new functions and uses of the new system. From as early as Le Clerq's mission in 1675, the Natives were used as couriers of letters to other priests.[31] Similarly, Maillard reported using Micmacs to deliver his letters to military officials. In another context, Maillard prepared transcriptions for the tribal government in his role as interpreter for the English. Aiding in the pacification of Micmacs after 1744 he transcribed the Treaty of 1752 into his Micmac roman script. Maillard sought their approval of the peace plan. As a trusted friend of the Micmac Santewi Mawio'mi, or Grand Council, Maillard presided at the ceremony and read the treaty to the assembled Indians. Through these exchanges, the Micmacs discovered the political significance of expanding their literacy repertoire. Furthermore, they were very impressed with the new mode of writing that enabled them to record the words and thoughts of the writer exactly.[32] Yet, Maillard refused to teach them alphabetic script and further forbade Micmacs from going to local English public schools.[33]

The English government sought literacy and education for Micmacs as the sword of assimilation. A century later, in 1842, the Nova Scotian government passed an act which provided for free tuition for Micmacs attending their schools; however, Micmacs were interested neither in having their children educated by others nor in the functions of English literacy. Government reports beginning in 1843 indicated Micmacs' growing interest in learning to read, although they were strongly adamant to transmit only their own culture through literacy in Micmac. The Micmacs' migratory lifestyle further prevented them from spending much time in school; thus literacy was taught at home by parents.[34]

By the time Reverend Silas Tertius Rand arrived among the Micmacs in 1845, they had already learned the fundamentals of how to read and write Micmac in the French roman script. In 1850, Rand reported Micmacs were in the constant habit of writing to one another in a script resembling English but sounding like French. Their only preserved literature was written in hieroglyphic characters.[35] Rand, a master of a dozen languages, believed in the power of reason achieved through literacy and Bible reading. He frequently criticized the French priests who, in seeking to prevent Micmacs from learning how to read and write letters, forbade them to go to school.[36] He wrote:

> Had their language been reduced to writing in the ordinary way, the Indians would have learned the use of writing and reading, and would have advanced in knowledge so as to be able to cope with their more enlightened invaders; and it would have been a more difficult matter for the latter to cheat them out of their lands and other rightful possessions.[37]

Rand's goals were to teach all Micmacs how to read and write, in a new script of his devising, and to develop literature for them to read. Finding no Micmacs willing to work with a Protestant minister, he relied upon a Frenchman, Joe Ruisseaux Brooks, who had lived among Micmacs most of his life and was fluent in Micmac as well as English and French. Rand's new Micmac roman script was based on English script and phonemes, using several diacritics to represent the unique Micmac sounds.

Hoping to show Micmacs the contradictions in Catholic dogma, Rand translated several sections from the Bible into Micmac and developed a Micmac dictionary and reading book. However, despite the courtesy Micmacs extended to Rand, neither he nor the Canadian government were able to dissuade Micmacs from their traditional habits and Catholic beliefs. Repeated governmental attempts to introduce Protestantism, Bible reading, and formal schooling into Micmac tribal society failed. But despite their refusal to accept the Protestant literature, Micmac literacy skills continued to grow through Rand's influence. Rand reported being pleased with the number of Micmacs who had learned to read.[38]

Micmacs became consumers of English- and colonial-made goods and vices, partly to convince the British that they were not different from them and they therefore need not be feared or oppressed. But the Micmac never cognitively assimilated English knowledge or values. They did not forget the tribal knowledge, history, or language, nor did they change their tribal rituals or lifestyle. Micmac society continually rejected the English language, the Protestant worldview, and its individualist society as demonic in nature. They believed that British society rested on the Protestant legacy of a losing fight against evil. Historical experience had confirmed this insight among Micmac people. The Micmac families fervently maintained their symbolic system, including the adopted Catholic teachings, and retained their traditional intellectual independence from European thought. Although the Micmac considered Reverend Rand as a threat to their faith, they admired his translation of the Gospel of Matthew and his First Reading Book in Micmac. When a Catholic priest demanded the burning of the Protestant books, the Natives refused.[39]

Experience had taught the Micmac that assimilation to colonial life did not advance their interest. The colonist in Canada would not permit them to acquire any of their confiscated wealth or enforce their legal rights. Despite numerous petitions to the Queen, the Governor General, and the Legislative Assemblies, the colonial system denied equal rights or opportunity for Micmacs. The Micmacs' civilized efforts to use roman script to petition the legal authorities to return their wealth were met with disdain and neglect.

The appearance in 1894 of Father Pacifique Buisson, better known as Father Pacifique, revived among Micmacs the religious rituals and traditions earlier established by Father Maillard. These religious rituals fostered the continued development of literacy, using the hieroglyphic literature of Father Maillard, and promoted the growth of letter literacy using Pacifique's new Catholic literature. Pacifique studied the various available Micmac publications and manuscripts, such as those of Maillard and Rand, before preparing his own script. Finding Maillard's script deficient in some respects, he modified it, adding capitals and punctuation and simplified the script to thirteen letters. Then he prepared a reading literature for it. Some contemporary commentators have maintained that Pacifique was responsible for spreading phonetic literacy among Micmacs;[40] however, Pacifique acknowledged that phonetic literacy was commonplace among Micmacs prior to his mission. He wrote: "They almost all know how to read and write in their own fashion. They teach each other from father to son long before they had schools."[41]

As mission priest for the annual Chapel Island mission, Father Pacifique noted the reverence and commitment of Micmacs to Maillard's literature and reinforced the already existing literacy traditions. In 1913, he published a catechism in his own modified script. In 1920 he reprinted the hieroglyphic prayers that had been printed in Vienna through the efforts of Father Kauder in 1866. The successes of the Christian literature among Micmacs suggested the need among missionaries to learn Micmac language and grammar. Thus in 1939, Father Pacifique had a Micmac grammar book published. The script was diffused directly through families as it had been in the past. In some communities, religious orders introduced Micmac literacy in the band schools, teaching them the fundamentals of the Catholic doctrines.[42]

ENGLISH LANGUAGE EDUCATION AS COGNITIVE IMPERIALISM

Micmac literacy was at its height in 1920 when Canadian governmental policy instituted English language in all Indian day schools and compulsory schooling for all Indian children from the ages of six to sixteen years. Both the Nova Scotia government and the federal government had found that their efforts from 1800 to 1920 to attract Micmacs to the White man's habits and to domesticated farming had been repeatedly rejected in favour of symbolic literacy and a traditional lifestyle.

By the early 1900's, however, the increasing public use of English among the Micmacs began to affect their language repertoire. In Prince Edward Island and Nova Scotia, the Micmacs were quickly adding English to their oral traditions. In 1914, 62 per cent were fluent in English; in 1915, 71 per cent; and in 1916, 82 per cent, while less than 1 per cent were fluent in French.[43] The ability to write English was also growing but at a much reduced rate: in 1914, 27 per cent of the population could write English; by 1915, it increased to 32 per cent; in 1916, 38 per cent could write English, while less than a handful could write French.[44]

Through the *Indian Act* of 1920, the Canadian parliament expanded its control over Indian lands and people by legislating regulatory provisions for Indian affairs. The administration of all schools for Indians was assumed by the Department of Indian Affairs, although some schools continued to be staffed by religious orders. In some communities, religious orders introduced Micmac literacy in the reserve day schools, using Pacifique's system for teaching the fundamentals of Catholic doctrines.[45] However, the Canadian government considered these schools ineffective.[46] "Effectiveness" of Indian schools was determined by their ability to transform the Indian. The commissioner of Indian affairs stated that the goal of federal education for Indians was "to give the rising generation of Indians such training as will make them loyal citizens of Canada and enable them to compete with their white neighbors."[47]

In 1930, the opening of residential boarding schools and the increased age for compulsory schooling to eighteen years led to a gradual decline in Micmac literacy. Although schools continued to be operated by the Catholic Church, the provincial curricula adopted in 1932 emphasized domestic tasks and farming.[48] But the schools failed to live up to their goals. Beginning with 286 students in 1930, only 158 students remained by 1935.[49] This was the lowest number of Micmac students in Nova Scotia since 1889, when 157 Micmacs were in school.[50]

The Shubenacadie residential school in Nova Scotia became a nightmare which continued into the middle of the 1950's. Micmac youths were forcibly taken to the boarding schools and, through strict discipline, corporal punishment, and rigid rules, were required to use only English in and out of school.[51] Children were not allowed to see their parents, and no letters or presents from parents were given to the children. Some children stayed in the school several years before being allowed home. Infractions of school rules sent children to isolation in darkened closets.[52] Perhaps the most traumatic effect of the residential school was not its language restriction but its destruction of the tribal family cohesion and its replacement with peer group allegiance.

After the Second World War, Canadian policies concentrated on creating individual Indians by further destroying Micmac family life. The federal government attempted to relocate the entire Micmac population from their ancestral homes in Nova Scotia to two centralized locations, Shubenacadie and Eskasoni. Promising houses, jobs, medical care, welfare, and other social services, the federal government began their relocation programme in the 1940's. In a further effort to dissolve the family base, government policy held that any Micmacs holding jobs off the reserves were "disenfranchised," thus destroying their right to live among other Micmacs. In the new central-ized location, Micmacs attended Indian day school staffed by nuns. English language policy was strictly enforced. After reaching the eighth grade, the Micmac males and females were separated from their parents and each other and sent to private Catholic schools in other provinces.

The implicit goal of federal education was the annihilation of Micmac history, knowledge, language, and collective habits, thereby making Micmac youths believe that Anglo-Canadian society was culturally and technically superior to Micmac society. Catholic residential day schools based their curriculum on teaching Micmacs to reject their traditional cultural ways in favour of the life of the individual in the dominant Canadian society. Inherent in this policy was the destruction of tribal identity and values along with the tribal soul. This educational process is called cognitive imperialism, the last stage of imperialism wherein the imperialist seeks to whitewash the tribal mind and soul and to create doubt.

Education became the tool of cognitive manipulation, used to disclaim tribal knowledge and values while validating the confiscation of tribal wealth to comfort the usurper's Christian conscience. Through false assumptions and interpretations of their history and purpose, Micmac students were led to accept their poverty and impotence as resulting from their cultural and racial status. The modern solution to their despair was described in terms of logical analysis and causal entailment, with the overriding burden being their being Micmac.

The displacement of a tribal worldview was justified by governmental interests. The gift of modern knowledge has been labeled the "banking" concept.[53] It views the students' minds as "containers" to be filled by teachers, thus allowing the imposition of one worldview over another, sometimes with a velvet glove. Knowledge is considered as

> a gift bestowed by those who consider themselves knowledgeable upon those who they consider to know nothing. Projecting an absolute igno-rance onto others, a characteristic of the ideology of oppression, negates education and knowledge as processes of inquiry. The teacher presents himself to his students as their necessary opposite; by considering their ignorance absolute, he justifies his own existence....Indeed, the interests of the oppressors lie in 'changing the consciousness of the oppressed, not the situation which oppresses them.'[54]

Into the late 1960's, federal policy continued its destruction of tribal language and culture. A survey of Canadian Indians in 1967 summarized the national policy of the federal government:

> As we have emphasized, the general aim of the federal government's present policy is based on the necessity of integrating Indians into Canadian society. Education is considered the principle means of achiev-ing this aim. The secondary aims are to provide Indians with a degree of economic and social welfare equivalent to that of non-Indians and to provide them with the knowledge which they will need to live ade-quately within their environment.[55]

No respect was accorded the Native languages or culture and the use of the Micmac language became a badge of servitude in Canadian society. Federal education, as the tool of cognitive imperialism, rejected Micmac knowledge, history, spirituality, culture, and language in their mission to create a Canadian individual. Justified by the myth of the illiterate savage, Canadian educators divided ideas, reordered events, and wrote fictitious accounts of past events.

The disruption of family socialization, along with the loss of their traditional land base with the government's centralization policy and the disenfranchisement policy, signalled the near demise of Micmac literacy. In 1969, the federal government proposed a final plan of assimilation and termination of Indian tribes. This White Paper was overwhelmingly rejected by Indian people throughout Canada. An alternate proposal by Indian leaders insisted upon the government developing a more positive and central role for language and culture in federal Indian programmes. The federal government responded by withholding the White Paper and entering into consultations with Indian bands and other tribal leaders.

The 1971 Subcommittee on Indian Education for the Standing Committee on Indian Affairs and Northern Development found that federal, provincial, and church schools alike had failed to educate Indian children.[56] Their report laid the foundation for Indian control of education, but while these efforts have ended some of the drastic unilateral measures of the DIA, no real Indian control exists in education.[57]

REVIVAL OF A FRAGMENTED MICMAC LANGUAGE

The initiation of Cultural Education Centres was the federal government's antidote to their attempts at destroying the cultural base. Based on the French language model of Quebec, Native Cultural Centres were established to support Native communities' efforts at developing culturally responsive educational materials. Eleven Micmac Cultural Centres were funded, each having its own priorities, needs and resources, but all were interested in preserving some aspects of the Micmac language and culture.

Research in the Micmac language occupied many of the Cultural Centres' initial efforts to find, collect, and adapt available materials to classroom learning. The existence of several writing systems, each considered linguistically deficient, led to community debates among Micmac Centres and among language specialists as to the best writing script in which to prepare educational materials. The major issue was whether it was better to promote literacy in the traditional orthography of Father Pacifique, despite its limitations, or to develop a fundamentally new writing script founded on current knowledge of linguistic principles.

In 1974, the Micmac Association of Cultural Studies, serving the Nova Scotia Micmac communities, developed their own script with the help of

Native and non-Native linguists. The system was initially met with resistance. Many elders feared the loss of the literacy traditions established by Pacifique and thus the loss of important cultural and spiritual traditions. When the Micmac Association of Cultural Studies finally brought the script to the Grand Council, explaining the merits of their system and seeking their acceptance, some Micmac communities adopted the script for their centres.

In some Micmac communities where loyalty to the Pacifique script was strong, modifications to it were sought. Mildred Millea, an energetic mother of eleven children and fluent Native speaker, began her linguistic and educational work without materials, except a language master reading machine and the prayer book from which her mother taught her to read. Without formal linguistic training, she launched a new modified Pacifique script and prepared Micmac language materials for the classroom. With as many conflicting views as there were linguists working on Micmac writing, Millea resolved to continue modifications of the Pacifique orthography until the issues were resolved.[58] Millea's work and her popularity as a teacher became well known among Micmac communities in New Brunswick and Nova Scotia. She was frequently recruited to conduct workshops and courses teaching others her new modified script.

In Micmac communities in Newfoundland and Quebec, other modifications of existing scripts prevailed. However, with most of the communities' efforts put into teaching uses for the new script, little progress was being made in materials development. By the beginning of the 1980's, four different roman scripts existed, each having its proponents. Because each programme had its script preference and had operated independently, duplication of efforts and lack of resource sharing has resulted in a general lack of sequential literacy materials among all groups and a lack of consensus over which script to use for educational purposes. Meanwhile, through 1979, high dropout rates and recidivism continued to characterize Indian education.[59]

The Charter of Rights and Freedoms in the *Constitution Act, 1982,* affirmed the rights of minority children to be educated in their own language. The charter cannot be interpreted so as to limit any of the aboriginal or treaty rights of Canada's Native peoples (section 25) and must be interpreted in a manner consistent with the preservation and enhancement of the multicultural heritage of Canadians (section 27). Thus, guarantees were affirmed of "customary right or privilege" acquired or enjoyed before the charter, especially for aboriginal people (section 22). While no new funding has been provided by Parliament for implementation, the guarantee of customary language rights of the aboriginal peoples is an important affirmation to help the Micmac people "preserve their culture and identity, their customs, tradition and languages."[60]

CONCLUSION

Carl Jung pointed out that the acquisition of human consciousness is a very recent and fragile experiment which has not achieved any reasonable degree of continuity and remains vulnerable to the fragmentation of the soul and mind.[61] He further asserted that the ability to fragment consciousness to concentrate on one thing cannot exclude the rest of consciousness—any more than an auto that disappears around the corner has vanished into thin air. Rather, the other realms of consciousness can arise from the repressed realms to influence our mind and our clarity.[62] Western sequential literacy has not erased Native symbolic literacy and consciousness, which has been developed over millennia. Symbolic literacy still affects the Micmac mind, soul, and conduct.

Just as symbolic literacy continues, so have coercive methods of cultural and cognitive assimilation continued in Western liberal education and literacy. Despite good intentions, the seemingly innocuous textbooks continue the mythical portrait of Micmacs and their society, when mentioned at all. Canadian history remains a fictitious history, a by-product of nineteenth-century European society, and the Micmacs and other tribal nations are merely bystanders in the flow and flux of European and Canadian history. Stripped of their wealth, Micmacs in eastern Canada carry the burden of history and modern economics while myths continue to erode their culture, language, and tribal identity. Micmac knowledge and tribal values receive barely a mention in new history texts. Micmac language is the least valued by educators despite the fact it sustains the feeling, emotions, and dreams of most Micmac youth and preserves the ancient ancestry. This psychological and cultural regime is substantially the same in provincial, federal, and most band-controlled schools.

The resiliency of early Algonkian literacy processes in Micmac consciousness has demonstrated that any system can function as long as the people value it and have use for it. The aboriginal forms of literacy served a function for Algonkian society: universal symbols represented concepts and ideas, and its legitimacy for contemporary tribal society has not been replaced. Rather, missionary and governmental education have attempted to assimilate Micmacs to the functions of cultural transmission of and adaptation to Canadian society. A contemporary assessment of Micmac education suggests the need for the continued development of traditional and contemporary functions of literacy and knowledge. Although the forms of literacy to which the Micmacs have been exposed have been intrinsically different, the symbolic literacy and its consciousness have persisted. Micmac literacy remains spiritual and family-based, rather than public. It continues to favour collective dialogue and ritual.

All forms of European literacy have been used to serve spiritual, cultural, and social needs of Micmacs, being maintained by tribal families for spiritual, secular, and personal needs of the people. Informal, supportive, but rigorous instructional contexts have characterized Micmac literacy. Micmac families have demonstrated that their culture and language provide strong bases of knowledge and methods of successful teaching.

Coercive methods of cultural assimilation through education and literacy must now be replaced with a Micmac education of cultural transmission and development of cultural adaptive strategies founded upon a choice of systems and knowledge. Bilingual, bicultural education must be the foundation upon which different knowledge bases and cultural processes are met with respect and chosen according to family preference.

NOTES TO CHAPTER TWO

1. Harvey Graff, "The Literacy Myth: Literacy and Social Structure in the Nineteenth Century" (Ph.D. diss., University of Toronto, 1979).
2. John Oxenham, *Literacy: Writing, Reading and Social Organization* (London: Routledge and Kegan Paul, 1981).
3. Sam and Joann Dauzat, "Literacy: In Quest of a Definition," *Convergence* 10, no. 1 (1977): 341; and Shirley Brice Heath, "Protean Shapes in Literacy Events: Evershifting Oral and Literate Functions," in *Spoken and Written Language: Exploring Orality and Literacy*, ed. Deborah Tannen (Norwood, New Jersey: Ablex Publishing, 1982), 91-117.
4. Michael Cole and Sylvia Scribner, "Literacy without Schooling: Testing for Intellectual Effects," *Harvard Educational Review* 40, no. 4 (1978): 448-61; and J.R. Clammer, *Literacy and Social Change* (Leiden: E.J. Brill, 1976).
5. Paul Copperman, *The Literacy Hoax* (New York: William Morrow and Company, 1978).
6. Bernard Spolsky, Guillermina Englebrecht, and Leroy Ortiz, *The Sociolinguistics of Literacy: An Historical and Comparative Study of Five Cases*, Final Report on Grant #NIE-G-79-0179 (Washington: National Institute of Education, 1982); Willard Walker, "Notes on Native Writing Systems and the Design of Native Literacy Programs," *Anthropological Linguistics* 2, no. 5 (1969); and Willard Walker, "Native American Writing Systems," in *Language in the U.S.A.*, ed. Charles Ferguson and Shirley Brice Heath (Cambridge: Cambridge University Press, 1981).
7. Graff, *The Literacy Myth*.
8. E.T. Hall, *The Silent Language* (New York: Doubleday, 1959).
9. D.G. Brinton, *The Lenape and Their Legends with the Complete Text and Symbols of the Walam Olum* (New York: AMS Press, 1884/1969), 217.
10. C.S. Rafinesque, *The American Nations* (Philadelphia, 1836); Brinton, *The Lenape and Their Legends*, 172-77.
11. Marion Robertson, *Rock Drawings of the Micmac Indians* (Halifax: Nova Scotia Museum, 1973).
12. Mircea Eliade, *Shamanism: Archaic Techniques of Ecstasy* (Princeton: Princeton University Press; 1964), 314ff.; see also Norman Feder, *American Indian Art* (New York: Abrahams, 1965), item 218, for an illustration of a section of the *Midewiwin* birchbark text of an initiation into the society. The illustration describes a certain stage or house, the knowledge totem, and how to set up and perform the ritual.
13. Roberto Mangabeira Unger, *Law in Modern Society* (New York: Free Press, 1976).
14. Montaigne, *Essayes*, Florio's translation, vol. 3 (Paris, 1580), 141.
15. *Collections and Proceedings*, Second Series, vol. 8 (Portland: Maine Historical Society, 1897).
16. William Ganong, ed. and trans., *New Relations of Gaspesia* (Toronto: The Champlain Society, 1910), 22.
17. Ibid., 23.
18. Reuben Gold Thwaites, ed., *The Jesuit Relations and Allied Documents*, vol. 3 (Cleveland, 1897), 73-74.
19. Martin Carnoy, *Education as Cultural Imperialism* (New York: Daniel MacKay, 1974); Paulo Freire, *Pedagogy of the Oppressed* (New York: Herder and Herder, 1971); Albert Memmi, *The Colonizer and the Colonized* (Boston: Beacon Press, 1965); and Marie Ann Battiste, "An Historical Investigation of the Social and Cultural Consequences of Micmac Literacy" (Ed.D. Diss., Stanford University, 1984).
20. Thwaites, *Jesuit Relations*, vol. 3; R.S. Mealing, *The Jesuit Relations and Allied Documents* (Toronto: McClelland and Stewart, 1963), 29-30.
21. For an exact replica of this wampum belt, see Plate 1 in David I. Bushnell, "Native Cemeteries and Forms of Burial East of the Mississippi" (Washington, D.C.: Bureau of Ethnology, Bulletin 71, 1920).

22. Ganong, *New Relations of Gaspesia*, 131.
23. Ibid., 126.
24. Frank Speck, *The Double Curve Motive in Northeastern Algonkian Art*, Memoir 42 (Ottawa: Government Printing Office, 1914); Frank Speck, "Wampum in Indian Tradition and Currency," *Proceedings of the Numismatic and Antiquarian Society of Philadelphia* 36 (1916): 121-30; and Frank Speck, "The Functions of Wampum among the Eastern Algonkian," *American Anthropologist* 4, no. 1 (1919).
25. Ganong, *New Relations of Gaspesia*.
26. Antoine Pierre Maillard, "Lettre de M. L'Abbé Maillard sur les Missions de l'Acadie et Particulièrement sur les Missions Micmaques," *Soirées Canadiennes* 3 (1963): 291-426.
27. Ganong, *New Relations of Gaspesia*; J.G. Shea, "Micmac or Recollect Hieroglyphics," *Historical Magazine* 10 (1861): 289-92; and John Hewson, "Micmac Hieroglyphics in Newfoundland," in *Language in Newfoundland and Labrador*, Preliminary Version, ed. H.J. Paddock (St. John's: Memorial University, 1977).
28. A.A. Johnston, *A History of the Catholic Church in Eastern Nova Scotia II*, (Antigonish, N.S.: Francis Xavier University, 1960).
29. J.B. Trend, *The Civilization of Spain* (London, 1944), 88.
30. Memmi, *The Colonizer and the Colonized*, 79-89.
31. Ganong, *New Relations of Gaspesia*.
32. Maillard, "Lettre de M. L'Abbé Maillard."
33. Henry Koren, *Knaves or Knights: A History of the Spiritan Missionaries in Acadia and North America 1732-1839*, (Pittsburgh: Duquesne University Press, 1962).
34. Department of Indian Affairs [DIA], *Annual Reports* [AR], 1843-73.
35. Silas Tertius Rand, *Micmac Tribe of Indians* (Halifax: James Bowes & Sons, 1850).
36. Koren, *Knaves or Knights*.
37. Silas Tertius Rand, *A Short Statement of the Facts Relating to the History, Manners, Customs, Language, and Literature of the Micmac Tribe of Indians in Nova Scotia and Prince Edward Island* (Halifax, 1849), 226.
38. Silas Tertius Rand, *A Short Statement of the Lord's Work among the Micmac Indians* (Halifax: W. MacNab, 1873).
39. Silas Tertius Rand, *A Brief Statement Concerning the Micmac Mission* (Halifax, 1880), 21.
40. Viviane Gray, "A Visit with Mildred Millea of Big Cove, New Brunswick," *Tawow* 2 (1976): 47.
41. R.P. Pacifique, *Quelques Traits Caractéristiques de la Tribu des Micmacs* (Quebec: Congrés International des Américanistes, 1907).
42. Phillip Bock, *The Micmac Indians of Restigouche*, Bulletin No. 213, Anthropological Series 77 (Ottawa: National Museum of Manitoba, 1966).
43. DIA, *AR*, 1914-16.
44. Ibid.
45. Bock, *The Micmac Indians of Restigouche*.
46. DIA, *AR*, 1927.
47. Ibid., 1918, 23.
48. Ibid., 1932, 1934.
49. Ibid., 1931-35.
50. Ibid., 1902.
51. "The Shubenagadie Residential School," *Micmac News*, August 1978.
52. Ibid., September 1978.
53. Freire, *Pedagogy of the Oppressed*.
54. Ibid., 58-62.
55. H.B. Hawthorn, et al., *A Survey of the Contemporary Indians of Canada* (Ottawa: Information Canada, 1967).
56. *Subcommittee on Indian Education* (Ottawa: DIA, 1971).
57. *Indian Self-Government in Canada*, Report of the Special Committee to the House of Commons (Ottawa: 1983), 23.
58. Milfred Millea, personal communication with author, June 1981.

59. *Survey of Indian Education 1971-1979*, Union of Nova Scotia Indians (Dalhousie University: School of Public Affairs, 1979).
60. *The Constitution and You* (Ottawa, 1982), 28.
61. Carl J. Jung, *Man and His Symbols* (London: Aldus Books, 1964).
62. Ibid., 17-26.

3

Education for Francization: The Case of New France in the Seventeenth Century

Cornelius J. Jaenen

As part of the efforts of the Bourbon bureaucracy and the Gallican church to build a viable French and Christian colony in North America in the seventeenth century, without at the same time "depopulating the mother country" or spending vast sums of money which could bring better returns if invested elsewhere, the education of Amerindian children was promoted with a view to "francizing" them and eventually assimilating them to the small French expatriate nucleus. The missionaries and religious women (including nursing and teaching nuns) and a few pious lay persons were assigned the task of achieving what proved to be almost unattainable objectives, namely, to convert and acculturate, Christianize and francize Algonkian and Iroquoian children.

THE CONCEPT OF FRANCIZATION

The concept of francization appears in an English dictionary as a verb meaning "to make French; to affect with French characteristics, as in manners, tastes, and expression."[1] A primary objective of French civil and religious contact with the Native peoples of North America was to incorporate them into New France and to convert and civilize them, concepts which again were founded on the conviction that they were without any religion, or pagans, or even devil worshippers, and on the conviction that they were brute savages, or barbarians. The Duc de Montmorency instructed Sieur de Monts in 1603 that his duty in Acadia was

> to seek to lead the nations thereof to the profession of the Christian faith, to civility of manners, an ordered life, practice and intercourse with the French for the gain of their commerce; and finally their recognition of and submission to the authority and domination of the Crown of France.[2]

The French would encourage a process of assimilation of the Amerindians until they would qualify for the seventeenth century equivalent of enfranchisement as described in article XVII of the Charter of the Company of New France (1627) which stipulated that

> the descendants of Frenchmen who will take up residence in the said country, together with the Natives who will have been brought to a knowledge of the Faith and will make profession thereof, will be supposed and reputed to be natural born Frenchmen, and as such will be allowed to come to live in France when it shall seem good to them, and to there acquire, negotiate, inherit and accept donations and bequests, just as the true subjects and original French, without being required to take out any letters of declaration or of naturalization.[3]

Francization, according to the company charter just cited, was evidenced by conversion to and practice of Catholicism, the King's religion. André Thévet had expressed the hope in the sixteenth century that once Native peoples had had more contact with Christians, "they will learn little by little to put off this brutishness to put on more civil and humane ways."[4] It was also made evident through the assumption of European manners and ways as seen in dress, deportment, habits, and so forth. The early Récollet missionaries kept insisting that they must "endeavour to make them men before we go about to make them Christians." Father Hennepin, a Récollet who had worked in the upper country, observed:

> Now in order to civilize them, 'tis necessary that the Europeans should mix with them, and that they should dwell together, which can never be done for certain till the Colonies are augmented....Yet before this be done, there's no way to convert these Unbelievers.[5]

Champlain assumed that through close contact with French colonists and "with the French language they may also acquire a French heart and spirit."[6] The outstanding evidence of their francization, apart from the adoption of

Catholicism, was the adoption by nomadic hunting, fishing and food-gathering bands of a sedentary, agricultural way of life. As Hennepin said, "But chiefly it should be endevour'd to fix the Barbarians to a certain dwelling Place, and introduce our Customs and Laws amongst them, further'd by the Assistance of zealous People in Europe, Colleges might be founded to breed up young Savages in the Christian Faith, which might in turn contribute very much to the Conversion of their Countrymen."[7] Thus francization seemed to mean conversion to Catholicism, adoption of sedentary agricultural or artisanal life, adoption of European manners, customs, laws and habits, and use of the French language in daily intercourse.

Francization was strongly supported in the early period of colonial exploitation for a number of nonreligious reasons as well. There was a desire to impose a cultural unity on the empire, to blend together not only the colonists from the various regions and provinces of Old France but also to blend in the Native peoples. Royal instructions issued in 1671 said:

> Always strive by all manner of means to encourage all the clergy and nuns who are in the aformentioned country to raise among them the largest possible number of the said children in order that through instruction in the matters of our religion and in our ways they might compose with the inhabitants of Canada a single people and by that means also fortify the colony.[8]

This was particularly attractive to the first minister of marine and colonies, Jean-Baptiste Colbert, who feared large scale emigration from France. Such a populationist view obviously encouraged the rapid assimilation of Amerindians to avoid metropolitan depopulation and to stimulate colonial demographic growth. Native peoples were to enter the French social scale at the lowest rung of the ladder, that is, as the equivalent of peasants. Francization was also seen as a vigorous means of promoting the Catholic work ethic. Intendant Jean Talon was instructed in 1665 to introduce manual labour early in the education of the Native youth because, according to Louis XIV's information, laziness in the children was the cause of most adult traits of weakness, and he had heard that the Amerindian men were particularly lazy.[9]

The educational programme designed to francize the Amerindian youth can be considered in four different aspects or phases. First of all, there was the attempt to educate the children in the mission field as a means of reaching the older generation and rearing up a generation of converts who would eventually rise to positions of influence in the band or tribe. Essentially, this was a programme of education for the conversion of families and, in the long run, of the creation of a Catholic community which would facilitate mass conversion. Secondly, there was the attempt to educate an elite, which would serve as Native examples and instructors, by sending chosen candidates to France. Thirdly, there was an attempt to educate the youth in the controlled atmosphere of the reserves under the guidance of the missionaries and converted Native chiefs and *dogiques* or catechists. Finally, there was the attempt to francize both girls and boys in the socially controlled atmosphere of the boarding schools. Examples of each of these approaches will serve to elucidate both the rationale and the strategies of such education.

PHASE ONE: EDUCATION OF CHILDREN IN THE MISSION FIELD

Education of the children in the mission field was attempted by all the missionaries. The Récollets made valiant attempts to instruct the young Hurons near the shores of Georgian Bay between 1615 and 1625 but met with little success. They also established a school for Cayuga youth near Fort Frontenac in the 1670's, but Father Hennepin reported (1679) that there was little hope of francizing them "till they be subdu'd by the Europeans, and that their children have another sort of Education." Nevertheless, when the Récollets left, these Iroquois "together with their Children, whom we had taught to read and write" lamented their departure.[10]

The secular Sulpician priests undertook to educate Native children at their mission at Quinté, but they were too embarrassed to admit upon receipt of Colbert's personal gift of 1,000 livres in 1677 for the education of these Iroquoian children that they no longer had any who came to them for instruction.[11] The Capuchins had operated a school for Micmac children at their mission station at La Hève in Acadia as early as 1632.[12]

The Jesuits as the chief missioners attempted to instruct the children among the nomadic Algonkian bands of Montagnais, Micmac, and Algonkins as well as among the sedentary horticultural Huron and Iroquois confederacies. The "wandering tribes" presented the greatest challenge, and the evangelists soon gave up sequential instruction. Among the settled village tribes, a much more sustained effort to bring about conversion of whole communities through instruction of the youth was attempted.

Father Jean Pierron, who laboured among the Mohawk, has left us a valuable account of a device he employed with great success to instruct Iroquoian children. He had already discovered that brightly coloured images were invaluable as instructional aids because, as he observed, "one must begin by touching their hearts, before he can convince their minds." Fear-inspiring images of the torments of hell and purgatory were useful tools in overthrowing what appeared to be Satanic domination. He had used "mildness and force, threats and prayers" to instruct and convert.

I had accordingly applied myself, for the space of a month, to the teaching of both of these (reading and writing) to the little children of the Iroquois; and some had already profited to such an extent that they wrote and read fairly well. But the small means that I have for furnishing rewards for the little ones,—which must be given to these children, in order to hold them to this pursuit—and the little time that remained to me for the essential duties of my Misson, at least obliged me to think of some other expedient, which should not be less efficacious.[13]

He devised a game to capture their attention and induce them to sustained effort because, he said, "gaming constitutes their whole occupation" and damnation, and so he would use it to instruct them and save their souls. This game was made up of emblems to represent the sacraments, the virtues, the commandments, the chief sins, and so forth, and was called "Point to Point" because it took the player "from the point of birth to the point of Eternity." It was more than a pastime, and even his students recognized this: "all our Savages have an extreme passion for learning it and playing it,—either because they display in it quickness in easily understanding things that are so difficult; or because they see clearly that this game instructs them, without difficulty, in what they must know in order to be saved."[14] Pierron sent his New World teaching aid to the mother country with the comment that "perhaps the Missionaries of France should use it with excellent results among the country people" there.

Nevertheless, Father Paul Le Jeune confided that this plan of action had failed:

> Father Lallemant begins to appreciate my reasons, for I assured him that we could not retain the little Savages, if they be not removed from their native country, or if they have not some companions who help them to remain of their own free will...when the savages were encamped near us, our children no longer belonged to us, we dared say nothing.[15]

Le Jeune wrote that "when we first came into these countries, as we hoped for scarcely anything from the old trees, we employed all our forces in cultivating the young plants; but, as the Lord gave us the adults, we are turning the great outlay we made for the children to the succor of their fathers and mothers....we still retain with us, however, some little abandoned orphans."[16] This conviction came at a time when nuns—Ursulines and two orders of Hospital Nuns—arrived in the colony. Le Jeune observed that the missionaries could continue to move into the far interior "where the sisters have no access," so the religious women could devote themselves to what he called "seminaries." The general conclusion of all the missionaries was that instruction of Amerindian children at the mission stations bore little fruit, and therefore it soon ceased to be a priority.

PHASE TWO: EDUCATION OF A NATIVE ELITE IN FRANCE

The Capuchins working in Brazil and Guiana had started sending young boys to France to be educated there in order to form a Native elite which on its return to America would help in the evangelization and francization of the tribal peoples. The same practice was adopted in Acadia and Canada with a view to training teachers and catechists, if not Native priests. Some young girls were also sent to France to be trained as teaching sisters. A case study will indicate both the motivations and the degree of success of such an undertaking.

In 1618, the Récollets had two boys who were "brought to France, baptized and put in boarding at the college of Calleville," one of whom was described as being "very well educated."[17] Two years later, they sent a Montagnais lad named Pastedechouan to France for five years of studies in French and Latin. When he returned to his native country he had forgotten much of his Montagnais tongue and had missed all the instruction in woodcraft, hunting, fishing, and so forth, necessary to survival among his own people. The Jesuits took him under their wing, had him instructed in his Montagnais tongue, and employed him for a brief period as a language teacher. He was a "lost soul" caught between two cultural worlds, in neither of which he felt at home. The *Relations* commented that "this poor wretch has become a barbarian like the others"; in fact, he had become an alcoholic, would enter into at least five unsuccessful marriages, and was a complete misfit among those the missionaries referred to as the "barbarians." It was reported that he had finally starved to death in the northern forests—a further indication of his inability to fit back into a traditional way of life.[18]

The Jesuits continued the Récollet policy for a few years. Father Paul Le Jeune informed the Provincial in Paris that it seemed to be the only practical approach at the time:

As to the children of the Savages in this country, there will be some trouble in keeping them [in schools]; I see no other way than that which Your Reverence suggests of sending a child every year to France. Having been there two years, he will return with a knowledge of the language, and having already become accustomed to our ways, he will not leave us and will retain his little countrymen.[19]

Would the Amerindians co-operate with such a plan? They were accustomed to offering some of their children, whom they loved dearly, as "presents" to friends and allies when sealing trading arrangements and military alliances. This custom seemed to have been confirmed in 1610 when Champlain sent a young Frenchman to live among chief Iroquet's people; in return, a Huron lad named Savignon accompanied Champlain to France. It is possible that the "giving" of children for a couple years to be educated abroad was understood in the same context by the Amerindian parents. When the Jesuits returned to Quebec in 1633, after a forced absence of four years, among the young men they instructed was one Sasousmay, who pleaded, "Take me to France to be instructed, otherwise thou wilt be responsible for my soul."[20] But not all were agreeable to having their children sent overseas. Of one young girl it was reported that "her father gave her to us only for two years on condition that she should not go to France."[21] No doubt, it was noted that only a small number of those who took this trans-Atlantic journey ever returned in good health; many died in France, even during the brief period spent there.

Of the few girls who were sent to France, some, like Brazilian girls in the previous century, were directed to the cloistered Carmelites. Two were baptized in the great convent of the Carmelites in Paris on 5 January 1637, and one survived to return to Canada.[22] In the fall of 1636, the ships returning to France took along an Iroquois woman, a little boy, and three little Montagnais girls. The Jesuit *Relations* informs us that "only two of them were to go, the third, who is baptized, began to weep so hard when she saw her companions leaving her, that she had to be sent with them."[23] As for the Iroquois woman, she was to live with and be instructed by Madame de Combalet, a wealthy patron of the missions. It was expected that she would return with the Hospital Nuns, who had asked to work in the Canadian missions, "for she would teach the little Savage girls, who will be with them, to plant Indian corn." The missionaries thought that she should be placed elsewhere than at Mme de Combalet's so that she could devote herself to gardening, otherwise "having too long tasted the sweetness of repose and the abundance of a great house, she should afterwards shun labor."[24] When some Hospital Nuns did come to Quebec in 1639, they brought with them a little girl named Louise who had done extremely well in her religious studies with the Hospital Nuns of Dieppe.

By 1639, however, this phase of education for francization came to an end. It was seen that sending select students to France for indoctrination and acculturation was not producing a Native elite capable of directing the work in the colony under the supervision of the missionaries. Scarcely a dozen had returned to the colony in one whole generation to assist the evangelizers. Father Lalemant had raised a couple of objections to this policy. First, he argued, there were the examples of Louis Amantacha, a Huron, and Pierre

Pastedechouan, a Montagnais, "two who have gone over and who have been ruined." Besides, "it will cost something to maintain these children in France, and the mission is poor."[25] But in 1639 a new centralized mission headquarters had been set up in Huronia, religious women involved in both teaching and hospital work were arriving at Quebec, a scheme to settle the island of Montreal with zealots was in the planning stage, and some money had been donated to start a reserve or "praying town" near Quebec. Since 1635, the Jesuits had a college at Quebec. So it was decided to bring the students in from the mission fields to the colony schools rather than send a select few to France, although some would still find their way to the mother country over the next century.

Had this experiment been a complete failure? Father Paul Le Jeune thought not. He offered the following evaluation:

> Let us come to our young Montagnais and Algonquins. These young lads, most of them between twelve and fifteen years of age, have taught us two admirable truths,—one is, that if animals are capable of discipline, the young Savage children are much more so; the other, that education alone is wanting in these poor children, whose minds are as good as those of our Europeans, as will be seen by what I am about to say.[26]

The problems to be overcome were clearly cultural; there was no question of intellectual inferiority. The Jesuits, as representatives of the intellectual elite of Europe, had made an important assessment.

PHASE THREE: DAY SCHOOLS ON RESERVES

The Jesuits who laboured among nomadic Algonkian peoples such as the Micmac, the Montagnais and the Algonkians soon became aware that their itinerant missions would not be satisfactory in holding the converts to the new faith and in francizing them through the combined influences of sedentary agricultural life, a parish church, schools and a hospital.

A small number of Montagnais and Algonkian children were gathered at Sillery, near Quebec, where converts were being relocated near a mission house and church to take up agriculture in proximity of a few French farmers. The Jesuits, as tutors of the Amerindians, obtained title to a seigneury, which was financed by Brulart de Sillery. This reserve or *reduction* was modelled on the closed settlements of Jesuit converts, started in Brazil in 1549, which enjoyed great success in Paraguay after 1588. Each community or reserve was administered by a couple of missionaries; agriculture and various trades were taught, and the Native converts owned as common property the products of their industry. As Father Le Jeune said, "if he who wrote this letter has read the Relation of what is occuring in Paraquais, he has seen that which shall some day be accomplished in New France."[27]

This attempt to educate the young in the controlled atmosphere of the reserve may have been promoted for nonreligious reasons as well. The Company of New France found that as some Montagnais overhunted their territories in a desire to obtain French trade goods, they became sullen and dependent on the company. The resettlement of these people on the St. Lawrence in a region suitable for agriculture seemed to be a solution advantageous to all concerned. The reserve eventually became a Huron reserve when refugees from the Huron-Iroquois war arrived in the vicinity of Quebec in great numbers. Another reserve was started near Montreal when Iroquois came to settle in 1667, again, not only for religious reasons but also to escape persecution by the pagan majority in their villages and to take advantage of the economic possibilities offered by close contact with the French. Later, reserves would be founded, as in the case of the Abenakis, to accommodate those whose lands had been usurped or hunting territories despoiled by English settlers. In all cases, however, the relocation consisted of attracting Amerindian peoples into the French tract of settlement with a view to francizing them and holding them to the Catholic religion and French allegiance. The reserve of the French regime was not a move to relocate Native peoples in order to make way for white settlement.

The reserve had been conceived as an institution of integration of the Amerindian population with the French. The Amerindians were to learn French ways by close contact with French neighbours, and the children would learn from their French companions in school. However, the reserve very soon became an institution of segregation, as was the case in South America, with the missionaries attempting to insulate their new converts from the "evils" of French contact, especially the nefarious brandy trade. Governor Denonville articulated the failure of francization on the reserves and concluded that segregation, although it might also promote a degree of retention of the Amerindian identity, was the soundest economic and military policy. He observed:

> It was believed for a very long time that domiciling the savages near our habitations was a very great means of teaching these people to live like us and to become instructed in our religion. I notice, Monseigneur, that the very opposite has taken place because instead of familiarizing them with our laws, I assure you that they communicate very much to us all they have that is the very worst, and take on likewise all that is bad and vicious in us.[28]

The reserve, from the educational point of view, was an attempt at total education, acculturation of not only the children but also the adults. The school was not a mere agency of socialization; it was part of the complexity of intended socialization. Indeed, education was part of a programme of social control and the imposition of Christian authority. The reserves were to become "republics" under the paternal authority of the missionaries and the Native catechists. A puritanical order was enforced by the *dogiques*, some of whom were women, not only on the professed converts but also on the pagans. The children came under particularly strict supervision, their education for a new French way of life (which was the objective the missionaries had in mind for them) consisting of constant supervision and correction at all times, not only in the classroom.[29] Although the children began to take on some French ways, especially in matters of dress and diet, it was quite clear that they were not being apprenticed with success in either agriculture or manual trades. They seem to have learned little, if any, French, and it was the missionaries who continued to learn the Amerindian languages and to translate catechisms and missals into the Native tongues.

By the mid-1640's, the Jesuits had decided to change the emphasis of their educational programme. They would concentrate on educating the youth in "seminaries" or boarding schools in the French towns, while on the reserves they would direct their efforts more towards the adults. The school for the Huron children at Sillery was closed down "because no notable fruit was seen among the Savages; our experience in beginning the instruction of a people with the children, has made us recognize this fact."[30] Two years later, the assessment was even more radical:

> God has confounded our thoughts and overthrown the foundations or the principles on which we were building. We watered, at the start, only the young plants,—despising, as it were, those old stumps which appeared incapable of bearing any fruit; but God has made them put forth green shoots again, to great advantage.[31]

The time had come to emphasize the fourth approach to the education of the Amerindian children.

PHASE FOUR: ESTABLISHMENT OF BOARDING SCHOOLS

The education of Amerindian children in "seminaries" or boarding schools was initiated in New France by the Récollet Fathers in 1620 at Notre Dame des Anges, near Quebec. Champlain had petitioned King Louis XIII for financial support.[32] The Récollets started with six Native and three French boys, all of whom received instruction together in catechism, reading and writing. But before long, the Native children found the regimen of studies too exacting, the curriculum often impractical, and the discipline and separation from their kin unbearable. Brother Sagard reported on the progress of the school:

> We had made a beginning of teaching them their letters, but as they are all for freedom and only want to play and give themselves a good time, as I said, they forgot in three days what we had taken four to teach, for lack of perseverance and for neglect of coming back to us at the hours appointed them; and if they told us that they had been prevented because of a game, they were clear. Besides, it was not yet advisable to be severe with them or reprove them otherwise than gently, and we could only in a complaisant manner urge them to be thorough in gaining knowledge which would be such an advantage to them and bring them satisfaction in time to come.[33]

When there were no more Native students, the Récollets closed their "seminary." This had taken place before they were forced to leave the colony in 1629.

It was the Jesuits who returned as chief missionaries in Canada in 1633, despite the efforts of Cardinal Richelieu's "grey eminence" to have Capuchins succeed the Récollets. The Jesuits planned to "erect a College for the education of the children of the families" and "to establish a Seminary for the little Savages, to rear them in the Christian faith."[34] Father Antoine Daniel was to bring down twelve boys from the Huron country to launch the project. At the last minute plans were upset because "when it came to separating the children from their mothers, the extraordinary tenderness which the Savage women have for their children stopped all proceedings, and nearly smothered our project in its birth." When Daniel reached Trois Rivières, the Jesuits awaiting the Huron party "were much surprised when we saw him with a single lad, already nearly grown." The missionaries did not lose courage but, in their words, "we had recourse to God and to men."[35]

The recourse "to God and to men" brought some results. Their religious propaganda in France brought more financial and material support, while the pressures put on the Huron elders resulted in the decision to send two more boys so that the Jesuit "seminary" could begin with three pupils. Unfortunately, two of the students died, both under somewhat strange circumstances, for one had been involved in a fistfight with a Frenchman and another had been struck by a sword during an altercation. These uneasy relations between the "races" did not bode well for the success of the school. However, more students came as the French sought to attract them. Le Jeune reported in 1637:

Behold, then, our Seminary begun under very great difficulties. These young men are pampered, are dressed in the French way, are furnished with linen and other necessary articles. They are lodged in the place selected for this purpose, with the Father who is to have the care of them. All seems to be going along peacefully. Our French people are pleased at seeing these young Savages anxious to live after the French fashion; all seemed very contented.[36]

The cost of this education was much greater than the missionary teachers had expected. They discovered that they virtually had to bribe the parents to obtain students and then they had to cater to the students' whims in order to retain them in the "seminary." Le Jeune continued:

When the Savages give you their children, they give them as naked as the hand,—that is, as soon as you get them you must have them dressed, and give their robes back to their parents. They must be well lodged and well fed; and yet these Barbarians imagine that you are under great obligations to them. I add still more; generally, presents must be made to their parents, and, if they dwell near you, you must help them to live, part of the time.[37]

The Jesuits soon began to clothe their young "seminarians" with "stuffs which originate among them" because these not only lasted longer, suited them better and protected them better from the winter cold, but they were less costly. However, this scarcely advanced the francization effort. They also started "using the money of the Country to save something for the benefit of these poor abandoned creatures," but their enemies soon accused them of being more interested in the conversion of beaver pelts than in the conversion of the Native children. The "seminary" was seen by Amerindians as a means of extracting material benefits from the French, and the missionary teachers were unable to extricate themselves from this dilemma if they hoped for any success.

We have no greater attractions for these poor people than their hope of getting from us some material assistance, and they never cease asking us for it. To refuse them is to estrange them. If we always give to them without taking anything in return, we shall soon be at the end of our string; and yet, if we take away from them the liberty of asking, they will never become civilized. What remains then?[38]

The Jesuits persisted and soon they had fifteen resident students and a number of day scholars who came to them for instruction, and they had to divide their classes into three linguistic groups—Huron, Algonkin, and Montagnais. Pious laymen began to take an interest in the education of Native children. A few boarded some students and sent the boys to the Jesuits to be educated. Orders from Versailles to both Governor and Intendant emphasized the need to press the francization policy on the missionaries and indicated that state officials might themselves set a good example by adopting Amerindian children and raising them in a French environment. The Iroquois gave Governor Frontenac four boys in 1674; he quickly placed two of them in the "seminary," and the other two he kept in his household but sent to the Jesuits daily for instruction. The Intendant Duchesneau took in three boys in 1680, but he had no sooner outfitted them with French clothes than they ran away. He took in two other boys and sent them to the Jesuits for instruction.

Bishop Laval opened a Minor Seminary in 1668 and recruited some Native students.

> As the King told me that he hoped we would attempt to raise in the manner of life of Frenchmen the little children of the Savages, in order to discipline them little by little. I have formed a seminary, into which I have taken a number of children for this express purpose; and in order to succeed better, I have been obliged to join with them some little French children, from whom, by living with them, the Savages could learn more easily both the customs and the language.[39]

He soon discovered that the Amerindians wanted their children at home in order to teach them the ancestral beliefs and way of life and in particular their responsibilities to their kinsmen and tribe. After two years, Laval admitted he had spent twice as much for the education of each Native child as for that of a French child and that the undertaking was "very difficult." He would continue to take those who were offered him by the parents, but in reality he had never founded a new school. He had provided board and room and had sent them to the Jesuits for instruction. By 1673 all his boarders had left, owing to their "inordinate passion" for liberty, and the only other attempt he made was to accept a Métis boy for a brief period in 1679.[40]

Among the children sent to the Jesuits in the 1630's were a number of girls. They boarded these Native children with devout French families in Quebec until the arrival of Ursuline nuns in 1639. Within four months of her arrival in the colony, Mother Marie de l'Incarnation had started teaching the first eight pupils.[41] By 1668 the Ursulines, who were always short staffed, limited their boarding school to taking in sixteen French girls and three Native girls. They had been offered seven Algonkian girls that year, but they had had to turn them away because they had insufficient funds to clothe, feed, and educate that number of students who contributed nothing to the cost of their education.

The number of students who remained for any length of time was quite limited, so that at all seasons of the year the Ursulines were able to accept a few new candidates as they presented themselves. Some of the students were captives taken from enemy tribes, a few were promising candidates for the sisterhood recommended by the missionaries, a few were intended brides for Frenchmen, and one or two were "hostages" offered by parents who wanted to please the French traders and military personnel. It is little wonder that many did not remain any longer than they were obliged to stay. Mother Marie de l'Incarnation commented on these inconstant scholars, saying:

> Others are here only as birds of passage and stay with us only until they are sad, something which savage humour cannot suffer; the moment they become sad, the parents take them away for fear they will die. We leave them free on this point, for we are more likely to win them over in this way than by keeping them by force or entreaties. There are others who go off by whim or caprice; they climb our palisade like squirrels, which is as high as a stone wall, and go to run in the woods. There are some who persevere and we bring them up as French girls; we then arrange their marriages and they do very well.[42]

By 1668, Mother Marie de l'Incarnation questioned the wisdom of the royal directives which said that the Jesuits should continue with the education for francization of boys and the Ursulines and other sisters with the francization of girls. She commented:

> It is however a very difficult thing, although not impossible, to francize or civilize them. We have had more experience in this than any others, and we have remarked that out of a hundred that have passed through our hands scarcely have we civilized one. We find docility and intelligence in them, but when we are least expecting it they climb over our enclosure and go to run the woods with their relatives, where they find more pleasure than in all the amenities of our French houses. Savage nature is made that way; they cannot be constrained, and if they are they become melancholy and their melancholy makes them sick. Besides, the Savages love their children extraordinarily and when they know that they are sad they will do everything to get them back, and we have to give them back to them.[43]

Thus the Ursuline efforts gradually diminished, and the nuns turned more and more to the education of French children. Amerindian girls were never excluded but few came.

The efforts of other religious orders were less intense than those of the Jesuits and Ursulines, but the failure was just as great. The Sulpician secular clergy of Montreal undertook the education of Amerindian boys at their reserve of La Montagne; a lay association founded by Marguerite Bourgeoys undertook the education of the girls. The *abbé* Souart convinced the foundress to accept four girls to be educated in their *petite école*. Eventually, two sisters taught the girls at La Montagne reserve. Neither the boys' school nor the girls' school proved successful.[44] The missionaries and lay teachers became increasingly concerned with holding the Native children to their Catholic convictions and abandoned an immediate programme of complete francization. In fact, church and state became concerned about a tendency for Frenchmen to adopt Native ways, a tendency which they interpreted as one of barbarization and colonial degeneration.

CONCLUSION

The education of Amerindian children was initially identified with a programme of francization by both church and state. Only gradually were the two strands separated and not consistently intertwined. The Jesuits had flirted with the concept of cultural relativism in their Huron mission. Later, largely as a result of the obvious failure of the francization efforts, education was offered without undue pressures to integrate the children into a French lifestyle. It was thought that assimilation would gradually impose itself. Although the civil officials never ceased to propound the thesis of francization, the teachers who were faced with implementing such a mandate felt it was impractical and increasingly said so.

Little by little, there was a realization on the part of the educators that Amerindian cultures were not easily eradicated, that traditional beliefs were well rooted, and that the colonial environment favoured many of the Amerindian customs and practices. There was some overt resistance to assimilation, but there were many covert factors inhibiting the progress of transformation of Native society into a European-type assimilated and subservient culture. Amerindians were a proud and independent people convinced of the validity of much of their culture. They did not deny the superiority of some aspects of French civility, especially the technological advantages the French enjoyed in some fields. On the other hand, they were not impressed by European concepts of authority, morality, property, and work. The critical acceptance of some aspects of French life, and the rejection of other aspects, had its effect on the Amerindian youth. As Father Le Jeune had remarked:

> The freedom of the children in these countries is so great, and they prove so incapable of government and discipline, that, far from being able to hope for the conversion of the country through the instruction of the children we must even despair of their instruction without the conversion of the parents.[45]

Consequently, the missionaries saw schooling as but one aspect of a multifaceted and long-range programme. Traditional European educational systems and philosophy, not to speak of methodology and curriculum, could not be imposed on such a novel and unique situation and be expected to produce the same results as in Old France. The objectives of this implanted education were alien to North America, and success for the Amerindian child meant alienation from the old way of life, disruption of traditional and ancestral sociocultural patterns, without at the same time offering a complete and equal opportunity to participate in a French society. Education as presented in the various mission fields made it clear that Catholicism was a European cultural institution which was unsuited to nomadic hunting bands. The authoritarian nature of the school, and the harsh discipline and great emphasis on time repelled the children, for these were elements not given much emphasis in their own cultures. The curriculum was scarcely adapted to Amerindian needs, at least initially, for the *Ratio Studiorium* and the study of classical languages were imposed. Sending children to France proved impractical and the results were often tragic because those who returned more often than not were misfits in both the French and Native worlds. Neither the reserve schools nor the "seminaries" or boarding schools turned out a significantly large number of competent pupils. There were no candidates for the priesthood, for the educational qualifications were never relaxed for Native candidates; and of the few novice nuns none survived long enough to influence her compatriots. The boarding school with its restrictions and regimentation was abhorrent to the pupils who seem to have suffered greatly in these institutions, in spite of the kind and well-meaning interest of the teachers. Little wonder the parents withdrew the children when they became aware of the loneliness, disorientation and humiliation the young experienced there.

In conclusion, it cannot be said that the educational programme espoused in New France in the seventeenth century was a success, whether viewed from the perspective of the colonial bureaucracy, the Gallican church, the zealous missionaries and teachers, or the Native peoples. Although the missionaries tended in time to distinguish between conversion and francization, it remained clear that to acquire an education, to rise to a state of civility, was inextricably related to European culture and thought. The Amerindians did not find that receiving a French education necessarily benefited them or assured them of a prominent or influential role in colonial society. Education was a domain where cultures clashed more often than converged. Education for the French remained essentially identified with formal schooling, whereas for the Amerindians it did not exist as a concept but was merely part of growing up and learning to take one's place in a traditional society by participation therein and imitation of one's role models.

NOTES TO CHAPTER THREE

* Revised from essay appearing in *Canadian Journal of Native Education* II, no. 1 (1983): 1-19.

1. It is given as francize and frenchify. George F.G. Stanley and Cornelius J. Jaenen have popularized the terms francization and frenchification in Canadian English.
2. W.L. Grant and H.P. Biggar, eds., *The History of New France by Marc Lescarbot*, vol. 2 (Toronto, 1907).
3. *Collection de Manuscrits contenant Lettres, mémoires, et autres documents d'historiques relatifs à la Nouvelle-France*, vol. 1 (Quebec, 1883), 70. Enfranchisement is a statutory term employed since 1859 to designate the accomplishment of sufficient "civilization" of a Native person to warrant his/her assumption of all the rights and privileges of ordinary citizens.
4. A. Thévet, *Les Singularités de la France Antartique* (Paris, 1555).
5. L. Hennepin, *A New Discovery of a Vast Country in America*, vol. 2 (London, 1698).
6. W.L. Grant, ed., *Voyages of Samuel de Champlain, 1604-1618*, vol. 1 (New York, 1917), 264, 323.
7. Hennepin, *A New Discovery*, 61.
8. Instructions to Talon, February 1671, Public Archives of Canada [PAC], MG1, Series B, III.
9. Instructions to Talon, 27 March 1665, PAC, MG1, Series B, I.
10. Hennepin, *A New Discovery*, 47, 57.
11. Colbert to Quéylus, 15 May 1669, 216-19, PAC, MG1, Series B, I.; P. Margry, ed., *Découvertes et Etablissements de Français dans l'Ouest et dans le Sud de l'Amérique septentrionale*, vol. 1 (Paris, 1879), 372.
12. C. le Nant, *Pages glorieuses de l'Epopée canadienne,* (Paris, 1927), 141-42.
13. R.G. Thwaites, ed., *The Jesuit Relations and Allied Documents*, vol. 57 (New York, 1959), 205-7.
14. Ibid., vol. 53, 211.
15. Ibid., vol. 6, 87-88.
16. Ibid., vol. 18, 79.
17. Margry, *Découvertes et Etablissements de Français*, vol. 1, 5-6.
18. Thwaites, *Jesuit Relations*, vol. 5, 107-13.
19. Ibid., vol. 6, 85. C. Le Clercq, *Premier Etablissement de la Foy dans la Nouvelle-France* (Paris, 1691), 367, 373; and G. Sagard, *Histoire du Canada* (Paris, 1866), 796-98.
20. Thwaites, *Jesuit Relations*, vol. 6, 109.
21. Ibid., vol. 9, 105.
22. Ibid, vol. 12, 95. Also see vol. 6, p. 109; vol. 7, p. 297; vol. 9, 223.
23. Ibid., vol. 12, 99, 125.
24. Ibid., vol. 11, 95.
25. Ibid., vol. 6, 87.
26. Ibid., vol. 16, 179.
27. Ibid., vol. 12, 221.
28. Denonville to Seignelay, 13 November 1685, 45-46, PAC, MG1, Series C:A, VII.
29. See Thwaites, *Jesuit Relations* vol. 57, 61.
30. Ibid., vol. 34, 103.
31. Ibid., vol. 39, 193-95.
32. Shea, vol. 1, 164-65.
33. G.M. Wrong, ed., *The Long Journey to the Country of the Hurons by Father Gabriel Sagard* (Toronto, 1939), 133.
34. Thwaites, *Jesuit Relations*, vol. 7, 265.
35. Ibid., vol. 12, 39-41.
36. Ibid., vol. 12, 45.
37. Ibid., vol. 12, 47.
38. Ibid., vol. 9, 77-79.
39. H. Tétu, *Biographies de Msgr Laval et de Msgr Plessis* (Montreal, 1913), 35.

40. Laval to Poitevin, 8 November 1668, 128, Archives de l'Archevéché de Québec, Lettres I; Laval to abbé de l'Isle-Dieu, 30 September 1670, PAC, MG18, E-9; and Histoire de Séminaire de Québec, fol. 3, 27-28, PAC, CCCXLV, A.S.M.E., Pt. I.
41. D.G. Oury, ed., *Marie de l'Incarnation, Ursuline (1599-1672). Correspondance* (Solesmes, 1951), 97.
42. Ibid., 801-2.
43. Ibid., 809.
44. Tronson to LeFebvre 6 June 1677, 106, Bibliothéque de Saint-Sulpice, vol. I, no. 32; Carton B. Mélanges, no. 28(b), 199, ibid.; Laval to abbé de l'Isle-Dieu, 30 September 1670, pp. 8-9, PAC, MG18, E-9.
45. Thwaites, *Jesuit Relations*, vol. 16, 251.

4

"No Blanket to be Worn in School": The Education of Indians in Nineteenth-Century Ontario

J. Donald Wilson

Some fifteen years ago, E. Palmer Patterson published a survey of Canadian Indian history since 1500.[1] It created quite a stir because it was the first attempt to write a history of the Canadian Indian since the arrival of the European. In the past decade a great deal more work has been done on various aspects of Canadian Indian history, including a major study by John Webster Grant, but relatively little has appeared on the topic of Indian education.[2] Studies by Jacqueline Gresko, Brian Titley, and James Redford are representative of the solid but infrequent work to date. Popular studies by Howard Adams and Harold Cardinal condemn the deleterious effects of White man's education of Indian people over a century and a half but make no effort to document the true nature of that education.[3] However dismal the record of church-run Indian schools in the nineteenth and twentieth centuries, it remains a fact that most of today's Indian-rights leaders are products of those very schools.

Throughout Canadian history from the time of Champlain's arrival in New France in 1608, there have been three basic views of Indian-White relations: integration or assimilation of Indians into the White culture which, although often a numerical minority, remained dominant because of its technological power over the Indian; biracial harmony or coexistence between the races by which both Europeans and "civilized" Indians would live in mutual co-operation; and segregation of the Indian from the White population by means of reserves. These views were all seriously contemplated and their implementation attempted at various times by the French before the British conquest in 1760. Extermination was never a serious policy consideration. Significantly, the same three views persisted during the "British" and "Canadian" periods of Canada's history. In the period with which this essay is concerned—nineteenth-century Ontario—all three views were considered by the British and Canadian authorities with the notion of assimilation dominant.

The Conquest of New France and the arrival of British settlers in large numbers, especially the influx of the Loyalists following the American Revolution, made it seem likely that since these settlers were intent upon permanent colonization, they would either dominate, oust, or conquer the indigenous population. In the case of Upper Canada, early relations with the Indian seem to exemplify what R.A. Schermerhorn calls "minimal" racism. In distinguishing between "minimal" and "maximal" racism, Schermerhorn says that "in its *minimal* form, racism defined darker peoples as backward or less evolved, different in degree but not in kind from their masters, therefore capable with training and education, to rise...to a status of equality with the ruling group."[4] The perceived need to make over Indians as Europeans for their own benefit is well expressed by John Webster Grant:

> [Humanitarians] agreed that a lower culture coming into contact with a higher one was doomed to extinction. Aborigines could hope to survive only by becoming Europeans, therefore, and it was the responsibility of missionaries and administrators to give them all possible help. Becoming like Europeans involved learning to cope with European technology, to adapt to European economic patterns, and eventually to adopt European manners and dress....It would also be necessary...to cultivate the European values of sobriety, frugality, industry, and enterprise.[5]

Christian humanitarianism was an important component of the civilization impulse. For Indians to be civilized or "reclaimed or their condition... effectively improved," the influence of Christianity was deemed absolutely necessary. They must, as a superintendent of Indian Affairs asserted in 1828, "shake off the rude habits of savage life, and...embrace Christianity and civilization."[6] For both Protestants and Catholics, a measure of literacy and familiarity with the English language was deemed essential. The process of conversion and civilizing was then dependent upon exposing Indian children to some form of schooling with all the inherent merits that schooling was seen to have for White and Native alike.

The major watershed in Indian-White relations in Upper Canada coincided with the 1830 transfer of responsibility for Indians from the military authority to the civil governors in each of the Canadas. Before that, governmental concern centred on the maintenance of Indian loyalty to the Crown "with almost the sole object of preventing their hostility and of conserving their assistance as allies." Once the Indian's usefulness as an ally had passed, his civilization became the ideal. The government then saw its duty to raise the Indian "from the debased condition into which he had fallen owing to the loose and pampering policy of former days." In announcing the policy, Sir George Murray, secretary of state for the colonies, stated that it was based on "the settled purpose of gradually reclaiming the Indians from a state of barbarism and introducing amongst them the industrious and peaceful habits of civilized life."[7]

EDUCATION AS A MISSIONARY BYPRODUCT

The first known Indian school in Upper Canada/Ontario to use English was set up by the Society for the Propagation of the Gospel (S.P.G.) for the Six Nations at the Bay of Quinté in 1784. Just as in the American colonies, the S.P.G. was the missionary arm of the Church of England, and one of its main concerns was the conversion of the Indians. On the Grand River, a teacher was maintained by the government from 1785, almost from the time of the arrival of the Six Nations Indians in Canada.[8] An interesting report in 1810 underscored the suspicion held by some Indian elders about the value of formal education.

> Many of the old men are not certain whether this School is of use or not—for some by learng [sic] to read not only become idle, but contract habits of Idleness which prevent them from excelling in the [hunt?]. They also object & this is a remarkable objection, that while they are under the care of the Schoolmaster their manners are neglected; & again that many who have learnt to read & write are not the better for it unless they continue to read after they have left school. This is an objection of a nature which I fear is but too common; for they cannot have any great number of Books: & it is needless to add that the improvement of those who cannot get access to these few, must necessarily be inconsiderable.[9]

At Fairfield on the Thames River in western Ontario, an Indian school was opened in 1793 among the Delawares by the Rev. David Zeisberger, a

Moravian missionary.[10] Both English and Delaware were taught, and books in both languages were read, including Zeisberger's Indian and English spelling book. In 1801, the Moravian missionaries at Fairfield petitioned the government for an Indian agricultural school, this being perhaps the earliest example of the "school-of-industry" concept. The aim was "to lead them [the Indians] on to a state of cultivation by keeping schools, teaching them to read, write, and cipher, and instructing them in agriculture, etc."[11]

By the 1820's, concern was increasing over the disposition and education of the province's Indian population. In 1826, Lieutenant-Governor Sir Pere-grine Maitland (1818-28) was responsible for setting up a village for the Mississaugas on the Credit River near York (Toronto). Skilled workmen and teachers were sent among the Indians to aid in their "civilization." The Rev. John Strachan, later Anglican bishop of Toronto, reported good progress being made by virtue of the fact that the Indians had "abjured intoxicating liquors."[12] The Rev. Peter Jones, a Native Methodist missionary, also remarked upon the apparent success of the settlement. The Indians there had comfort-able houses, furniture, "window curtains, boxes and trunks for their wearing apparel, small shelves fastened against the wall for their books, closets for their cooking utensils, cupboards for their plates, cups, saucers, knives and forks; some had clocks and watches."[13] The lessons of "civilization," though superficial, were obviously taking effect.

Strachan himself played his part in promoting Indian education. Besides encouraging Maitland's work, he appealed to the Church Missionary Soci-ety (C.M.S.) for aid in a programme of educating Indians. He wanted his proposed university, King's College, to extend its benefits to Indians so that they might be trained as missionaries and then return to their people to teach. He also hoped some White students at King's would learn Indian languages so that they might be able to minister to the Indians. In answer to Strachan's request for assistance, the C.M.S. granted $100 annually for the maintenance of two scholarships and $100 for a professorship of Indian languages.[14] Not much came of these grand ideas, in large part because Strachan's King's College never got off the ground.

Typical of C.M.S., Strachan believed that the Gospel (conversion to Christianity) and the arts of civilization should be taught simultaneously. He advised that teacher-missionaries should work side by side with Indians in the fields

> for the Indians, if not incouraged [sic] in this way would become dis-gusted, whereas the assistance of their masters and superiors would be of great excitement. In many cases, the Indians, even those who are partially civilized, think it beneath them to perform drudgery when the example has not been set by the employers.

Generally speaking, Strachan was optimistic about the Indians. He reported them all to be "anxious to have their children educated," even if it meant leaving them behind while the men went off hunting. "These children are found as apt to learn as those of Whites, and acquire the common branches of instruction and expertness in the Mechanical arts with equal facility."[15] Strachan's report commented on their ready adaptability to the White man's ways, once they had been shown the desirability of these ends: "they are found to be docile...and very soon become clean and tidy in their persons." The use of the children to reach the parents—a common assimilative device used by the nation-state in the following hundred years—found Strachan's approval: "the Church can reach the parents through the children, and even should she be less successful with the adults, she can gradually get possession of the rising generation, and, in half an age, the tribe becomes Christian."[16] Two decades earlier, Maitland had made the same point: in civilizing and Christianizing the Indians "little perhaps can be expected from grown-up Indians"; rather success "will chiefly depend upon the influence" to be "acquired over the young."[17] Reflective of the "civilizing" role of the school was the rule which adorned the wall of the Credit River School in 1830: "No Blanket to be Worn in School."[18]

Methodist missionaries and clergymen were also active in this early period. The celebrated Peter Jones was one of the Methodists' most effective missionaries among the Mississaugas, along with the Indian preacher John Sunday. The ubiquitous Egerton Ryerson cut his teeth as a missionary among the Credit River Indians, where in his usual diligent fashion he learned their language. Ryerson carried this experience with him in his efforts to establish the Methodist Upper Canada Academy in Cobourg. While he was in England in 1836 trying to obtain a Royal Charter for the college, an Academy prospectus spoke of the need "to educate the most promising youth of the recently converted Indian tribes of Canada, as Teachers to their aboriginal countrymen."[19] Ryerson's optimism regarding Indian education is likewise evident in the pages of the *Christian Guardian*, which he edited at this time:

> There may be instances where parents are indifferent as to the schooling of their children....But this is not generally the case. A great majority of the Indians ardently desire the improvement of their off-spring; and many of them make sacrifices, and suffer inconveniences which undeniably prove that they are by no means indifferent to the subject of education.[20]

Of all the Christian churches, the Methodists had the most missionaries assigned to Indian tribes in Upper Canada. In the late 1820's and throughout the 1830's, the pages of the annual reports of the Missionary Society of the Methodist Episcopal Church reveal the extent of Methodist involvement in Indian education. The annual reports leave no doubt that the Methodist schools were primarily intended for converting the Indians to Christianity. "Nothing, in our opinion," an early report stated, "can rescue this people, but the power of the gospel."[21] A later report made the same point about religion being a necessary base for true education: "the principles of true religion are the foundation of every other improvement, and all that is noble and excellent in the character of man." After conversion, the main purpose of educating Indians was to tender moral instruction. Indians must be led away from their uncivilized and depraved ways, especially their proclivity to slothfulness and drunkenness. By 1830, the Methodists had established an extensive educational mission among the Indians with eleven schools, eleven teachers, and 400 students, of whom 150 "can read in the New Testament." "It was a sight most novel," one report concluded, "and to the friends of improvement very animating, to witness the tents of a tribe of pagan Indians pitched about the school for the purpose of affording to their children the means of education."[22]

Another reformer of the period who, amongst his diverse humanitarian interests, numbered the education and training of Indians was Thaddeus Osgood. Born in Massachusetts in 1755, Osgood was educated at Dartmouth College, licensed to preach in 1804, and ordained a Congregational minister in 1806.[23] Three years later, he came to Canada and began to distribute tracts designed "to make amusement and instruction friends" for thousands of little children. A decade or so later he launched a society called The Central Auxiliary Society for Promoting Education and Industry in Canada, whose main responsibility was to aid in the establishment of schools among Indians and destitute settlers.[24] Most of the Indian schools mentioned by Osgood in his annual reports for the Society were serviced by missionaries sent out by the Missionary Society of the Methodist Episcopal Church. In all cases the monies were directed to the erection or support of Schools of Industry. These schools were designed primarily to teach Indian boys useful trades. Beyond the normal "civilizing" and "moralizing" benefits of such schools, there were additional practical advantages relating to the acquisition of useful skills such as shoemaking, carpentry, and cabinet-making, which would prepare Indian boys to engage in productive activity.

By the end of the 1820's, Osgood, the inveterate optimist, was looking forward to the establishment of some kind of school for training Indian teachers. "The plan of training up Teachers from among the Indians and Emigrants," he reported, "appears so very important that they warmly recommend the opening of a Seminary, as soon as funds and a suitable

Instructor can be procured."[25] Despite Osgood's plans, however, the Society came to an end in 1829.

CIVILIZATON AS GOVERNMENT POLICY

In 1830, the imperial government decided to alter its Indian policy. From a policy based upon using the Indians as military allies, it was deemed preferable to convert them from their state of "barbarism" and "savagry" to a state of civilization through education. The Indian Department intended to promote civilization through religious instruction, basic literacy training, and an elementary training in agriculture pursuant to settling the Indians on farms. For Indians to be permanently settled became one of the necessary prerequisites for the programmes of acculturation which were soon inaugurated.

Both lieutenant-governors of the 1830's became actively involved in promotion of the new policy. The government settlement and education policies for Indians under Sir John Colborne (1828-36) were typified by the Coldwater and Lake Simcoe Narrows experiments. The Indians (Chippewas) would be settled at these two locations northwest of Lake Simcoe well removed from York/Toronto. After building a road between the two settlements, the Indians were to clear land for farming purposes, each family receiving a sixteen-acre lot. White farmers and skilled workers would instruct the Indians in clearing and farming and would build houses for them. Thus, the Indians' former nomadic occupation of hunting and fishing would be replaced by permanent residence as farmers and carters carrying supplies between Penetanguishene and Orillia. Missionaries and schoolmasters were brought in to instruct the Indian children. Colborne was ecstatic about the success of the assimilation policy:

> All the Indian Tribes in Canada are collected in Villages....Schools are instituted for their Benefit...they are placed under the Care of Persons interested in their Welfare...few cases of Intoxication now occur, except among the visiting Indians chiefly resident in the United States.[26]

However, the Coldwater establishment was abandoned in 1837.[27]

Colborne's successor, Sir Francis Bond Head (1836-38), was not at all convinced of the alleged achievements with the Indian settlements. Having completed an inspection tour in the summer of 1836, Bond Head wrote to Colonial Secretary Lord Glenelg, ridiculing as a "complete Failure" the "Attempt to make Farmers of the Red Men." Secondly, the idea of "congregating them for the Purpose of Civilization [had] implanted many more Vices than it [had] eradicated." As a proponent of segregation, he concluded that "the greatest Kindness we can perform toward these intelligent, simple-minded People, is to remove and fortify them as much as possible from all communication with the Whites"[28] — in other words, to carry out the responsibility of "protecting" the Native peoples. His major project in this respect was the scheme to collect various Indian tribes living in the vicinity of Lake Huron and the Thames River and move them to Manitoulin Island in Lake Huron after turning over their own lands. Although a number of Indians were moved to Manitoulin Island, the scheme was soon afterwards abandoned as Bond Head's attention was diverted by the events leading to the 1837 Rebellion and his departure for England the following spring. In its 1839 *Report on the Indians of Upper Canada,* the London-based Aborigines' Protection Society denounced Bond Head as typical of White intruders and the champion of "avaricious speculator[s] in land."[29] For their part, the Indians found repellent the formalized and paternalistic nature of the forced settlement.[30]

One of the central issues associated with Indian education during these years was the question of the language of instruction. Was it preferable to teach in the Indian or the English language? For the Methodists in the 1820's, it was considered wise to use English, "there being so few translations into the Indian tongue." Once English was known, it would be "no difficult task to learn [sic] the scholars to read their native tongue."[31] As more translations in Indian languages became available, the controversy became more heated.[32] The Mohawk Indians at Tyendinaga (Bay of Quinté, east of Belleville), for example, requested of Bishop Strachan in 1843 to be allowed to have a school where the Indian language would be used, as well as a second one with English. They even offered to pay for the cost of printing Indian books for use in the school. The opposing view was expressed by Captain T.G. Anderson, a superintendent of Indian Affairs. He disapproved of Indian Testaments being used as text books "because the intercourse of the rising generation must be with the whites and it therefore appears to me that teaching them in their own language is time and labour lost."[33]

EDUCATION FOR ASSIMILATION

After converting the Indians and teaching them to pray and read and pursue "moral" lives, the missionaries and reformers soon realized this was not enough. The Indians must be introduced to "industrious labour" and "the acts of civilized life." Prompting this concern was a realization that the Indians' traditional mode of livelihood had been disrupted by the material advance of White society and the decline of the fur trade. Upper Canada's population tripled between 1825 and 1842 to 450,000 and would more than double again by 1851.[34] As Strachan phrased it in 1837, "they could no longer live by hunting as the settlements were extending through every part of the Province and unless something was done to induce them to alter their mode of life they must inevitably" face destruction and ruin.[35] A decade later this contention was verified by the Indians themselves. The Mohawks of the Bay of Quinté, in an address to a general council of tribes at Orillia, stated:

> Let us sound the shell, and summon every Red man from the woods; let us give up the chase of the Deer and the Beaver; it is unprofitable. The White man's labour is fast eating away the forest, whilst the sound of his Axe in summer and his Bells in winter is driving the game far away from their old haunts; it will soon be all gone.[36]

Maitland's plan to put Indians in village settlements had been a move in the right direction, but efforts must now be made to introduce "the various arts of mechanism among this people."[37] Few Indians had enough new skills to compete in the White man's world. Cooperage, shoemaking, chair-making, cabinet-making, blacksmithing, tailoring— these were the useful skills to be taught to young men; while girls would learn sewing, knitting, cooking, washing and laundry work.

Schools of Industry were set up at Grape Island, Credit River, Alderville (Alnwick) near Rice Lake, and Mohawk village on the Grand River.[38] The conference minutes of the Wesleyan Methodist Church in 1837 record adoption of a recommendation for the erection of a Central Manual Labour School for Indian youth where their "religious, literary, mechanical and agricultural education" might be undertaken.[39] "The great work must be unweariedly persevered in," the recommendation continued, "until...the practices of paganism cease to exist, habits of industry be formed, and peace and tranquility dwell in the midst of this people."[40] The additional advantage of a central school would be the removal of the Indian children "from their imperfectly civilized parents" and their placement "under the exclusive direction of their religious and secular Instructors." At the 1836 general council, Captain Anderson emphasized that the point of establishing schools of industry was to enable Indian children to "forget their Indian habits, and be instructed in all the necessary arts of civilized life, and become one with [their] White brethren." Children would be well taken care of, fed and clothed. Parents would not be forced to relocate if they did not desire to, but "their children must go to the Schools."[41]

In 1845, the Rev. Peter Jones, one of the most energetic missionaries among the Indians, collected enough money to establish the Mount Elgin Industrial Institution at Munceytown Reserve, whose aims and objectives closely paralleled those of the superintendent of the Choctaw Academy for

Indians in the United States.[42] The object of the institution was "to Christianize and elevate the Indian youth of our country, to teach the boys useful trades, viz. shoe-making, carpentering and cabinet-making, as well as the correct principles of farming; and the girls, sewing, knitting, spinning and general house work." As to their moral and civic education, "the greatest care is taken to inculcate habits of industry and frugality, which are essential to the future prosperity and happiness of our Indians."[43] Similarly, the Choctaw Academy superintendent considered "that nothing will tend more rapidly to promote civilized habits among that unfortunate race of people (in addition to even a moderate English education) than the encouragement of the mechanical arts."[44] The problems of adjustment to White society, it was thought, could best be met if Indians learned to hold and respect the same values as the White man, and these values were contained in the words "industry and frugality." Added to the benefits of this type of instruction was the advantage of the residential nature of these schools. Removed from parental influence and the perceived deleterious milieu of the reserve, Indian boys or girls would receive that sort of education that would eventually enable them to return as "effective emissaries of Christian civilization among their people."[45]

The essentially voluntary aspect of Indian education in the first half of the nineteenth century was being replaced by a more and more insistent appeal that all Indian children, whether willing or not, should acquire "White" values and a minimum of industrial skills. Thus, as the century progressed, the "civilizing" mission of church and state was succeeded by the schools-of-industry concept with its aim of making Indians both useful and reasonably self-sufficient and thus "amalgamating" them, as Rev. E.F. Wilson put it, into the White economic system.

SYSTEMATIC ASSIMILATION THROUGH RESIDENTIAL EDUCATION

In the years following Confederation, the necessity for an official policy on Indian education became a priority. By the terms of the British North America Act, Indians were made wards of the dominion/federal government. With the acquisition of Rupert's Land and the North West Territories and the entry into Confederation of Manitoba and British Columbia, their numbers tripled to 100,000 or more. Treaties for the surrender of Indian lands on the Prairies began to be signed from the early 1870's, and among their most frequent provisions was the promise to provide schools.

Within the decade, it became clear that the day schools which formed the bulk of facilities in Ontario, Québec and the Maritimes would not suffice in the West, where the Indians had had far less contact with Europeans. By

1880, the dominion/federal government had committed itself to a policy of residential education similar to that already being put in place across the United States. Two types of institutions came into existence: small boarding schools intended for young children, and large industrial schools designed to educate their older siblings. The latter schools were considered the ultimate tool for assimilating the young Indian into White society. Again, boys concentrated on learning trade or farming skills (there was ideally a garden or farm at each school) while girls acquired domestic skills. On the Prairies, the industrial schools were jointly administered by the department and the various church authorities, but the actual management of the schools was the responsibility of the churches. The department provided the land, constructed the building, and contributed to the operating expenses in the form of an annual per capita grant ranging from $110 to $145. By 1890, fourteen industrial schools were in operation, four of them in Ontario.[46]

Two of the Ontario schools predated Confederation. Representative of the more recent establishments was the Shingwauk Industrial Home for Indians near Sault Ste. Marie, created out of the missionary effort of an English-born Anglican clergyman named Rev. Edward F. Wilson. Born in 1844 into a solid Evangelical and upper-middle class home, Wilson came to Canada in 1868 to serve in the Sarnia area under the auspices of the Church Missionary Society (C.M.S.). This organization was primarily interested in converting Indians to Christianity, but Wilson found both here and three years later in the Lake Superior region that most Indians had already been converted through the prior efforts of Methodists, Roman Catholics and, to a lesser extent, some Anglicans. He therefore left the C.M.S. in 1872 and set his mind to "amalgamating" the already converted Indians into Canadian society. The vehicle for this transformation in Wilson's mind was to be the residential industrial school. For him the overall goal of Native education was "the civilization, education, and Christian training of Indian children." The Shingwauk Industrial School, named after an Indian chief at the Garden River reserve and founded near Sault Ste. Marie in 1873, served as his model. It was intended "to wean our [Indian] boys altogether from their old savage life; to instill into them civilized tastes, to teach them English thoroughly, to encourage their intercourse with white people, and in fact to make Canadians of them."[47] Wilson veered from his policy of amalgamation briefly in the mid-1870's when he proposed setting up at Batchawana Bay north of Sault Ste. Marie a model community composed of Shingwauk graduates. "Supposing this plan to succeed," he argued, "there is no reason why in time all the present Indian Reserves which are looked upon as blots in the country should not be gradually effaced — as the old people die off." But by 1877 Wilson once again held "that it will be of more advantage to them [our boys] in after life to become incorporated with the white population than to be living on land specially set apart for them."[48]

Ultimately, Wilson's goal of rescuing the Indian youth of the Lake Superior region can be equated to the work at much the same time of Dr. Thomas Barnardo among the children of London's poor. In fact, he consciously patterned himself after Barnardo: "Our desire is simply to do the same for the Indian children of Canada that Dr. Barnardo has been doing for the street children of London and other English cities."[49] Wilson's faith in the transforming power of education is underscored in a letter he wrote to the Superintendent of Indian Affairs:

> I believe that there is through Canada a *kindly feeling* towards the Indian race, that it is only their dirty habits, their undisciplined behaviour, and their speaking another language, that prevents their intermingling with the white people. I believe also that there is in the Indian a perfect capability of adapting himself to the customs of the white people...but he wants the advantages given him while young, and he requires to be drilled into the use of those advantages.[50]

The first Shingwauk building, with sixteen boys in attendance, was completed on 22 September 1873. Six days later it mysteriously burned to the ground. In August 1875 a new building was opened on the outskirts of Sault Ste. Marie some ten miles from the reserve. Four years later a school for girls located at Sarnia, called Wawanosh after an old Ojibway chief of the Indians, was founded about two miles away from Shingwauk. The Shingwauk School was built for seventy boys, but in the early days never more than fifty attended. The school was mainly supported by voluntary contributions, and most students were maintained by various Church of England Sunday Schools across Ontario. Maintenance included the supplying of clothing or money to purchase the institution's uniform, which consisted of a grey cloth military coat with black facings, red trimming, and "Shingwauk buttons."[51]

Indian boys admitted to the school ranged in age from ten to eighteen. Sociologist David Nock estimates that the average age of entry was 11.88 years and that the average stay of pupils was less than two-and-a-half years of what was supposed to be a five-year programme. Most children in attendance ranged from twelve to fifteen years of age. Wilson regretted the late age of first entry to school relative to White children. Indian parents seemed reluctant to release their children to Wilson much before puberty, and consequently, he complained, "we are obliged to pass over young intelligent looking children whom we feel sure would benefit far more by receiving a course of instruction."[52]

During the first two years pupils spent their days at school. During the third year they were half at school, half at trades. In the last two years they were full-time apprentices. Trades training was conducted in the smaller buildings which surrounded the residence: carpenter shop, laundry, printing office (for the *Algoma Missionary News*), tinsmith shop, bootmaker's and tailor's shops, and farm buildings. In November 1877, the following intended occupations of Shingwauk boys were noted: missionary (1), teacher (2), medicine (2), tinsmith (2), carpenter (3), bootmaker (3), tailor (3), printer (3), blacksmith (1), and farming (3); the remaining boys were all under twelve years old. Eventually a sash factory was begun "in the hope that it may prove a source of profit to the institution, and also be a means of affording employment to some of our ex-pupils and fit them for making their living by engaging at other factories when they leave us."[53]

As can be seen, most of the boys were to become tradesmen; only the better students were trained as missionaries and teachers, "as it is thought," reported Wilson's bishop, Frederick Fauquier, "that they, when properly prepared, will be able to live with their red brethren, and work more effectively among them, both for their *evangelization* and *civilization*, than white men can be expected to do." However, whether teachers or tradesmen, Shingwauk graduates were not to go back to "their old way of living." Except for the missionaries, "we want them," Wilson asserted, "to become apprenticed out to white people and become in fact Canadians."[54]

To help effect the "amalgamation" desired, only English was used at Shingwauk except at tea-time between six and seven P.M., when Ojibway was allowed. Wilson explained:

> We make a great point of insisting on the boys talking English as, for their advancement in civilization, this is, of all things, the most necessary. Twice a week we have English class. The more advanced boys sit with their slates and write out definitions of English words; the rest of the boys form lines in two classes and are taught *vive voce*, besides being put through certain manual exercises such as shutting the door, putting a slate on the bench, pulling down the blind, etc.; the object being to teach them to understand, and obey promptly, directions given in English.[55]

An ingenious method was devised to discourage the students from using their Native tongue. Every week buttons were distributed to the children, with more going to the newer arrivals who spoke little English. If a child spoke Ojibway (except at tea-time), his closest partner was allowed to demand a button. At the end of the week, the buttons per student were tallied up and those with the most received nuts in return. Proper assimilation, of course, demanded fluency in English, and so to discourage the use of Ojibway in this way was considered quite a justifiable course of action. In 1884, Wilson proudly reported: "Not a word of Indian is heard from our

Indian boys after six months in the institution. All their talk among themselves while at play, is in English."[56]

The process of cultural replacement extended beyond language and religion. As at Hampton Institute and Carlisle Indian School in the United States, non-Indian games and sports, with the exception of lacrosse, shared the spotlight. The boys played cricket, baseball, soccer, and marbles and also had available a swing, climbing pole, horizontal bars, and a covered skittle alley. In their new baseball uniforms, one report noted, the Indian boys "really looked exceedingly nice, 'quite like English boys' as some one remarked." Likewise, the boys were taught British and European musical forms, in particular British patriotic, religious, popular, and folk songs. In the 1880's, a brass band was organized and regularly played in Sault Ste. Marie. In this respect, the band and the baseball team were expected to encourage interaction between Indian and White children and youth. Of course, there was also a boys' choir for church services. On overhearing a choir practice, a visitor to Shingwauk noted "we could almost imagine we heard the strains of some surpliced choir in England."[57]

The children at Wilson's schools lived a very regimented life, marked off at regular intervals by the ringing of bells. The boys were awakened at six A.M., had breakfast at seven, and at eight A.M. half went to work, the other half to class after bed-making and a half-hour play period. Class continued till noon, when dinner was served. The two halves of the school traded places for the afternoon. Tea was at six, and evening prayers at seven followed by singing or school work. Bedtime varied from 7:15 P.M. to 9:15 P.M. depending on the age of the boy. The routinized nature of life at Shingwauk not only contributed to the smooth operation of the school but also helped the students to prepare for their eventual integration into White society. Wilson was both proud and optimistic about the results of such a regimented school life. "Our apprentice boys work ten hours a day, six days a week, and very rarely ask for a holiday. Having once become accustomed to regular work, they like it, and will stick to it as well as any white man."[58]

Very little corporal punishment was meted out of Shingwauk. Instead peer pressure and shame were utilized to ensure good conduct. Two cards were hung up to public view. The one listing those students who displayed good conduct was headed "Certificated List"; the other was the "Black List." Principal Wilson concluded with pride: "these two cards seem to have a very good moral effect on the boys."[59]

The need to make the school residential and to locate it away from the reserves was apparent to both Wilson and his superior, Bishop Fauquier. Wilson believed adult Indians were bad influences on their children. The church's task was difficult enough "to try and break them of their old instincts inherited from their fathers, and to make them care for a civilized and respectable life." "Many of the old [Indian] people," he continued, "are even quite averse to their children being educated, they think it unfits them for hunting and fishing." Bishop Fauquier concurred:

> Since if it be for the advantage of the red men that they should give up the roaming habits of their forefathers, and acquire the habits of industry which are peculiar to civilized life, this can only be effected by training up the children and forming their habits of life—by teaching them and instructing them, ere other habits are formed, in useful trades and agricultural pursuits, and gradually weaning them from their wild and idle ways.

In desperation over the failure of many of his students to return to Shingwauk after the summer vacation, Wilson even advocated compulsory attendance enforced by federal or provincial statute. Indians had been prevented the use of "firewater," Wilson argued. "Might they not be further benefitted if some wise laws were enacted requiring the attendance of their children at school during a certain age."[60]

Most boys who arrived at Shingwauk could neither read nor write. Most had never seen a book, especially those from "up Lake Superior," and could hardly speak a word of English. The "ignorance" of some, to quote Mme Capelle, the English superintendent of Wawanosh, the nearby Indian girls' school, even extended to not knowing how to hold a broom when asked to sweep the lavatory. In time, however, as she conceded, they finally did learn how to clean the kitchen, wash dishes and their own clothes, and even bake bread. Mme Capelle's direct comparison between Canadian Indians and U.S. Blacks is worth noting:

> They are in general very lazy, even more so than the negroes, who have a great heat as their excuse; but the Indians living in the most healthy climate of the world, in a bracing air, have only neglected their mental as well as their bodily powers, and a good discipline is wanted to change them in a lapse of time to really useful working people.[61]

Punctuality, cleanliness and politeness were attributes accorded special attention at both schools. One of Wilson's favourite boys whom he took with him on fund-raising tours of Southern Ontario, John Maggrah, recounted a story with an obvious moral.

> Once a man wanted to choose out a boy among a crowd of boys to work for him. He got them to come into his office one by one. Some came in without shutting the door, and did not seem to care how they spoke. The

last boy came; before opening the door he cleaned his feet, knocked at the door, shut it quietly, and took off his hat. The man at once noticed how the boy acted and for this reason he choosed [sic] him. The boy was polite.[62]

The overall importance of cleanliness and tidiness is underlined in a typical passage from the teacher of another school, namely the Colonial and Continental Church Society school on Manitoulin Island. With entering students there was an immediate need to "disentangle, or unweave, or shear...human hair which had been matted for years, and never felt a comb, or...scour with soap and brush...skin which from infancy had been covered day and night with cloth rags or a tattered blanket."[63]

When the Shingwauk Home was opened, it was intended to have both boys and girls in the same institution. The *Algoma Missionary News* reported rather cryptically that "the trial was made; but eventually it was found necessary to have separate establishments."[64] In 1876 a *Pamphlet on the Wawanosh Proposal* was circulated in Britain by the "English Committee." The pamphlet was explicit that the present arrangement was "most undesirable" since it "necessitates the dwelling under one roof of young persons of both sexes, only recently removed from a life of barbarism in the forest."[65] Like Shingwauk, the Wawanosh Home for Indian Girls, with room for thirty girls, was intended to "give them a good Christian education, and fit them for domestic service, by teaching all that is necessary in household work, and training them to be industrious, cleanly and tidy." Since it was intended that Wawanosh girls would marry Shingwauk boys, it followed that they had a "noble mission" to fulfil by assisting their husbands "to continue in the way in which they have been brought up at Shingwauk." Moreover, such married couples had the added responsibility "by their good conduct, and tidily kept cottages [of] prov[ing] living recommendations to the benighted ones among whom their lot may be cast."[66]

The curriculum at Wawanosh emphasized reading, writing and housework including cooking, sewing, and laundry. The girls arose at 6:30 A.M. "as they do all the work of the Home, to prepare them for making good servants."[67] Before getting married, it was expected most Wawanosh girls would enter domestic service. This said, it was not surprising that Indian school officials, generally and not just at Wawanosh, began relying upon student labour to keep the school operating. At Hampton Institute, for example, in 1883 the matron described the work routine for Indian girls as follows:

All of the Indian girls, from eight to twenty-four years old, make their own clothes, wash and iron them, care for their rooms and a great many of them take care of the teachers' rooms. Besides this they have extra work, such as sweeping, dusting, and scrubbing the corridors, stairs, hall, sewing-room, chapel, and cleaning other parts of the building.

The linkage between formal education and the world of work for Indian girls was clearly understood by school officials in both the United States and Canada. In an 1881 report, Captain Pratt of the Carlisle Indian School wondered, "Of what avail is it that the [Indian] man be hard-working and industrious, providing by his labor food and clothing for his household, if the wife, unskilled in cookery, unused to the needle, with no habits of order or neatness, makes what might be a cheerful, happy home only a wretched abode of filth and squalor?"[68]

The strict routine of Wilson's schools when matched with months of separation from their homes and loved ones often left Indian students contending with bouts of homesickness, and Wilson and his staff often faced the problem of runaways. Wilson expounded on the situation as follows: "Some of them, when homesick, seemed to lose all control over themselves and made an unearthly noise; others would watch their opportunity and run away." Wilson devoted a whole chapter in his memoirs to this problem.

> One day three boys were missing; nobody could tell what had become of them; the bush was scoured, and messengers dispatched to the Sault to try and gain some clue to their whereabouts. After a time it was discovered that some bread and other things were missing, and it became clear that they had decamped. Their home was 300 miles away.

In this case the search proved successful. Some twelve days after their disappearance, the boys were picked up on an island on the Lake Superior shore north of Sault Ste. Marie. Their eventual return by boat to Shingwauk led to "dancing on the dock" by all the boys who were "greatly edified to see the return of the runaways."[69]

Wilson blamed the "downpull" of reserve life for student discontent of this sort. Attendance was always sharply down in September after the summer holidays, and Wilson often had to make personal visits to nearby Indian communities to round up the delinquents. In his memoirs, he complained the Indians "seem to care little whether their children are in their place at class or roving about the bush with a bow and arrow."[70] The elders were often of little help, and in fact some were opposed to Wilson's work. "Many of the old men think," he complained, "that we are spoiling the children by educating them." One solution which Wilson proposed (but did not act on) was to implement a year-round school year with no summer vacation. The extent of Wilson's frustration is perhaps best summed up in his contention that "Indians for their real advancement require to be held with a somewhat firmer hand and...if they will not see what is good for them that they should be made to do so."[71] On the other hand, Wilson did receive support from some important quarters. Chief Augustin Shingwauk of the Garden River reserve, after whom the boys' school was named, asserted: "The time is passed for my people to live by hunting and fishing as our forefathers used to do; if we are to continue to exist at all we must learn to gain our living in the same way as the white people."[72]

With some notable exceptions, graduates of Shingwauk and Wawanosh failed to attain that equal footing with their White neighbours which was held out as the objective of this sort of schooling. A factor which Wilson and his associates could not control was, of course, the receptivity of Indians, even industrial school graduates, by White society. Most graduates found themselves forced back onto the reserve to face a traditional tribal life for which they were no longer prepared.[73] Facing the reality of all this, industrial school advocates like the Methodist Rev. Thompson Ferrier seemed satisfied with evidence of minor success. The homes of Methodist boarding and industrial school graduates, he reported in 1906, are "neater and better cared for and more abundantly supplied with light and air. They have also more personal tidiness."[74] Such attainment was a far cry from the original aim of the "amalgamation" of the Indian people with the mainstream of Canadian society.

FROM ASSIMILATION TO INDIAN AUTONOMY

At least as late as 1886, as is evident in his memoirs, Wilson was still very optimistic about the prospects for assimilation.[75] In June 1888, a branch home called Washakada was opened in Elkhorn, Manitoba, southwest of Brandon. "As a result of my visit to Ottawa with thirty Shingwauk pupils in 1887," Wilson reported, "the Government [of Canada] made us a grant of $12,000" for completion of buildings and furnishing of Washakada.[76] One of Wilson's sons eventually became principal of this school. Wilson's fascination with prairie Indians extended further west. Construction began on a large Indian Home in Medicine Hat in the autumn of 1890 with a projected opening the following summer, but "this home was never opened," Wilson admitted, "as I gave up my Indian work the following year [1892]—and deeded the property to the Bishop of Calgary, who put it to some other purpose."[77]

By the early years of the next decade, Wilson had completely reversed himself and began talking about the need for "Indian autonomy." In his last annual report on his schools at Sault Ste. Marie in 1892, he conceded: "that the results have not been greater I must confess that I am disappointed."[78] In a series of articles he authored under the pseudonym "Fair Play" in *The Canadian Indian* in the spring of 1891, Wilson condemned policies designed to "un-Indianize the Indian, and make him in every sense a white man." "Why should we expect that Indians alone," he asked, "should be ready quietly to give up all old customs and traditions and language, and adopt those of the aggressor upon their soil?" "The change which we expect the Indian to make...is a far greater one than is required of immigrants to Canada from Germany, Sweden, France and Italy." Instead, he suggested that White North Americans should be prepared to accept "an independent Indian community" that should have its own government with its own lieutenant-governor and parliament.[79] "Would it not be pleasanter," Wilson argued, "and even safer to us, to have living in our midst a contented, well-to-do, self-respecting, thriving community of Indians, rather than a set of dependent, dissatisfied, half-educated and half-Anglicized paupers?"[80] Such a solution resembles the notion of biracial harmony mentioned at the outset of this chapter as a means of conflict regulation between the races. Interestingly, it also resembles the self-government proposals of some contemporary Indian groups, such as the Déné nation.[81]

That Wilson finally turned his back on "amalgamation" as the solution of the Indian problem in Canada sets him apart from the mainstream of thinking on the subject in his day. Most missionaries, churchmen, politicians, and Indian Affairs officials continued past the turn of the century to sing the praises of assimilationist policies. Rev. Thompson Ferrier, a leading Methodist spokesman, was convinced that "the only hope of the Indian race is that it should be finally merged in the life of the country....Our nation, if it is to be a nation at all, must be homogeneous."[82] To the Toronto *Globe*, the great Canadian melting pot must also include Native Indians, once civilized.

> Englishman and Frenchman, Scot, Irishman, German and Swede, are content to yield up their boasted nationalities, and mingle in the common Canadian stock. They are not exterminated by becoming Canadians; and neither need the civilized Indian be exterminated, though he share in the same lot, and merge in the common stock of our Canadian people. The Indian tribes of Wyandotte, or Ottawa, Mississaugas, Mohawks, or Cayuga, will indeed disappear; but not by extermination or extinction. They will simply be merged into the common stock of the Canadian people, like the clan McNab, the Seaforth Mackenzies, or any other body of emigrants who have cast their lot among us, and won thereby a share in the common prosperity of our Province and Dominion.[83]

CONCLUSION

A new shift in federal government Indian policy marked the turn of the century. It featured a general shift away from assimilation toward segregation. Much as Wilson had already done, federal authorities would lay the blame for previous failures on the inability of educated young Indians to enter the dominant society. In 1910, a more frugal educational policy was adopted, which officially changed the function of Indian schooling as being intended "to fit the Indian for civilized life in his own environment."[84]

Throughout the nineteenth century, most colonial and church officials held that the problems of Indian adjustment to White society could best be met if Indians learned to hold and respect the same values as the White man—in other words, a policy of assimilation. A minority, like Sir Francis Bond Head, favoured outright segregation of Indians from White society. A few others, like Wilson in later life, clung to the possibility of biracial harmony by which both Europeans and "civilized" Indians would live in mutual co-operation.

But assimilation, the major thrust, was not to be, for its principles were founded upon a suffocating paternalism, the dangers of which were perceived as early as 1841 by Governor Lord Sydenham of Canada when he spoke of "the general truth that a government undertaking to assume a parental relation to adult men and women is sure to do itself and them unmixed harm."[85] In effect, most often the graduates of schools such as Shingwauk and Wawanosh became marginalized beings, lacking the necessary skills of both White and Indian cultures, confused over their identity, and left to their own devices after their failed school experience. The impact of residential schools on students' parents and communities can only be imagined. Certainly the graduates themselves most often neither fitted into White industrial society nor could they return with ease to their own culture.[86] The long-lasting sense of alienation and frustration felt by many Indians towards Canadian society today is in part a product of the educational system to which they were subjected during the nineteenth century.

NOTES TO CHAPTER FOUR

* The first three sections of this article are a revised and updated version of an article by the same title which appeared in *Histoire sociale/Social History* 7, no. 14 (November 1974): 293-305. The journal has granted permission to reprint the article in this much expanded form.

1. E. Palmer Patterson, *The Canadian Indian: A History Since 1500* (Toronto: Collier-Macmillan, 1972).
2. John Webster Grant, *Moon of Wintertime: Missionaries and the Indians of Canada in Encounter Since 1534* (Toronto: University of Toronto Press, 1984). For two excellent bibliographic surveys, see Robert J. Surtees, *Canadian Indian Policy: A Critical Bibliography* (Bloomington: Indiana University Press, 1982), and James W. St. G. Walker, "The Indian in Canadian Historical Writing, 1972-1982," in *As Long as the Sun Shines and the Water Flows: A Reader in Canadian Native Studies,* ed. Ian A.L. Getty and Antoine S. Lussier (Vancouver: University of British Columbia Press, 1983), 340-457. For representative work on Indian education, see Jacqueline Gresko, "White 'Rites' and Indian 'Rites': Indian Education and Native Responses in the West, 1870-1910," in *Shaping the Schools of the Canadian West,* ed. D.C. Jones, N.M. Sheehan and R.M. Stamp (Calgary: Detselig, 1979), 84-106; James Redford, "Attendance at Indian Residential Schools in British Columbia, 1890-1920," *BC Studies* 44 (Winter 1979-80): 41-56; E. Brian Titley, "Duncan Campbell Scott and Indian Educational Policy," in *The Imperfect Past: Education and Society in Canadian History,* ed. J. Donald Wilson (Vancouver: University of British Columbia Curriculum Centre, 1984), 141-53.
3. Howard Adams, *Prison of Grass: Canada from the Native Point of View* (Toronto: New Press, 1975), and Harold Cardinal, *The Rebirth of Canada's Indians* (Edmonton: Hurtig, 1977).
4. R.A. Schermerhorn, *Comparative Ethnic Relations* (New York: Random House, 1970), 73-74. He continues: "The key notion in *maximal* racism becomes the inherent superiority of peoples with lighter color, together with its obverse, the inherent inferiority of the darker colored. In this view, the rule of the former over the latter is therefore inevitable, not arbitrary."
5. Grant, *Moon of Wintertime,* 75.
6. Rev. Dr. Alder to Lord Glenelg, 14 December 1837, in *Documentary History of Education in Upper Canada* [DHE], ed. J.G. Hodgins (28 vols., Toronto: L.K. Cameron, 1893-1904), vol. 4, 123. Maj. Gen. Darling (Superintendent of Indian Affairs) to Dalhousie, 1828, in "Report of the English Aboriginal Society, 1839,"[DHE], 128.
7. Duncan C. Scott, "Indian Affairs, 1763-1841," in *Canada and its Provinces,* ed. Adam Shortt and A.G. Doughty, 23 vols. (Toronto: Glasgow, Brook and Company, 1914), vol. 4, 695, 724. See also Robert S. Allen, *The British Indian Department and the Frontier in North America, 1755-1830* (Ottawa: Indian and Northern Affairs, 1975).
8. R. Mathews to Nepean, 8 April 1785, Public Archives of Canada [PAC], Q, Series, 24(1), 71.
9. "The Educational Problems of the Confederacy about 1810," in *The Valley of the Six Nations,* ed. Charles M. Johnston (Toronto: Champlain Society, 1964), 245.
10. For an account of the Fairfield settlement and Zeisberger's work among the Indians, see John Morrison, ed., "Extracts from the Journal of David Zeisberger," Ontario Historical Society, *Papers and Records* 12 (1914): 178-98, and Elma E. Gray, *Wilderness Christians* (Toronto: Macmillan, 1945), part 2.
11. Petition of United Brethren (Moravians) at Fairfield, 1 May 1801, Ontario Bureau of Archives, *Sixth Report* (Toronto, 1911), 206.
12. Strachan to Church Missionary Society, 27 February 1827, Archives of Ontario, Strachan Papers.
13. "Report of the Committee on Aborigines," *Parliamentary Papers,* 1836, vol. 7, 47-48. For details on the Credit River settlement and Peter Jones, see Donald B. Smith, "The Mississauga, Peter Jones and the White Man: The Algonkians' Adjustment to the European on the North Shore of Lake Ontario to 1860" (Ph.D. Diss., University of Toronto, 1975).

14. Church Missionary Society to Strachan, 16 March 1827, Strachan Papers.
15. Strachan to Bishop McDonell [sic], n.d. 1827, Strachan Papers. Other observers concurred with this contention. An 1845 report on the "Condition and Education of the Indian Tribes in Upper Canada," commissioned by Lieutenant-Governor Bagot in 1842, found that although Indian attendance was very irregular, "their ability in acquiring knowledge was in no way inferior to that of the White children." In *DHE*, vol. 5, 293.
16. J. Strachan, "A Charge Delivered to the Clergy of the Diocese of Toronto at the Triennial Visitation...(1844)," cited in *John Strachan: Documents and Opinions*, ed. J.L.H. Henderson, Carleton Library series, 243-44 (Toronto: McClelland and Stewart, 1969).
17. Maitland to Lord Bathurst, 29 November 1821, in Johnston, *Valley of the Six Nations*, 289.
18. Report by William L. Mackenzie based on visit to Indian settlement at Credit River in December 1830. In *DHE*, vol. 2, 122.
19. Ibid., p. 241.
20. *Christian Guardian,* 19 July 1837.
21. Canada Conference Missionary Society Methodist Church [CCMSMC], *Annual Report* [*AR*], 1825, 7. The Annual Reports of the Canadian Conference Missionary Society of the Methodist Episcopal Church in Canada beginning in 1825 are housed in the United Church Archives in Toronto. In 1833 the name was changed to the Missionary Society Wesleyan Methodist Church in British North America.
22. CCMSMC, *AR*, 1829, 5; 1827, 7; 1829-31, 3; and 1826, 5.
23. Biographical details are taken from *Appleton's Cyclopaedia of American Biography* (New York: D. Appleton and Company, 1888), 601. For a more extensive account, see W. P. J. Millar, "Thaddeus Osgood," *Dictionary of Canadian Biography*, vol. 8 (Toronto: University of Toronto Press, forthcoming 1985). My thanks to the author for allowing me to read this biography in advance of publication.
24. *York Gazette,* 14 November 1810. In Edith Firth, *The Town of York, 1793-1815* (Toronto: Champlain Society, 1962), 210-11. See petition from Osgood to Maitland, Upper Canada Sundries, 19 December 1826, PAC.
25. Second Annual Report, Central Auxiliary Society for Promoting Education and Industry in Canada, 16, cited in George W. Spragge, "Monitorial Schools in the Canadas, 1810-1845" (D. Paed. Diss., University of Toronto, 1935), 212.
26. Report of Captain T.G. Anderson, 24 September 1835, in Colborne to Glenelg, 22 January 1826, *Parliamentary Papers* 1839, p. 336, cited in L.F.S. Upton, "Indian Policy in the Canadas during the 1830's" (Unpublished Ms., October 1972).
27. See R.J. Surtees, "The Development of an Indian Reserve Policy in Canada," *Ontario History* 61 (1969): 94.
28. Head to Glenelg, 20 November 1836, cited in George K. Mellor, *British Imperial Trusteeship, 1783-1850* (London: Faber and Faber, 1951), 389.
29. As cited in Ruth Bleasdale, "Manitowaning: An Experiment in Indian Settlement," *Ontario History* 66 (1974): 149.
30. Egerton Ryerson's critique of the Manitoulin Island scheme was typical of the sort of opposition Head encountered. See *DHE*, vol. 4, 126.
31. CCMSMC, *AR*, 1829, 3.
32. Two examples of such texts can be seen at the Toronto Central Library. *Spelling for the Schools in the Chipeway Language* (York: Printed for the Canada Conference Missionary Society, 1828), and *A Hymnbook in Ojibwa Language prepared by Peter Jones* (Boston: Printed for the American Board of Commissioners for Foreign Missions by Crocker & Brewster, 1836). Jones himself had an Ojibway mother.
33. Indians at Tyendinaga to Bishop of Toronto, 7 September 1843; T.G. Anderson, S.I.A., Manitowaning, to Col. S.P. Jarvis, C.S.I.A., Kingston, 4 March 1863, Strachan Papers.
34. R. Cole Harris and John Warkentin, *Canada before Confederation* (Toronto: Oxford University Press, 1974), 118.
35. "Paper on the Religious State of the Indians in Upper Canada," 2 December 1837, Strachan Papers.
36. *DHE*, vol. 5, 297. The council met 21 July 1846.
37. Peter Jones to Strachan, Grape Island, 31 January 1828, Strachan Papers.

38. During one two-week period, the students at Alderville manufactured 172 axe handles, 6 scoop shovels, 57 ladles, 4 trays, 44 broom handles, and 415 brooms. This fine effort was acknowledged by having the articles sent on a travelling exhibition to the United States. G.F. Playter, *History of Methodism in Canada* (Toronto: William Briggs, 1862), 343.

39. Minutes of the *Annual Conferences of the Wesleyan-Methodist Church in Canada, 1824-1845* (Toronto: Anson Green, 1846), 160. The 1837 meeting was held on 14-24 June in Toronto.

40. *Christian Guardian*, 19 July 1837.

41. Rev. Dr. Alder to Lord Glenelg, 14 December 1837, *DHE*, vol. 4. 122, vol. 5, 296.

42. Founded in 1825 by a United States senator from Kentucky in co-operation with the Baptist General Convention, the Academy might be improved, its superintendent argued in 1832, by "a few workshops, embracing life: say a blacksmith, shoemaker, and wheelright who understood stocking ploughs; or any other which would seem best calculated to suit the present condition of the Indians." Robert H. Bremner, ed., *Children and Youth in America: A Documentary History*, 2 vols. (Cambridge: Harvard University Press, 1970), vol. 1, 554.

43. Cited in George H. Cornish, *Cyclopaedia of Methodism in Canada* (Toronto: Methodist Book and Publishing House, 1881), 551.

44. Bremner, *Children and Youth in America,* 555.

45. Grant, *Moon of Wintertime,* 86.

46. Department of Indian Affairs [DIA], *AR*,1889/90, 219-35.

47. *Algoma Missionary News and Shingwauk Journal,* April 1877; November 1877, 35. This paper was printed and bound by Indian boys at the Shingwauk Home. The cover page of each issue contained a half-page illustration of a horse and sleigh breaking through the ice with their passengers. This action was framed by an immobile Indian, two snowshoes, three wigwams, and overhead a beaver perched in a maple tree. The title was represented as covered in snow and ice.

48. Wilson to Superintendent General of Indian Affairs, 8 November 1877, quoted in David Nock, "E.F. Wilson: Early Years as Missionary in Huron and Algoma," *Journal of the Canadian Church Historical Society* 15, no. 14 (December 1973), 91.

49. *Algoma Missionary News,* 1 July 1885, 90.

50. Wilson to Superintendent of Indian Affairs, 2 August 1877, quoted in David A. Nock, "The Social Effects of Missionary Education: A Victorian Case Study," in *Reading, Writing, and Riches: Education and the Socio-Economic Order in North America*, ed. Randle W. Nelsen and David A. Nock (Kitchener: Between the Lines, 1978), 237.

51. *Algoma Missionary News,* July 1877; April 1877. The Wawanosh girls' uniforms which were supplied from England were blue serge trimmed with scarlet based on a design by Bishop Fauquier's wife. Edward F. Wilson, *Missionary Work Among the Ojibway Indians* (London: S.P.C.K., 1886), 225.

52. Nock, "The Social Effects of Missionary Education," 245; Wilson to Superintendent of Indian Affairs, 2 August 1877, quoted in ibid., 247.

53. Dominion of Canada, *Sessional Paper*, no. 3, 1884 (Ottawa, 1885), 24.

54. *Algoma Missionary News*, November 1877, 35; August 1877, 11.

55. *Fourth Annual Report of the Shingwauk and Wawanosh Homes* (Sault Ste. Marie, 1877), 20.

56. *Sessional Paper*, no. 3, 1884, 24.

57. "Letter to the Sunday Schools," *Our Forest Children* (1890); *Algoma Missionary News*, February 1886, 21. Wilson made two trips to the Carlisle Institute in Pennsylvania in 1887 and 1888 for discussions with its principal, Captain Pratt, and at least one visit to the Hampton Institute in Virginia in 1887. E.F. Wilson, "From Barnsbury England in 1868 to Barnsbury Canada, 1908" (illustrated diary/journal), n.p. (1887, 1888). Xerox copy at Victoria, Provincial Archives of British Columbia.

58. "A Day at the Shingwauk," *Our Forest Children* (Christmas, 1888), 15-16; *Fourth Annual Report of the Shingwauk and Wawanosh Homes*, 23.

59. *Algoma Missionary News,* April 1877.

60. Ibid., September 1877, 23; January 1878, 54; September 1877, 24.

61. Ibid., August 1877, 14. Interestingly, Mme Capelle lasted only a few days at Wawanosh. Wilson reported that she was "a decided failure." Wilson, "From Barnsbury England in 1868 to Barnsbury Canada, 1908."

62. Dominion of Canada, *Sessional Paper*, no. 16, 1888 (Ottawa, 1889), 23.
63. Quoted in Grant, *Moon of Wintertime*, 178-79.
64. *Algoma Missionary News*, December 1877, 47.
65. Quoted in David Nock, "The Social Effects of Missionary Education: A Victorian Case Study" (typescript, April 1975), 26.
66. Report signed by Bishop F.D. Fauquier, *Algoma Missionary News*, December 1877, 47-48; April 1881, 18.
67. Ibid., January 1882 2.
68. Robert A. Trennert, "Educating Indian Girls at Nonreservation Boarding Schools, 1878-1920," *Western Historical Quarterly* 13, no. 3 (July 1982): 277, 278.
69. Wilson, *Missionary Work*, 164, 166, 170.
70. Ibid., 90.
71. Wilson to Superintendent of Indian Affairs, 2 August 1877, PAC, RGIO, vol. 2023, quoted in Nock, "The Social Effects of Missionary Education," 246.
72. Wilson, *Missionary Work*, 12.
73. A similar type of failure on the part of industrial schools has been noted in the United States. Margaret Connell Szasz concludes that "the most convincing criticism was that many Indians who attended the schools 'returned to the blanket.' " Szasz, *Education and the American Indian: The Road to Self-Determination Since 1928* (Albuquerque: University of New Mexico Press, 1977), 10.
74. Thompson Ferrier, *Indian Education in the North West* (Toronto: Department of Missionary Literature of the Methodist Church, 1906), 35, 37.
75. Wilson, *Missionary Work*, 243-45.
76. Wilson, "From Barnsbury England in 1868 to Barnsbury Canada, 1908."
77. Ibid.; *The Canadian Indian* 1, no. 4 (January 1891): 118-19.
78. Nock, "E.F. Wilson," 9.
79. "Fair Play" [E.F. Wilson],"The Future of Our Indians," no. 4, *Western Canadian Journal of Anthropology* 6, no. 2 (1976): 60; no. 3, 57; no. 2, 56; no. 4, 61.
80. "Fair Play" [E.F. Wilson] "The Future of Our Indians," *The Canadian Indian* 1, no. 6 (March 1891): 160.
81. René Fumoleau, the Dene Nation, *Denendeh: A Dene Celebration* (Toronto: McClelland and Stewart, 1984).
82. Cited in Grant, *Moon of Wintertime*, 184.
83. "Our Indian Reserves," *The Globe*, 5 March 1872, quoted in David Nock, "A White Man's Burden: A Portrait of E.F. Wilson, Missionary in Ontario, 1868-1885" (M.A. thesis, Carleton University, 1973), 67.
84. Duncan C. Scott, "Indian Affairs, 1867-1912," in *Canada and Its Provinces*, ed. Shortt and Doughty, vol. 7, 616.
85. Cited in George Mellor, *British Imperial Trusteeship, 1783-1850*, 413.
86. For a comprehensive account of Indian industrial schools in Western Canada, see E. Brian Titley's chapter in *Schools in the West: Essays in Canadian Educational History*, ed. Nancy M. Sheehan, J. Donald Wilson and David C. Jones (Calgary: Detselig, 1986). See also Kenneth Coates, " 'Betwixt and Between': The Anglican Church and the Children of the Carcross (Chooutla) Residential School, 1911-1954," *BC Studies* 64 (Winter 1984-85): 27-47.

5

Creating Little Dominions Within the Dominion: Early Catholic Indian Schools in Saskatchewan and British Columbia

Jacqueline Gresko

According to the interpretation of Indian educational history sketched by Harold Cardinal and George Manuel, the residential schools established by nineteenth-century missionaries in Western Canada uniformly oppressed young Indians and attempted to wipe out their languages and cultures.[1] From these schools they barely escaped with their lives. Now, their descendents send their children to provincial or Native-run schools and struggle to revive their languages and culture.

Yet a study of two Catholic Indian Schools active during the late nineteenth and early twentieth centuries—Qu'Appelle at Lebret, Saskatchewan, and St. Mary's Mission at Mission, British Columbia[2]—show that neither the missionary educational efforts nor the Native responses were this simplistic.[3] Comparison of these two Oblate mission schools reveals that educational efforts and Native responses varied according to the Native culture, the particular school programmes, and the nature of White settlement.[4]

The general response of the Cree to Qu'Appelle School and of the Salish to St. Mary's School were very similar. In both cases, Natives resisted or rejected much of the school's programmes, instead retaining and developing their own cultural institutions in the form of dancing groups and traditional gatherings. The relatively good economic position of western Canadian Indians as seasonal labourers and the weakness of government and missionary acculturation programmes assisted this process of rejection. Ironically, so did such strengths as had the missionary schools. The brass bands, sports teams, and school spirit of Qu'Appelle and St. Mary's laid the foundation for such present-day Indian cultural institutions as the Qu'Appelle Pow Wow and the Mission War Dance Festival. When the Qu'Appelle Indian Residential School celebrated its centennial in 1984, the Indian social and sports events took precedence over Roman Catholic religious observances. When St. Mary's Indian Residence closed in 1984, Native dances by Native staff were part of the chapel liturgy.

TRADITIONAL NATIVE CULTURE

Ancestors of the Indian children who would attend the Roman Catholic mission school at Lebret included Cree, Salteaux, Assiniboine, and Sioux. Of these, the Plains Cree were the major linguistic and cultural group. Traditionally, they had no special educational institutions. Rather, the "*social group as a whole* was the school of every growing mind. . . .The practical and the religious, the manual and the intellectual, the individual and the social flowed as one complex integrated function within the Indian group."[5] When ethnographer David Mandelbaum recorded descriptions of Cree life in 1936, his oldest informants' memories stretched back to the 1860's and 1870's. He noted that the traditional Cree way of life continued on from the time "before the buffalo had disappeared."[6] Gatherings of families and bands for the buffalo hunt preceded the largest and most important meeting of the Cree year, the late June or early July sun dance. There, one or "several bands converged... together for two weeks or even longer."[7] The dance encampment included the main religious "thirst" dance, social dances, gambling, games, display of horses, and visiting. After the dance meeting, bands dispersed, travelling to traditional territories to fish or to hunt and gather food for winter.

Ancestors of the children who would attend the Oblate mission school in southern British Columbia were similarly dominated by one linguistic and cultural group, in this case the Coast Salish. Their Stalo, or river groups, like those of the Plains Cree, had no formal educational institutions. When anthropologist Wilson Duff gathered materials in the early 1950's for his ethnography of the Upper Stalo, his informants described the lives of extended families of the mid-nineteenth century, who were grouped in permanent winter villages along the river.[8] Their annual lifecycle included spring to fall migrations of some or all of the families to camp for root gathering, fishing, or berry picking, and then winter hunting trips. Most work was done in groups, not by individuals. Grandparents often cared for children while parents worked at food gathering. Grandparents also imparted the life skills and lore of the Stalo.

Unlike the Plains Cree, the Stalo social structure did not emphasize powerful tribal chiefs. Instead, co-operation and kinship in social and economic activities were stressed. However, like the Plains Cree, Stalo band or village units congregated for annual sacred and social rituals. The rainy winter season saw large gatherings for spirit dances, which were religious and social in nature, and for potlatches, which were social, economic and ceremonial occasions.[9] Among Pacific Coast Indians, a potlatch was a formal gathering of a host group, with guests present to witness and validate some change in the social status of host group members, such as birth, puberty, marriage, or burial. Guests were treated with gifts, feasting, oratory, and displays of family or personal spirit power in dance or song. Both potlatches and spirit dance gatherings might include gambling, canoe races, visiting, and displays of material wealth.

WHITE CONTACT

By the 1860's and 1870's, when Oblate priests established missions and schools among the Cree and Salish, Native cultures had been changed by contact with fur traders and the growing White settlement. The Plains Cree and their territories were included in the Hudson's Bay Company land grant transferred to Canada in 1870. To ensure peaceful settlement, Canada quickly made treaties with the Indians of the North West Territories, as the area later encompassing Saskatchewan and Alberta was known. Treaty Four, signed with the Cree, Saulteaux, and Assiniboine peoples around Fort Qu'Appelle in 1874, provided for Indian reserve lands, annuities, and schools. Schoolmasters were not sent out to the Indians until the latter took up residence on their allotted reserves. This did not happen until the buffalo disappeared late in the decade. Annual migrations to and from hunting, and especially to dancing sites, continued despite White settlement and the establishment of missions and Indian agencies.[10]

In parallel fashion, the Stalo experienced several decades of contact with fur traders at Fort Langley before the gold rushes brought White settlement, colonial government, and missions. The Stalo, like the Plains Indians, acquired guns, tobacco and alcohol early. The Stalo salmon fishery was not, however, wiped out as the buffalo had been. At the same time, the Stalo religious system was perhaps more affected by fur trade influences: as early as the 1840's, a Native prophet near Agassiz was preaching such Catholic concepts as confession, prayers, and hymns.[11]

The gold rush boom which began in 1858 brought the Stalo into a new British colony as part of the New Westminster civil district of British Columbia. Its colonial government did not make Indian treaties; thus it did not commit itself to provide schools.[12] When British Columbia entered Confederation, the terms of union continued this policy. Only in the 1880's were federal policies and programmes extended to the Indians of British Columbia. Until that time, missionaries provided the main impetus for establishing schools. The New Westminster *Mainland Guardian* of 28 May 1873 lauded Roman Catholic missionary effort when reporting the attendance of their brass band pupils among 2,500 Indians at the Queen's Birthday celebrations in the city.[13]

In both the Fraser Valley and in southern Saskatchewan, the new towns distracted Indians from the missions. Salmon canneries, lumber mills, warehouses, wharves, and farms needed Indian seasonal labour. Indian wages from these activities, which were often performed by groups working together, contributed to the continuity of Stalo winter dance gatherings and potlatches. These persisted despite the 1880's installation of federal agents, federal backing for mission schools, and prohibition of dances and potlatches.[14]

QU'APPELLE SCHOOL

The first Oblate missionary school at what is now Lebret had been established by Father Hugonnard before the Plains Cree signed Treaty Four in 1874. Like other nineteenth century French Oblates, young Joseph Hugonnard was of humble background: a labourer's son with teaching and hospital experience in France. Full of zeal for the missions, he saw schools as the civilizing part of the Christianizing process.[15] By the late 1870's, the federal government moved to establish Indian schools not only to fulfil treaty promises and missionary requests for aid, but also to make up for the demise of the buffalo by turning Indians into self-sufficient farmers. Prime Minister John A. Macdonald sent his friend, lawyer-journalist Nicholas F. Davin, to report on American industrial boarding schools for Indians. He recommended the establishment of similar schools under contract to churches in each treaty area of the North West Territories. Davin was struck in particular by the success of such schools among the five civilized Cherokee tribes. Their schools had promoted agricultural self-support, Indian administration of education, and Indian local government. These Indian communities constituted "five little republics within the Republic." Davin looked forward to little dominions within the Dominion.[16]

Qu'Appelle Industrial School would be one of the first Catholic Oblate-operated schools established in the North West Territories. The federal government, the Catholic hierarchy, and the local school principal laid careful plans drawing on Davin's report and on accounts of other schools in Ontario and the United States.[17] The work of Captain Richard H. Pratt at Carlisle in Pennsylvania particularly impressed the organizers. Pratt, a former cavalry officer, had been taking Western Indian boys and girls, particularly the Sioux, off reservations to Carlisle. There, he immersed them in Christian civilization. Pratt taught not only English and the three R's but also trades, farming, and housework during half of each day. His graduates went on outings as apprentices before being sent out into the lower rungs of the mainstream of American life as factory workers and parlour maids.[18]

Although Qu'Appelle Industrial School, built in 1884, was a Canadian government-funded school run by Catholic Oblates, it closely resembled its American counterparts of the same period in physical appearance, programmes, and intended results. The three brick buildings housed residences, classrooms, shops, hospital, heating plants, staff quarters and a chapel. The school stood on 509 acres and maintained its own farm.[19] Photographs in the Department of Indian Affairs *Annual Reports* displayed model pupils in tidy uniforms alongside parents in traditional clothing; and ex-pupils' homes juxtaposed with ordinary reserve housing.[20] Newpapers and travel diaries reported Indian pupils on excursions to fairs or band trips intended to expose them to civilization.[21] The programme of studies, which ran eleven months of the year, included six standards or elementary grades.[22] The curriculum emphasized the three R's with some attention to geography and history at higher levels. The celebration of such 'civilized' feasts as Christmas and Dominion Day rounded out formal studies.

Although planned for male Indians, Qu'Appelle quickly acquired a female wing run by the Grey Nuns. Their offer of labour could not be refused by the government, since it so economically complemented Oblate efforts. The girls' lives and programmes were similar in all but trades training and outdoor sports. They were taught not in the farm fields and shops but in the garden, hen yard, dairy, kitchen, laundry and sewing room. The sisters provided sewing and knitting machines, as well as swings, croquet mallets, and jumping ropes for outdoor recreation.[23]

The weekday schedule of Qu'Appelle Industrial School pupils, male or female, went as follows:

5:30	Rise
6:00	Chapel
6:30-7:15	Bed making, milking, and pumping
7:15-7:30	Inspection to see children are clean and well
7:30	Breakfast
7:30-8:00	Fatigue [Chores] for small boys
8:00	Trade boys at work
9:00-12:00	School, with a 15 minute morning recess
12:00-12:40	Dinner
12:40-2:00	Recreation

2:00-4:00	School and trades for older pupils
4:45-6:00	Fatigues [Chores], sweeping, pumping, and so forth
6:00-6:10	Preparing for supper
6:10-6:40	Supper
6:40-8:00	Recreation
8:00	Prayer and retire

Then on Sundays: "Usual fatigues, morning church parade to Lebret Parish Church: 2:30 P.M. Vespers with Choir: 5:00 to 6:00 P.M. Principal gives talk on behaviour and moral instruction—in winter he does this an hour a day."[24]

Significantly, the reports sent to the government by Father Hugonnard, principal of Qu'Appelle from 1884 to 1917, omitted the Cree and Sioux catechism classes which he held. Nor did he report that he asked the sisters, some of whom managed to learn Cree, to teach new pupils first in Cree then in English.[25] The assimilationist Ottawa bureaucrats were not concerned with sending home bilingual ex-pupils as missionary auxiliaries.[26] Nor did Indian Department officials encourage Hugonnard to develop dual language (English-Cree) primers.[27] As well, unlike Hugonnard, they wanted to restrict parental visits, because they were seen as encouraging retention of Indian languages and Indian habits. Hugonnard's divergence from government policy was both religious and personal. He intended to promote parental conversion through school visits. He was conscious of and sensitive to the Native culture, with its close familial links, so similar to that of his own milieu in France. Consequently, he interpreted the government dictate that only parents could visit Indian schools in the old French sense of the word "parents" as being relatives.[28]

Other special features which Father Hugonnard developed for Qu'Appelle drew government approbation. These included arranging marriages between ex-pupils and showing concern for their welfare back on the reserve. His work, along with that of the principals of Protestant schools at File Hills and Regina, led to the development of an ex-pupil colony at File Hills in the early 1900's. This separate, on-reserve farming community of twenty self-sufficient families seemed like the fulfilment of the industrial school designers' dreams.[29]

However, Father Hugonnard was forced to change his programmes during his tenure as principal. Shifts in federal policy toward greater economy and centralization of control, especially under the Liberals after 1896, meant close and harsh evaluation of the industrial school system. Bureaucrats judged industrial schools expensive, contentious, and inefficient in assimilating Indian youth.[30]

Protestant and Catholic principals, always short of staff and funds, competed against each other for pupils in order to obtain or maintain grants. Within denominations, principals of less expensive boarding schools located on reserves competed with industrial schools for pupils. In all schools, epidemic diseases and tuberculosis decimated the student population. Most importantly, ex-pupils were not living up to expectations by taking up individual farming.[31]

By the time a fire destroyed the Qu'Appelle school in 1904, the federal government had already begun to revise its industrial school policy. Although Qu'Appelle would be rebuilt, it would, like other missionary-managed residential schools, find its grants cut, technical programmes reduced, and the half day of practical instruction turned into what even Oblate principals would call "child labour," necessary to support the institutions.[32] The industrial schools would become residential schools seen by young Indians as prisons more than educational institutions.[33] The Oblate order would send new young Irish Canadian or French Canadian staff who did not know Indian languages. These men would follow government funding requirements to teach in English only, and Father Hugonnard's Native language catechism classes and ongoing links with parent groups would wither. Federal government stinginess and strictures on mission school management would cause their Oblate superior to remark: "La position de nos pères dans ces écoles est certainement difficile."[34]

ST. MARY'S MISSION SCHOOL

The early history of Oblate mission schools in British Columbia shares many similarities with schools in the North West Territories. St. Mary's mission and school was originally planned by the Oblate bishop, D'Herbomez, as a *reduction*, or model Christian village community similar to those used by the Jesuits in seventeenth-century Paraguay to Christianize and civilize the Indians. The Oblates, who came from France in the 1840's to assist Quebec missions on the Pacific coast, had discussed this concept with neighbouring Belgian Jesuits in the American Oregon territory. By the time of the gold rush of 1858, the Oblates had moved north into the new British colony.[35] There, as on the Prairies, they would be the major Catholic mission force.

The Stalo came under their St. Charles Mission, centred at the mainland colonial capital of New Westminster. The evils of that gold rush city were a major reason why the Oblates pushed formation of temperance societies and reductions along with catechetical programmes. In the North West Territories, by contrast, reductions were never promoted to any great extent.[36]

In 1861, Father Leon Fouquet began a mission upriver from New Westminster in the Fraser Valley.[37] Two years later, Father Florimond Gendre started a manual labour boarding school on this site. It was named St. Mary's, and it began with forty-two boys. Father Gendre taught them religion, reading and writing in English, gardening and farming. He also took the pupils on such excursions as the celebration of the Queen's Birthday in New Westminster.[38] Father Gendre visited Indian homes, studied their character, and used his knowledge to improve classroom discipline. He created little dignities similar to those of Native life for his pupils: watchmen of behaviour, cantors, sweeper, captain of the tools. He had the bishop present awards on the first school prize day, such as "Captain of the Holy Angels" and a flag with blue and red stars and the words "Jesus Christ Rex Angelorum." Father Gendre then sent the boys home for summer holidays to act as catechists for their families.[39] By 1870, another young Oblate schoolmaster, Father Denis Lamure, impressed the pupils, their parents, and White city dwellers by obtaining brass band instruments and starting a school band.[40]

In the 1880's, St. Mary's was still an Oblate boarding school receiving only minimal funds. Young seminarian A.G. Morice described the school, where he revived the brass band, as smaller than it had once been: only about twenty-five male pupils attended, and some of these were half-breeds. They learned English, the three R's, geography, and history from Brother Henry de Vries, a former steamboat captain. They spent half days working on the farm or at the bakery or flour mill.[41]

As at Qu'Appelle, the Oblate fathers at St. Mary's had secured an order of nuns, the Sisters of St. Ann, to run a girls' residential school beside the boys'.[42] These Lachine based sisters, who arived in 1868, included French and Irish Canadian teachers accustomed to frontier towns of British Columbia but not specially trained for Indian mission work. Their programme for the thirty to thirty-six Indian girls varied little from that offered White girls in the order's Victoria and New Westminster convents: the three R's, housekeeping, gardening, sewing, and catechism. Conditions in their "rough lumber convent" remained less refined than those of the town schools. The male Oblate superiors added to the French Canadian nuns' labours by imposing English conversation on them.

When the federal government decided to extend industrial schools west of the Rockies in the early 1890's, the Oblate bishop, Paul Durieu, was quick to respond.[43] A French farmer's son, he had risen in the Oblate order to become coadjutor for, then successor to, the ailing Bishop D'Herbomez.[44] He intensified the temperance society and the existing system of indirect control of Indian villages. These efforts, like the offer of government assistance for more effective industrial schools, were seen by Durieu as necessary to meet competition for Indians both from neighbouring Protestant schools and from wage labour employment opportunities.[45]

According to missionary and government reports, the aims and programmes at St. Mary's in the 1890's and early 1900's paralleled those of Qu'Appelle. Oblate principals, such as Fathers Chirouse, Tavernier, and Bedard, sought to convert the Indians to Christian, civilized lives. St. Mary's, which stood on

360 acres of land donated by the Oblates, consisted of two frame buildings housing boys' and girls' schools, shops, and staff and pupil residences.[46] The Oblates and the Sisters of St. Ann "strictly adhered to" government requirements by teaching students the six elementary standards, sewing, gardening, farmwork, carpentry, shoemaking and bookkeeping. As well, they provided brass band and sports teams instruction.[47] The school day included classes from 9:00 to 11:30 A.M. and 2:00 to 3:00 P.M. as well as half an hour of evening catechism. Indian pupils spent early morning and late afternoon periods doing farm or household chores, studying, or at recreation. Boys played baseball and football; girls, croquet or handball. The Oblates contributed as much or more as the Indian Department to supply staff, equipment or repairs. Its funding requirements made English mandatory in classrooms. However, Oblates well versed in Indian languages and retired from active duty, like Father Leon Fouquet, did help out with the schoolchildren and with local Indian parish work.[48] Oblate teachers made some allowance for the Indian students' culture. They recognized that these proud pupils should not have harsh punishments but instead should write lines or lose play periods.[49]

Visits to public occasions in towns or at other missions publicly displayed the missionaries' work and the educated, civilized pupils. For example, in 1890 the Agricultural Society of New Westminster engaged the St. Mary's Boys Band to play during its exhibition and in 1896 displayed the girls' handiwork.[50] Photographs of the pupils in the Indian affairs *Annual Reports* show them working on the farm and in the carpentry shop, studying in classes, and posing with their brass band instruments.[51]

Unlike Qu'Appelle, no ex-pupil colony existed. Early Oblate missionaries had hoped that a colony would grow up at Matsqui across the river, but lack of a longterm principal worked against its formation.[52] Oblate missionaries did, however, co-operate with Indian agents to establish Seabird Island Reserve in 1879 as an amalgam of various bands. Missionaries praised ex-pupils who taught in Indian village day schools, and agents lauded those whose lifestyle and work opportunities had been improved.[53] Government agents happily assisted missionary efforts to replace Salishan peoples' traditional gatherings of dances or potlatches with the celebration of Eucharistic Congresses and Passion Plays. The Vancouver *Province* of 1 June 1901 reported on the front page how two thousand Indians had gone to Chilliwack for a week to attend religious services and to present a Passion Play. At the Passion Plays of the 1890's and 1900's, pupils, ex-pupils, and relatives of St. Mary's Mission school took prominent parts.[54] Traditional canoe races, use of Indian languages, and visits among pupils and large groups of Indian relatives were part of these events in British Columbia just as they did in Saskatchewan. Such activities fit with missionary goals but not with assimilationist government policies.

In the early 1900's, when the federal government changed industrial school programmes by cutting funds, staff, and trades training, no strong defender of the existing system—like Qu'Appelle Principal Hugonnard—stood out at St. Mary's. In British Columbia, as in Saskatchewan, a new generation of Oblate mission school staff were coming to replace the original Frenchmen and Irishmen, who had humble backgrounds and missionary fervor. The new men would still be concerned with Indian education and would still make sacrifices to keep it going in times of government restraint, but most of the new staff would speak English and would not learn Indian languages.[55] There might be some use of Chinook jargon, but the pioneer priests with their appreciation of Indian languages were gone. Government funding requirements continued to stress using English only in Indian schools. In surrounding communities where Indians found jobs, English replaced Chinook in the workplace.[56] Oblates came to serve local parishes, both Indian and White, in English.[57]

NATIVE RESPONSE

Native response to both Qu'Appelle and St. Mary's was mainly negative, though some Indians welcomed the missionary concern for their well being in a time of government and societal indifference. Native people were not aware of the increasingly assimilationist government regulations for school staff, nor of the financial burdens borne by missionary groups to keep schools open. Indians did appreciate smallpox vaccine, early missionaries' use of Indian languages, the grand missionary celebrations, and priests' accommodation to Cree or Stalo lifestyles. Some Native people did want their children to learn to read or farm.[58]

At the same time, most of the Oblate mission school programmes were not welcomed. Native parents in the North West Territories and in British Columbia disliked the conversion and "civilization" of their children in distant residential schools, the stress on English, and the teaching of women's chores to young men. Father Hugonnard found recruiting pupils for Qu'Appelle Industrial School particularly difficult after the North West Rebellion because parents feared his exercise drills were an attempt to make their children into soldiers.[59] Piapot's people resisted agency and mission staff invitations to have children attend off-reserve boarding schools run by a religion other than their own.[60] These Cree and the neighbouring Standing Buffalo Sioux and Pasqua's Saulteaux would not support on-reserve day schools either, so these were closed in the mid-1890's, and the children were sent to Qu'Appelle and Regina industrial schools.[61] There Indian boys rejected the hard labour of farm training or feminine tailor training for carpentry, blacksmithing, and butchering. Those jobs fit Native traditional patterns of life.[62]

Coastal as well as Plains Indians often refused to send their children to school, sent them irregularly, or sent only expendable youth: the orphaned, mixed blood, female, or ill.[63] Indians played off denominations and kinds of schools against one another, or tricked agents to prevent children from going to school or to promote their removal. In both the Qu'Appelle and Fraser Valleys, Protestant industrial and Catholic and Protestant boarding and reserve day schools existed by the 1900's.[64] A school like the Oblate-run St. Mary's in British Columbia had to compete with salmon cannery and lumber mill employers for pupils. The Brownsville, Musqueam, and Semiahmoo bands who resided near canneries and mills, however, managed to complain to the Indian agents that St. Mary's did not have enough room for their children or that education had not been provided close to home.[65] Attendance at Qu'Appelle was healthy for a time, owing to Hugonnard's diplomatic exertions, yet attendance there only amounted to 25 to 30 per cent of potential pupil numbers.[66] Bishop Durieu had to acknowledge in 1898 that St. Mary's had only eighty-eight pupils, both boys and girls, from a Catholic Indian population of roughly two thousand.[67] Neither administrator liked to admit how truancy added to problems of managing schools dependent on per pupil grants. The childhoods of Indian children who did not attend school were characterized by freedom "even during the most sacred rites" of their people. As well, children continued to migrate with their bands and to be cared for more often by grandparents than by parents, just as in precontact times.[68]

At both Qu'Appelle and St. Mary's Schools, health conditions limited recruitment, cut pupil populations and hurt home-school relations.[69] Tuberculosis was a particularly difficult problem. Mission school staff did care for ill pupils as best they could. Smallpox vaccines and cough remedies were available. The Grey Nuns and Sisters of St. Ann were often experienced in home and in hospital nursing, but antibiotics did not yet exist, and tubercular disease was believed to be hereditary rather than infectious. Indeed, the living conditions of Native peoples in Saskatchewan and British Columbia in the late nineteenth century contributed to the spread of tuberculosis.

Ex-pupils of both schools, including residents of File Hills Colony and Seabird Island, persisted in returning to their old cultures.[70] Former pupils of Qu'Appelle joined their bands in communal seasonal wage labour more often than they chose to farm individually. Men harvested for White farmers, and women worked as domestics or dug seneca root.[71] Then the tribes went off to sundance gatherings or staged pow wows for exhibitions in towns. Both kinds of occasions continued from pre-mission days, often under the cover of missionary gatherings and fairs or stampedes.[72] In southern Saskatchewan and Alberta at the turn of the century, fair promoters were seeking out Indians to dance in traditional costumes.[73] Unwittingly, these Whites provided opportunity for the Old Men of Cree tradition again to inspire the young.[74] Also at this time, ex-pupils of St. Mary's worked as wage labourers in fisheries, on steamboats and at sawmills; the jobs were easier and more profitable than farming. Furthermore, as an Indian agent remarked, they loved "working in batches together."[75]

Later, opportunities in hop picking, berrying, harvesting, and lumbering were chosen over individual farming.[76] Indian earnings provided costumes for the chiefs invited to greet vice-regal visitors to New Westminster, or for the brass bands, or the Honour Guard of the Sacred Heart at missionary pageants at Squamish and Sechelt.[77] Gambling, canoe races, and displays of Indian wealth went along with missionary celebrations and royal visit performances. Such occasions as the dedication of new churches or the burial of prominent individuals, like Bishop D'Herbomez, resembled precontact potlatches.[78]

Ex-pupils of St. Mary's also attended Native potlatches and joined spirit dancing groups.[79] Anthropologist Wayne Suttles argues that such groups persisted under cover of public ceremonials and with the aid of continued seasonal seminomadic labour patterns. There is some irony here in that the Native parents and pupils who rejected the Oblate-run schools accepted much of Oblate religious adult education programmes and the grand mission gatherings.[80]

There is also irony in the Native response to Oblate-operated Qu'Appelle Industrial School. Ex-pupils began to use methods taught by the Whites to defend their Native civil right to freedom of religion, including attendance at dance gatherings. In the 1900's, ex-pupil involvement in Native dances drew the ire not only of Qu'Appelle Principal Hugonnard but also of Methodist and Presbyterian principals and Indian agents. On their recommendation, the Department of Indian Affairs opposed test cases on the legality of dances in 1904 and on legal petitions for "feasts, and sports and thanksgiving promenades" in 1906 and 1907. Significantly, it was Daniel Kennedy, the Assiniboine Qu'Appelle graduate, who helped his elders get legal advice about sending the petitions to Ottawa.[81] In pre-reserve days, Native elders had educated their young men by sending them to live with chiefs and learn their skills in hunting and warfare. The products of industrial school were, in effect, reincorporated into the Indian social system and then used in defiance of White domination.

Life histories of early ex-pupils of Qu'Appelle and St. Mary's illustrate the Native response.[82] Daniel Kennedy's autobiography, *Recollections of an Assiniboine Chief*, contends that he was "lassoed, roped and taken to the

Government school at Lebret" in 1886 at the age of twelve. He found school routines and the cutting of his long braided hair shocking. However, Father Hugonnard's genial personality won the young Kennedy as a friend. Kennedy credits him and Father Lacombe with arranging for advanced Indians to attend eastern colleges such as St. Boniface free of charge. Kennedy speaks of being there in 1895 but does not dwell on his post-college career; rather, his memoirs stress the traditions of the Assiniboine people.

When he returned from college, the Department of Indian Affairs employed Kennedy as interpreter and assistant farmer, while his Assiniboine elders invited him to traditional dance gatherings. They used him as a spokesman in their struggles to hold dances under cover of sports days or festivals. Through legal petitions to Ottawa, Kennedy led a fight to entrench Indian civil rights to traditional religious and social ceremonies in the Treaty Four area. During the boom times of western development in the 1900's, the wages Kennedy and his fellow Indians received as labourers paid the legal bills. Kennedy persisted in his traditional Indian cultural and social activities throughout his adult life.

In the 1930's, anthropologist David Mandelbaum found the "older men" insisting "that they perform the [Sun or Thirst Dance] ceremonies" despite opposition of agents and of "every other non-Cree." One of the agents commented that the Indian children were in school "all the year round, but as soon as they [came] to the Sundance [they were] Indians again!" Mandelbaum says that during the dance, "participants not only felt themselves in touch with something more than mortal,...but they felt themselves essentially Plains Cree. They found their identity there."[83]

This finding is backed up by K.J. Tarasoff's studies of the 1960's Sundances of the Cree and Saulteaux of the Lebret area. His informant, Feelix Ponipekeesick a Saulteaux ex-pupil of Qu'Appelle Residential School, had organized Sundances since 1911, when he was 24.[84]

St. Mary's ex-pupil Henry Pennier entitled his autobiography *Chiefly Indian.*[85] Although he and his orphaned siblings were halfbreeds, they identified with the Indian community and were admitted by the Oblates to St. Mary's. He was, like Kennedy, nostalgic concerning the Oblate staff at the school, and said of leaving school at age thirteen in 1917, "things were never quite so nice again." In Pennier's case, mission schooling did help him to obtain employment and begin farms, but it did not end his association with Indian patterns of life. Annual brass band competitions in Vancouver with ex-pupil musicians, Dominion Day sports gatherings for Catholic and Protestant Stalo on the Chilliwack reserve, and Indian participation in lacrosse teams reinforced Indian identity. Even ex-pupils who did not return to spirit dancing could easily persist in Indian social and cultural patterns—working in groups and celebrating together.

Cornelius Kelleher provides a more contemporary comparison for Daniel Kennedy than does Henry Pennier.[86] Kelleher never published his memoirs himself, but he was often interviewed. Born in 1872, he was the son of an Irish father and a Nooksack Salish woman from Washington state. After his father's death in 1879, young Kelleher went to St. Mary's Mission School. He remembered "lots of work but...lots of fun all the same," and "good wholesome food." His teachers included Brother "Captain" Henry, but were "mostly French teachers trying to teach us English," like old Father Peytavin. The school boys skipped out of his class to ride the first C.P.R. locomotive to pass by the school in 1882. They evaded their night supervisors to snitch apples from the orchard. They went happily on band trips up river as far as Lytton with Brother Morice and down to New Westminster with the Fathers. They went to the Corpus Christi celebrations at Sechelt in 1881. They saw canoes arrive en masse, enjoyed the greeting of the local mission band, saw the Indian tent encampment, and observed services involving use of Chinook, Stalo, and Sechelt languages. Kelleher also remembered Passion Play performances and his friendship with retired Father Fouquet. He commented little on chores or trades training except for the St. Mary's flour mill. After leaving school, Kelleher farmed and worked on the railroad. He also joined neighbours both White and Indian in fishing for salmon and sturgeon in the Fraser River; for the latter he made his own net, just as Native neighbours did.

Cornelius Kelleher did not send his daughter Irene, born in 1901, to a church school. She contends that it was because he considered the education poor and the religion overemphasized. Yet he regaled her with stories of Passion Plays at St. Mary's Mission, even though he joined Rosicrucians in his later years.

St. Mary's School, unlike Qu'Appelle, did not send graduates to institutions of further education like St. Boniface College. Four Indian girls from St. Mary's did attempt to begin a novitiate at a teaching sisterhood in 1897, but all became homesick and returned to their Stalo villages. Yet many other ex-pupils became watchmen or supervisors of these Durieu mission villages and members of the civil police. Many ex-pupils joined spirit dance and potlatch groups. All could afford to do so, given the seasonal and casual labour opportunities of the turn of the century in the Fraser Valley.

Ex-pupils and Roman Catholic Indians such as Simon Pierre of Katzie were prominent among anthropologists' informants in the twentieth century.[87] Recent anthropologists like Wayne Suttles and Pamela Amoss remarked on the revival of interest in Coast Salish winter dances or spirit dances in the Fraser Valley and Washington state. Amoss finds the growth in the 1970's of the dances among the Washington state Nooksack as not only religious but also economic and social in character. Amoss agrees with Suttles and with

Michael Kew, a student of the Musqueam of British Columbia, that the dances, like the bone game cycle of festivals and the summer canoe races, not only perpetuate intervillage ties but also maintain village/reserve solidarity. Furthermore, as the "market for Indian labour" declined since the First World War, the "winter ceremonial activities" reaffirmed individual worth "in a milieu from which whites are excluded."[88]

CONCLUSION

Native response to two Oblate Indian schools in western Canada varied according to the nature of their Native cultures, the particular missionary programme, and the pattern of White settlement. The Native peoples played an important part in the historic development of the schools. Treaty Four Indians persisted in their own educational institutions, specifically dance gatherings, despite Father Hugonnard's dynamic and diplomatic management of Qu'Appelle Industrial School from 1884 to 1917, and despite the establishment of White farming settlements. The Salishan peoples of the Lower Fraser Valley continued to migrate to seasonal employment and to hold winter dances and potlatches, despite instruction at St. Mary's School. There was no direct parallel to longterm principal Hugonnard, but Father E.C. Chirouse, Jr. did serve at St. Mary's Mission from 1879 to the 1920's, providing continuity of instruction. St. Mary's educated mainly Coast and Interior Salishan children. It also furthered their social contacts and group identity. Family visits to the school for grand religious gatherings enhanced this process. These events involved ceremonial proceedings not unlike the aboriginal potlatches and allowed for continuity of canoe races and games. Native people rejected the school's assimilationist programmes but accepted the missionary adult education programme since it fit traditional lifestyles.[89] Neither Oblate school achieved its goal of Indian assimilation; in both cases, a high degree of resistance to change in indigenous cultural patterns persisted.

Over the long run, industrial schools like Qu'Appelle and St. Mary's aided the preservation of Indian cultural patterns, stimulated resistance to missionary and government assimilative efforts, spread a pan-Indian identity, and eventually brought about the generation of modern Indian rights movements and cultural/educational activities. The Cherokee anthropologist R.K. Thomas has pointed out how the modern pan-Indian movement in the United States is linked to the "boarding school experience of nineteenth and twentieth century Indians."[90] It educated young Indians about one another and politicized them about their place in the larger society. The mission residential school experience became part of the Canadian Indian identity, even though not all Native people experienced it. Many Native leaders and authors did so, from

Senator James Gladstone and Andrew Paull through to Harold Cardinal and George Manuel.[91] Modern Indian rights leaders seem to share a continuity with the industrial school system.[92] George Manuel made an effort to send his son to high school at St. Mary's when he might have attended a local public school.[93] Qu'Appelle Valley Natives in 1973 established an all-Indian high school in the former Oblate residential school, and in 1984 the Stalo Indians leased the former St. Mary's Mission residence for an Indian training centre.[94] Here in the fate of these two schools lies the fulfillment of Nicholas Davin's dream to create little dominions within the Dominion.

NOTES TO CHAPTER FIVE

1. Harold Cardinal, *The Unjust Society: the Tragedy of Canada's Indians* (Edmonton: M.G. Hurtig, 1969), 51-61; and George Manuel and M. Polsuns, *The Fourth World: An Indian Reality* (Don Mills: Collier Macmillan, 1974), 63-68.

2. Terminology on Indian schools has been simplified by referring to Qu'Appelle Industrial School up to 1917 and Lebret or Qu'Appelle Residential School thereafter, as these are the names by which it was formally known. In the case of St. Mary's, which bore various titles, including "industrial," "Boarding," "Industrial," and in the twentieth century "Residential," its most common name, St. Mary's Mission School, has been used.

3. J.J. Kennedy [Gresko], "Qu'Appelle Industrial School: White Rites for the Indians of the Old North West" (Master's Thesis, Carleton University, 1970); and J.J. Kennedy [Gresko], "Roman Catholic Missionary Effort and Indian Acculturation in the Fraser Valley, B.C. 1860-1900" (B.A. Honours Essay, University of British Columbia, 1969).

4. The standard ethnographies are D. Mandelbaum, *The Plains Cree* (Anthropological Papers of the American Museum of Natural History, 1940), and W. Duff, *The Upper Stalo Indians of the Fraser Valley, British Columbia* (Victoria: King's Printer, 1952). Compare E.B. Titley, "W.M. Graham: Indian Agent Extraordinaire," *Prairie Forum* 8, no. 1 (Spring 1983): 25-42. Titley remarks, 39, "The Indians had been merely pawns in the grandiose schemes with which Graham attempted to enhance his reputation and advance his career."

5. J. Collier in introduction to E. Adams, *American Indian Education* (New York: King's Crown Press, 1946), xi.

6. Mandelbaum, *Plains Cree,* 167. Compare E. Tootoosis's commentary on D. Mandelbaum, "The Plains Cree Remember," in *Proceedings of the Plains Cree Conference*, 1975 (Regina: Canadian Plains Research Centre, 1979), 21.

7. Mandelbaum, *Plains Cree,* 203-4. See also L. O'Brodovich, "Plains Cree Sundance 1968," *Western Canadian Journal of Anthropology* 1 (1969); and K.J. Tarasoff, *Persistent Ceremonialism: the Plains Cree and Saulteaux* (Ottawa: National Museum of Man Mercury Series, 1980, Canadian Ethnology Service Paper no. 69).

8. Duff, *Upper Stalo.* It should be noted that Stalo children also attended other mission schools, such as Oblate Kuper Island, Methodist Coqualeetza, and Anglican All Hallows or St. Georges.

9. Ibid., 88, 108.

10. Kennedy, "Qu'Appelle," 173-227.

11. Duff, *Upper Stalo,* 121-22.

12. R. Fisher, "Joseph Trutch and Indian Land Policy," *BC Studies* 12 (Winter 1971-72): 3-33. It is interesting to note Trutch's comments on Indian education (from Barry M. Gough, *Gunboat Frontier British Maritime Authority and Northwest Coast Indians, 1846-1890* [Vancouver: University of British Columbia Press, 1984], p. 258n 3, citing Trutch to the secretary of state for the provinces [Joseph Howe] 26 September 1871, in British Columbia, *Papers Connected with the Indian Land Question 1850-1875* [Victoria: Queen's Printer, 1875], 99). Trutch "felt the missionary pressure to be unwarranted and of considerable nuisance value. He noted that only two missions, Metlakatla and St. Mary's (later Mission), had shown any notable success, while there were many failures."

13. *British Columbian,* New Westminster, 29 April 1865; 27 May 1865; and 24 May 1866.

14. Kennedy, "Roman Catholic," 66-68, 77-78.

15. G. Carriére, *L'Apétre des Prairies: Joseph Hugonnard, o.m.i. 1848-1917* (Montreal: Rayonnement, 1967), 7-35. Compare J.W. Grant, *Moon of Wintertime: Missionaries and the Indians of Canada in Encounter since 1534* (Toronto: University of Toronto Press, 1984), 176-79.

16. N.F. Davin, "Report on Industrial Schools for Indians and Half-Breeds, to the Right Honourable the Minister of the Interior. Ottawa, 14th March, 1879." Printed copy in Public Archives of Canada Library. See also C.B. Koester, *Mr. Davin M.P.* (Saskatoon: Western Producer, 1980).

17. Kennedy, "Qu'Appelle," 42-48, 64-74.

18. Ibid., 57-63. See also R.M. Utley, ed., *R.H. Pratt Battlefield and Classroom*, (New Haven: Yale University Press, 1964).

19. Department of Indian Affairs [DIA], *Annual Report [AR]*, 1903, 395-96.
20. See DIA, *AR*, 1895-1904, for examples.
21. See, for example, F.H. Abbott, *The Administration of Indian Affairs in Canada* (Washington DC, 1915), and G. Binnie-Clark, *Wheat and Woman* (London: William Heinemann, 1914, and University of Toronto Press, Social History of Canada Series reprint edited by S. Jackel [1979]), also Winnipeg *Free Press*, 2 October 1891.
22. DIA, *AR*, 1894, 246-49.
23. Kennedy, "Qu'Appelle," 68-69, 106-7; and DIA, *AR*, 1891, 149; 1893, 89-91. See Bettina Bradbury, "The Fragmented Family," in *Childhood and Family in Canadian History*, ed. Joy Parr (Toronto: McClelland and Stewart, 1982), for an account of contemporary nuns, the Sisters of Providence, at St. Alexis Orphanage in Montreal.
24. DIA, *AR*, 1893, 173.
25. Kennedy, "Qu'Appelle," 79, citing *Petites Annales* (Paris) 22 (1912): 265; and Hugonnard à Rev. Mére Filiatraut, Soeurs Grises Supérieure Générale, 11 July 1891, Soeurs Grises Montréal film 70, Oblate Historical Archives, Ottawa.
26. *Missions de la Congrégation des Missionnaires Oblats de Marie Immaculée* (Paris: A. Hennuyer 1862-1900; Rome: Maison Générale 1900-29), 1889,150.
27. Kennedy, "Qu'Appelle," 105.
28. H. Reed, Indian Commissionaer N.W.T. to the Deputy of the Superintendent General of Indian Affairs, 20 May 1891, Public Archives of Canada [PAC], RG 10, Black 11, 422-4; also A. McGibbion, Inspector to the Indian Commissioner, Regina, 28 February 1889, "Indians visiting the school to see the children...are swelling up to large proportions, the number in November was 165, in December 202, and in January 271...," PAC, RG 10, Black 50, 744-10.
29. DIA, *AR*, 1904, 177, 345-46; E. Brass, "The File Hills Ex-pupil Colony," *Saskatchewan History* 6, no. 2 (Spring 1953): 66-69; and Titley, "Graham."
30. Kennedy, "Qu'Appelle," 150-72; see also D. Leighton on Vankoughnet, and D.J. Hall, "Clifford Sifton and Canadian Indian Administration 1896-1905," in *As Long as the Sun Shines and the Water Flows*, ed. D. Getty and A. Lussier (Vancouver: University of British Columbia Press, 1983).
31. Kennedy, "Qu'Appelle," 82-83, 156ff.
32. H. Dunlop, O.M.I., "The Residential School," paper read at the Meeting of Residential School Principals, Vancouver, 26 February 1962.
33. Kennedy, "Qu'Appelle," 150-72. Also see E.B. Titley, "Duncan Campbell Scott and Indian Education Policy." After 1910, Scott phased out industrial schools by lessening their differences with boarding schools. By 1923 the term residential school was in vogue.
34. *Missions*, 1920, 279.
35. J. Gresko, "Louis Joseph d'Herbomez," *Dictionary of Canadian Biography* 11, 401-2; J. Gresko, "Roman Catholic Missions to the Indian of British Columbia: a Reappraisal of the Lemert Thesis," *Journal of the Canadian Church Historical Society* 24, no. 2 (October 1982): 51-62.
36. Kennedy, "Qu'Appelle," 18-19.
37. Kennedy, "Roman Catholic," 38-58.
38. *Missions*, 1865, 290-95.
39. D'Herbomez Conseils Centraux de la Propagation de la Foi, from New Westminster, 12 October 1864, Oblate General Archives, Rome, File: D'Herbomez (Information supplied courtesy of Father G. Carriére, O.M.I.).
40. J. Gresko, "Some Research Notes: Roman Catholic Indian Brass Bands, 1866-1915," *British Columbia Historical News* 16, no. 2 (Winter 1983): 12-15.
41. *Missions*, 1881, 387-95; 1873, 335; and 1879, 416. It is interesting to note a comment in the last reference that the Oblate fathers at St. Mary's "cherchent à imiter les Péres Bénédictions d'Australie; ils se font à leur exemple, agriculteurs, industriels et commerçants." It is also interesting to note Superintendent I.W. Powell's comment, DIA, *AR*, 1882, 167, that St. Mary's pupils included halfbreeds.
42. Mary Margaret Downs, *A Century of Service* (Victoria: Morriss, 1966), 62-63; Sister Marie Rollande, "S.S.A. in the life of Mére Marie Angéle", 182-85, quoting the notes of Soeur Marie de Bonsecours (Microfilm Oregon No. 30, Oblate Historical Archives, Ottawa). See

also DIA, *AR*, 1881, 1882 and 1884 on St. Mary's and also 1886-88. The sisters' authorship of these reports reflects staff shortages experienced by Oblates. They had to serve Indian villages and White settlements as well as staff the school. The Sisters of St. Ann would take over most of the classroom teaching at St. Mary's by the 1900's. See J.A. Bedard, O.M.I. in DIA, *AR*, 1899, 388-89.

43. Kennedy, "Qu'Appelle," 85; *Missions,* 1893, 406, for Durieu's report to the General Chapter meeting of the Oblate Order; DIA, *AR*, 1894, 258, St. Mary's Mission *Industrial* School [underlining mine].

44. Gresko, "Roman Catholic."

45. Kennedy, "Roman Catholic," 74-77.

46. DIA, *AR*, 1901, 409.

47. DIA, *AR*, 1897, 296; 1899, 388-89; 1900, 417-19; 1902, 409-11; also *Missions,* 1893, 396, on staffing requirements. Besides three teaching brothers, St. Mary's required teachers for shoemaking, blacksmithing, and carpentry.

48. Leon Fouquet lived out his retirement years 1899-1912 at St. Mary's Mission. G. Carriere, O.M.I., *Dictionnaire Biographique des Oblats de Marie Immaculée au Canada,* vol. 2 (Ottawa, 1977), 42-43.

49. DIA, *AR*, 1896, 390-92 and G. Forbes O.M.I., "Indian Education in British Columbia," *Oblate Missions* 14 (December 1948): 15-17, re: Father Martinet, Oblate Superior General speaking against the use of school manual labour periods as child labour.

50. DIA, *AR*, 1890, 128-29; 1896, 390.

51. DIA, *AR*, 1895-1904.

52. *Missions,* 1879, 417.

53. *Missions,* 1880, 372-73; DIA, *AR*, 1900, 242.

54. *Missions,* 1893, 151-56, on St. Mary's Passion Play.

55. J. Speare, ed., *The Days of Augusta* (Vancouver: J.J. Douglas, 1977), 37, on Shuswap-speaking early priest. See also M. Whitehead, *Now You Are My Brother* (Victoria: Provincial Archives of B.C., 1981), *Sound Heritage* 34, which says some mid-twentieth century Oblate Missionaries did learn Indian languages.

56. Compare N.W. Lidster, "Fraser Teamed With Salmon, the Language Was Chinook," *British Columbian,* 11 March 1972, an interview with 88 year old E.K. DeBeck on his summer job at a Steveston (Fraser River) salmon cannery in 1899: "Chinook was the language used to knit" the multicultural workforce of Asians, Indians and Whites together; and Sister Patricia as cited in Whitehead, *Now You Are My Brother,* 53, on how English was the language of work fifty years later.

57. *Missions,* 1905, 277. Newly arrived young missionaries from Liége, Rome and Hunfield spent several months at St. Mary's learning English.

58. See J. Redford, "Attendance at Indian Residential Schools in British Columbia, 1890-1920," *BC Studies* 44 (Winter 1979-80): 41-56. See also Indian Superintendant Powell's report for 1882. DIA, *AR*, 167, re: B.C. Indian requests for schooling.

59. Kennedy, "Qu'Appelle," 77.

60. Piapot quoted in Hugonnard Taché, 17 fevrier 1887, cited by Carriére, *L'Apétre,* 58.

61. DIA, *AR*, 1896, 188-90.

62. DIA, *AR*, 1902, Tabular Statements, 48-49; 1886, 140.

63. Kennedy, "Qu'Appelle," 182; DIA, *AR*, 1894, 258-59, stating St. Mary's Mission Industrial School had twenty-eight male and thiry-eight female students; DIA, *AR*, 1900: St. Mary's forty-three boys and forty-four girls. See also Speare, *Days of Augusta,* 18, re: Augusta's memories of being "dumped" at St. Joseph's School, Williams Lake, in 1892 at age four. This halfbreed child remained there until age thirteen. Her parents visited three times a year "but they never missed us while I was small and useless." See also Whitehead, *Now You Are My Brother,* for interview with M. Englund, and I. Orchard, *Growing up in the Valley* (Victoria: Provincial Archives of British Columbia, 1983), *Sound Heritage* 40, on orphan and halfbreed students at St. Mary's Mission school.

The high rate of intermarriage between settlers and Fraser Valley Indians is reflected in local histories such as D. Sleigh, *Discovering Deroche* (Abbotsford: Abbotsford Printing, 1983), 6, 13, 23, 31. Some interesting comments on why halfbreed and/or orphaned children were sent to mission schools appear in M. Mitchell and A. Franklin, "When You Don't Know the Language, You Listen to the Silence: An Historical Overview of Native Indian Women in British Columbia," in *Not Just Pin Money* ed. B.K. Latham and R.J. Pazdro (Victoria: Camosun College, 1984), 22-25. Mitchell and Franklin say that in the patrilineal Salishan communities, halfbreed offspring were considered "illegitimate and shameful," deprived of the "more important and paternal half of their birthright." Halfbreed and Indian ex-pupils often asked to be readmitted to school as "school life frequently offered more security and stability...than home life did." Pupils would be orphaned by epidemics, parents working away from home, family illness, poverty, or other family dislocations.

64. Kennedy, "Qu'Appelle," 81-182; compare *Missions,* 1890, 206; on St. Mary's see Durieu's report, *Missions,* 1893, 396, and DIA, *AR,* 1899, 225-34, on complaints received by agent. Examples of boarding schools: File Hills Saskatchewan, and St. Paul's, North Vancouver, B.C. Examples of industrial schools: Regina, and Coqualeetza at Sardis, B.C.

65. DIA, *AR,* 1899, 389 and 225-34.

66. Kennedy, "Qu'Appelle," 173-74; compare S. Cuthand, "The Native People of the Prairies in the 1920's and 1930's," in *One Century Later,* ed. I. Getty and D. Smith (Vancouver: University of British Columbia Press, 1978), 37. Cuthand says that in the 1930's, despite the low cost of education in church run schools, "less than half of the children of school age were enrolled in any school."

67. *Missions,* 1898, Durieu's report to the General Chapter of the Oblate Congregation.

68. Mandelbaum, *Plains Cree,* 243-44. On the Fraser Valley Indians see DIA, *AR,* 1886, 80-81, and H. Pennier, *Chiefly Indian* (Vancouver: Graydonald, 1972), 16, re: Indians berrying at Hatzic and hop picking at Agassiz.

69. Kennedy, "Qu'Appelle," 82-83; *Missions,* 1867, 19, on Fraser Valley Indian deaths; compare Duff, *Upper Stalo,* 28, on Indian population decline 1839-1915. F. Goodfellow (née Agassiz) remembers White teachers and students at Angela College, Victoria, circa 1868-70 suffering tubercular disease and later dying from it, see her *Memories of Pioneer Life in B.C.* (n.p., n.d.), 27. J. Wherrett, *The Miracle of the Empty Beds* (Toronto: University of Toronto Press, 1977), provides interesting background, but the author is uncritical of the Indian Department.

70. On File Hills colonists, see Kennedy, "Qu'Appelle," 193; on Seabird see E.B. Leacock, "The Seabird Community," in *Indians of the Urban Northwest,* ed. M. Smith (New York, 1949), 192.

71. DIA, *AR,* 1901, 208. N.W.T. Commissioner Laird, an oldtimer in the Indian service, listed the Qu'Appelle Agency Indians as the nearest to self-supporting. See also DIA, *AR,* 1898, 280-81; 1899, 152-53; 1900, 166-75; 1904, 173.

72. Kennedy, "Qu'Appelle," 191-200. See also Principal Hugonnard's comments, DIA, *AR,* 1903, 398; and 1904, 380: "Usually the dance was the first downward step of ex-pupils, as when they became dancers, progressive ideas and actions [were] abandonned."

73. Kennedy, "Qu'Appelle," 219.

74. E. Ahenakew, *Voices of the Plains Cree,* ed. R. Buck (Toronto: McClelland and Stewart, 1973), 24; and Kennedy, "Qu'Appelle," 223-25.

75. DIA, *AR,* 1881, 166; P. McTiernan on Fraser Agency. See also G.B. White, "A History of the Eastern Fraser Valley since 1885" (Master's thesis, University of British Columbia, 1937), 135-37 and 125. Of 21,000 acres of reserve land, only 10 per cent were cultivated. On the persistence of Indian dances and potlatches, see Albert Drinkwater's interview in Orchard, *Growing Up in the Valley,* 70. Drinkwater, born in 1888 and a resident of South Langley and Surrey, B.C., remembers seeing every summer how Indians passed his home en route "to a big pow-wow or potlatch at Semiahmoo." He found it wonderful to see the Indians "all dressed in their fancy clothes [and] the best blankets they owned....There must have been,...two or three different tribes or villages that went together."

76. DIA, *AR,* 1886, 80-81. Indians went to Washington state to pick hops and consorted with gamblers and liquor dealers there. Lerman, *Folktales of the Lower Fraser Indians,* 181, says the berry and hop fields were important areas of cultural exchange and cultural continuity. I. Orchard, *Floodland and Forest: Memories of the Chilliwack Valley* (Victoria: Provincial

Archives of British Columbia, 1983), *Sound Heritage* 37, 28, says farming settlers employed Indians during haying and harvesting.

77. *Missions,* 1888, 82-83; *British Columbian* 21 September 1912, "ROYAL CITY PAYS HOMAGE TO CANADA'S GOVERNOR-GENERAL...FRASER INDIANS' FEALTY."

78. *Missions,* 1874, 304-6. St. Mary's Mission Indians went with the Oblates to attend Queen's Birthday Celebrations in New Westminster in 1873, then to church, then to canoe races. Also *British Columbian,* 5 June 1890, on the death of Bishop D'Herbomez.

79. *Missions,* 1886, 480-83; P. Amoss, *Coast Salish Spirit Dancing: the Survival of An Ancestral Religion* (Seattle: University of Washington Press, 1978), vii-viii; W. Suttles, "The Persistence of Intervillage Ties Among the Coast Salish," *Ethnology* 2 (1963): 513-25.

80. See references on C. Kelleher, note 86.

81. J. Kennedy, "White 'Rites' and Indian 'Rites' " in *Western Canada Past and Present,* ed. A.W. Rasporich (Calgary: McClelland and Stewart West, 1975), 176-78.

82. D. Kennedy, *Recollections of an Assiniboine Chief* (Toronto: McClelland and Stewart, 1972). DIA, *AR,* 1893, differs from Kennedy's memories in that its "Report Showing Status of discharged pupils from Qu'Appelle Industrial School up to June 30th, 1893," 95, shows Kennedy as eight in 1885, completing a commercial course at St. Boniface College, and returning to the Qu'Appelle School in 1893. See Kennedy, "White 'Rites' " and Indian 'Rites.' "

83. D. Mandelbaum, "The Plains Cree Remembered," 12, 14, 15.

84. K.J. Tarasoff, *Persistent Ceremonialism,* 4, 77, 209.

85. H. Pennier, *Chiefly Indian,* 20-21, 113.

86. Kelleher's biography is drawn from *Fraser Valley Record* (Mission, B.C.), 13 November 1957, 8, "Presentation of Passion Play: Early Days at St. Mary's School Related by a Pupil of the 80's"; *Where Trails Meet* (Abbotsford: Matsqui-Sumas-Abbotsford Centennial Society, 1958), 30-33; Orchard, *Growing Up in the Valley,* 21-26.

87. W. Suttles, *Katzie Ethnographic Notes* (Includes D. Jenness, "The Faith of a Coast Salish Indian" (Victoria: Provincial Museum Memoir no. 2, 1955), 5. In 1952, Suttles checked Jenness's 1936 Manuscript with Simon Pierre, son of old Pierre, Jenness's informant. Simon Pierre had a deep knowledge of his own culture and of English. He was not famed as his father was for "possession of supernatural powers" but his "interest in the supernatural is intense. In his youth, as one of the few literate men of his generation, he showed great promise. He visited London as secretary to a delegation of Native chiefs petitioning the Throne." On p. 6, Suttles says he might have had a career in the White world "if his white spiritual advisors had not discouraged such worldly ambitions." Sometimes he condemned the Christian Church but he "continues to participate in its services." Simon attended the Roman Catholic church in his early manhood, in the 1880's and 1890's. In his father's family, the Catholic priests took the three "surviving older brothers away." One became an assistant preacher at Lillooet, one a police chief on New Westminster reserve, one a policeman at Harrison Mills. The New Westminster brother's family all died of tuberculosis. Both of the last two mentioned "were killed by bad Indian doctors because they put people in jail."

In M. Whitehead, *Cariboo Mission* (Victoria: Sono Nis, 1981), 118, there is the description of the four Stalo girls going to begin a trial period with Sisters of the Child Jesus at William's Lake, St. Joseph's School.

On Kelleher's daughter, Irene, see M. Ravicz et al. "Rainbow Women of the Fraser Valley," in *Not Just Pin Money,* ed. B.K. Latham and R.J. Pazdro, 14-47.

88. Suttles, "Persistence"; and Amoss, *Coast Salish Spirit Dancing,* vii-viii, 28, 162-63.

89. Amoss, *Coast Salish Spirit Dancing,* 23. In contrast with American Nooksack Indians whose parents were pro schools even if children were homesick, Amoss's Canadian-raised informant "reports that her family and peers were indifferent or even hostile to schooling for children."

91. R.K. Thomas, cited in E.P. Patterson, *The Canadian Indian* (Don Mills: Collier Macmillan, 1972), 8. Compare S. Shack, "The Education of Immigrant Children During the First Two Decades of this Century," Historical and Scientific Society of Manitoba, *Transactions III,*

no. 30, (1973-74): 30-31. Shack makes an interesting point: stories of strict discipline are always told by male immigrant ex-pupils.

92. W.T. Stanbury, "The Education Gap: Urban Indians in British Columbia," *BC Studies* 19 (1973): 33. The "Indian non-Indian 'education gap' depends strongly on the age group." In the 45-64 age group of his sample, 90 per cent had only elementary education compared with 39 per cent of B.C. and 50 per cent of Canada in the same category (1971 statistics).

93. See E.P. Patterson on A. Paull in *One Century Later,* and compare M. Boldt, "Canadian Native Indian Leadership," *Canadian Ethnic Studies* 12, no. 1 (1980), 24, on the symbiotic relationship between traditional elders and young, educated leaders. A. Paull was G. Manuel's mentor, see *Fourth World.*

94. H. Dunlop, O.M.I., interview with J. Gresko, 13 December 1984. Compare Manuel, *Fourth World,* 61, on early harmony between Christian Church membership and traditional way of life: "For a long time becoming a Christian meant going to Church on Sunday and accepting the services of the priest at births, deaths, and marriages. It did not mean giving up the traditional understanding of the world that shaped our day-to-day lives."

6

Separate and Unequal: Indian and White Girls at All Hallows School, 1884-1920[1]

Jean Barman

During the first decade of this century, Indian education in Canada underwent re-evaluation. Previously, federal policy had been directed toward the immediate assimilation of educated young Indians into the dominant socio-economic order. But, so the Department of Indian Affairs argued, most pupils were returning home to their reserves rather than settling down in White society. In 1910, the department's goal became "to fit the Indian for civilized life in his own environment" rather than "to transform an Indian into a white man."[2] The move away from assimilation altered the course of Indian history in Canada and so merits explanation. The federal government argued that educated young Indians were themselves responsible for the shift because of their unwillingness or inability to make the transition. A close examination of the policy shift within the context of a specific school admitting both Indian and White pupils suggests that the failure of government policy became inevitable because of federal parsimony and White prejudice. The case in point is All Hallows School in British Columbia, in existence for a third of a century between 1884 and 1920.

ORIGINS

All Hallows School developed as a result of similar interests between Christian missionaries and the federal government in the late nineteenth century. Almost as soon as the first White settlers arrived in British Columbia, the major denominations began demarcating spheres of influence for the purpose of Indian conversion.[3] The Anglican claim to the southwestern interior was consolidated with the arrival from England of the first bishop of the diocese of New Westminster in 1880.[4] Bishop Sillitoe quickly became convinced that the establishment of schools not only was essential to carry out God's work among the three thousand Indians in the Yale district but was also deeply desired by the Indians. His travels about the mission showed him "examples enough of self-improvement under the present very limited opportunities to warrant the highest expectations" if schools were begun.

> When we shall have been allowed to accomplish this, we shall have wrought a social revolution in the land, for we shall have elevated the people from the servile condition of hewers of wood and drawers of water and given them an equal chance in the race of life.[5]

To this end, he enticed out from England both missionary clerics to establish a boys' school and Anglican nuns to work with Indian girls.

Unfortunately, by the time three sisters of the order of All Hallows arrived in British Columbia in October 1884, the diocese's finances were in disarray, the bishop's enthusiasm having far outstripped resources, which were limited to a small endowment and voluntary contributions from Britain.[6] The sisters had come on the understanding that financial support for a boarding school would be forthcoming but instead found themselves isolated at Yale, "forced to take in washing to make ends meet."[7] The community, nestled in the steep mountains of the Fraser canyon, had originated a quarter of a century before, during the gold rush, and had received its second life as a construction centre for the transcontinental railroad. Now it was "gradually decaying."

Despite their onerous condition, the sisters immediately began a day school, but irregularity of attendance soon confirmed the absolute necessity of a boarding school.[8] The bishop proposed an expedient. Among projects initiated in his original spate of energy had been two church schools for White girls, intended to counter the non-denominationalism of the province's public system.[9] Neither was self-supporting. If the sisters would also commit themselves to take on this work, then funds granted by an English mission society for their capital costs could be used at Yale.[10] The sisters acquiesced, and White boarders began to be accepted alongside Indian girls. Additional funds still had to be raised, however. Bishop Sillitoe turned to the Department of Indian Affairs, which he had first approached without success at the time of the sisters' arrival.[11] In June 1888, an agreement was concluded to subsidize up to twenty-five pupils and construction of a dormitory.[12] Thus All

Hallows was established, with enrolment eventually reaching thirty-five Indian and forty-five White pupils, the latter almost all the daughters of Anglican families in the New Westminster diocese.[13]

REASONS FOR ATTENDANCE

Pupils were attracted to All Hallows for a variety of reasons. Since young Indians were not legally compelled to attend school, they had to decide themselves if they wanted a formal education. By the time of All Hallows's foundation, Indians in the Yale district had experienced a quarter century of White contact, and lifestyles were changing. Thus, according to a contemporary, while few "parents can read or write (the mothers certainly cannot)," many families accepted the utility of offsprings learning English, becoming literate, and acquiring some familiarity with White culture.[14] As one All Hallows pupil explained, she was sent "to learn White people's ways."[15] From the late 1890's, All Hallows had little difficulty attracting sufficient pupils and was compelled more than once to refuse applications for lack of room. To quote the order's magazine in 1897:

> The present difficulty is not to secure children for the school, as in former years, when we had to go to the Indian Reservations to coax the parents into sending their children to school and the children into coming but to find room for those who are desirous of admission.[16]

The local Indian agent reported in 1900 that Indians of the Yale band "take a good deal of interest in the education of their children and are anxious in this respect to see them on a par with their white neighbours." The same year a local chief expressed his pleasure to the sisters that Indian pupils were now "growing up together" with "the children of the white people." A decade later, another elderly chief in the area "complained" to the local Indian agent that their "children were not taught enough": "We wish our children taught the same as the whites. They go to school, maybe, five, six, seven years. They learn read [sic] a little. That's all. Not much use."[17]

In some cases the local Anglican cleric urged attendance. The Yale district contained about twelve hundred baptized Indians. More than one family must have agreed because the request that their children attend the school came from a representative of the church. An Indian pupil recalled how the local cleric would regularly "pick up girls that wanted to go to school." As remembered by another, who in 1894 at the age of eight joined her older sister and cousins at All Hallows, "Archdeacon Small, you see, was in charge of that part of the parish, and it was him that got these girls in and finally talked mother into letting me come."[18]

Family dislocation also brought pupils to All Hallows. For example, during Holy Week 1901 a "very pale thin child, with a care worn face," appeared on the school's doorstep, volunteering only that her name was "Tuchsia." Some time later a telegram arrived from her mother, a former Indian pupil not remembered for her academic ability: "I sent my little girl to you pecause [sic] I am dying. Dake care of her, make her to pe goot." Among the Indian girls Tuchsia joined at school was "a loving soft dumpling" named Grace who had arrived a year earlier at age two after her mother, also an ex-pupil, died. Grace was still too young to understand when a few months later her father was killed in a mine explosion.[19] No data exist to determine the proportion of Indian girls who came to All Hallows as a result of family dislocation. The sole surviving school register, for the years 1910-18, contains only partial information, but it indicates that many girls had only one living parent or that parents were separated.[20]

Another reason bringing Indian pupils to All Hallows was lack of educational alternatives. According to the Department of Indian Affairs, only "in a few instances" across Canada could "Indian children attend the white children's schools." For a time a handful of exceptions existed in British Columbia, but in 1911 came the observation that "a very marked prejudice exists, I might say, generally among the whites against association with Indian children." The next year, pupils in several schools were told to discontinue attendance. The All Hallows register for 1910-18 notes only two occasions where a pupil also attended a public school.[21]

PHYSICAL SEPARATION OF PUPILS

The peculiar circumstances of All Hallows's creation offered a unique opportunity for young Indians and Whites to learn to live together in a physical environment relatively isolated from the larger society. But such was not to be the case. Originally, a certain amount of contact existed. So long as only a handful of White boarders enrolled at what was in essence an Indian school, they could not remain apart, nor did they. Indeed, in March 1888 Bishop Sillitoe commented approvingly that "no prejudice seems to exist among white parents against sending their children to the same school." Christmas 1889 was celebrated, to quote a participant, by "twenty of us Indians and half-breeds, and only two young ladies," one of whom was "going to be Father Christmas, and she is followed by four Christmas spirits."[22]

Then came physical separation. Late in 1890, an anonymous letter appeared in the New Westminster newspaper "raising the question of mixed classes" at All Hallows. While denouncing the letter as "abusive and slanderous," Bishop Sillitoe in effect acquiesced, as is evidenced by his statement that "there are certainly two classes of children in the Yale School." He went on to assure present and prospective parents that the school's seven White boarders were, or would be, treated in a manner consistent with their station in life and thus were lodged separately: "Even in the play ground they only very occasionally mix with the other children." The visiting examiner that spring commented that "the school is, it may perhaps be well to note, having regard to racial and other prejudices, entirely distinct from the Indian Mission work of the All Hallows Sisterhood."[23]

Such arrangements continued. On Christmas 1895, as two of seven white girls remaining at school alongside twenty-five Indian pupils reported somewhat wistfully, no common events occurred, as had been the case previously:

> At midnight [on Christmas eve] there was a celebration of the Holy Communion in the school chapel, to which the Indian children and about sixty Indians went. We were not allowed to go to this, but from our dormitory we tried to listen to the singing.

Two days later, a party was held around "the Indian Christmas-tree."

> We were not allowed to go to it, only to peep in through the open door for a little while, and I will tell you what I saw .... The Indian children of the school stood on the platform at one end of the room singing carols. They all wore dark frocks and red pinafores and looked very nice.

A report to the order's Mother Superior in England summed up the new arrangements: "In accordance with the wishes of the English parents, the white children and the Indians do not mix." Eventually the only activity shared by all the girls was the daily religious services. Even then they attended as two separate groups. As a thirteen-year-old White girl explained, "the seats are on either side, and the Indian school in red caps and pinafores sit on one side, and the Canadian school in white veils on the other."[24]

Pupil recollections confirm the entirety of separation. As put by an Indian girl at school from 1894 to about 1900, "We didn't mix at all." However, to defend the sisters, whom she deeply admired, she put the case in favour of separation: "I think the sisters were very wise in keeping us separate because we didn't begin to have the nice things the other children had because our people couldn't afford it." The only time she recalled talking with a White girl was once when they both happened to be folding linen. According to a

White pupil at All Hallows from 1909 to 1914, "Whites and Indians were never together, that I can tell you." "We didn't think about mixing in those days." Another has summed up, "There was no contact at all." And another, "We weren't allowed to speak to them." A fourth White girl has made the same point: "We weren't allowed to look at the Indian girls, were not even supposed to look at them in chapel which was the only time we ever saw them."[25]

PHYSICAL SEPARATION BUT EDUCATIONAL PARITY

While the physical separation existing at All Hallows between Indian and "Canadian" girls was significant enough on its own terms, its consequences would have been immeasurably compounded if accompanied by inequality. In All Hallows's first years, inequality remained relative, with parity existing to the fullest extent possible given the assumptions of the age. The churches believed, and the Department of Indian Affairs concurred, that Christianity and civilization were coterminous and, more specifically, that civilization was a White prerogative. To Christianize an Indian was to civilize him, and to civilize him was to socialize him into the dominant culture.

Thus Indian girls arriving at All Hallows at age five or seven or nine, from an affectionate environment without restraints or punishments, familiar only with the world of their family and band, and very probably knowing no English, were immediately thrust into a closely regulated alien environment. Family clothing had to be exchanged for garments provided by the school, consisting in winter of chemise and drawers of unbleached cotton, heavy red or grey flannel petticoat, long woollen stockings, high leather boots, dark blue serge longsleeved dress, red pinafore, and red cloak for ouside. New pupils had their own sleeping area, in order "to acquire habits of cleanliness and order" before moving to a dormitory housing eight to twenty-five girls. Thereafter came a relentless routine whose infringement brought such traditional European punishments as being "sent to bed early, put in the corner," or deprived of "Sunday pudding." Once in school, Indian pupils had little choice as to whether or not they wished to be "civilized."[26]

A second critical assumption of the nineteenth century held that status at birth was decisive in determining status in adulthood. A principal function of education lay in preparing each individual for his place in the socioeconomic order as foretold by his conditions of birth. Thus, in an English orphanage also under the auspices of the sisters of All Hallows, poor White girls were "trained for domestic service, were confirmed, and were employed in performing the household chores of the main school, whose pupils were also orphans but of the Upper Class."[27] Similarly, the Protestant Orphans'

Home in Victoria, British Columbia, taught its female residents "to wash clothes, scrub floors, wash dishes and attend young children and all domestic work as a most important part of their education."[28]

White pupils at All Hallows in Yale, born into the middle or upper class, had by force of circumstance to be suitably prepared to assume that lifestyle. On the basis of their birth, All Hallows's Indian pupils had not even attained the bottom rung of the White socioeconomic order. Their education must therefore have as its first goal that achievement, which meant training not unlike that meted out to most White orphans of the day. The Department of Indian Affairs assumed that "semi-industrial" schools like All Hallows would give "domestic training in cooking, housework, laundry, waiting, gardening and needlework."[29] In part for reasons of economy, All Hallows's Indian pupils had always been expected to "assist in the domestic arrangements of the house." As the school grew with the admission of more and more White boarders, the Indian girls, as part of their training, became responsible for all household duties, including food preparation.[30] As summed up by a White pupil, "They were the servants; they did the work."[31]

Consequently, Indian girls rose earlier than did their White counterparts in order to do an hour of "House work" before the joint chapel service at 7:30. Whereas White pupils spent the hours from 9 A.M. to 3 P.M. wholly in the classroom, Indian girls interspersed classes with another hour of housework. When White girls went "up to dress for dinner," their Indian counterparts set the tables and lit the lamps. At the end of the year, on Prize Day, both groups received awards for academic performance and conduct, but Indian girls were also commended in such areas as "bread-making" and "laundry-work." The only work activities performed by All Hallows's White pupils appear to have been making their beds each morning after chapel and darning their stockings on Friday evening.[32]

Originally, inequality in work was offset by parity in the classroom. While bound by the assumptions of the age, the concept of assimilation nonetheless foresaw some opportunity for individual advancement beyond the bottom rung of White society. The potential in education was perceived as enormous, not only by Bishop Sillitoe but also by federal authorities. "The Indian problem exists owing to the fact that the Indian is untrained to take his place in the world. Once teach him to do this, and the solution is had." Individual ability would make the difference, and some would do better than others. In 1892, the Department of Indian Affairs commented on "the prospects of being considered fit for promotion to schools of a higher type, seeming to act as a stimulus to the pupils to excel." Already "the Indian race of Ontario has its representatives in all the learned professions, as well as in every other honourable occupation," and "no doubt the same satisfactory results will in time follow" elsewhere in Canada.[33]

No question exists but that the sisters of All Hallows considered their Indian charges to be academically capable human beings. The external examiner of spring 1887 spoke of

> the careful and successful teaching; of the readiness and accuracy with which my questions were almost invariably answered; of their quickness of apprehension and the clear understanding of the subjects treated of in the examination....The children seemed to brighten up and look pleased when I laid aside the books and appealed to their intelligence rather than to their memories.

A year later, the bishop himself held "a very rigid examination" and discovered "the answers in all respects being equal, and sometimes superior, to anything that could be expected from white children of the same age."[34] From 1893, federal authorities required that the academic level of Indian pupils be assessed annually. In British Columbia Indian residential schools in general over half the pupils were in two lowest grades, just 14 per cent in grades 5-6; at All Hallows, 45 per cent were in grades 1-2 and fully 28 per cent in 5-6.[35] As summed up by an Englishman visiting All Hallows in 1897, "Education goes on in much the same methodical routine as in England, only at Yale it is rather two schools under one roof."[36]

Individual pupils made great strides. For example, " 'Mary' came to us three years ago, not knowing her letters nor a word of English; she is now in the 'Third Canadian Reader,' and in the compound rules, weights and measures in arithmetic; she can also say the Church catechism perfectly." During her holidays Mary wrote a long letter to the sisters which suggests her progress:

> It was raining very hard when I got off the train. I got so wet, and my poor little dolly was wet too, because she had no hat on....Oh, Sister dear, if you can't find my Communion little catechism book, I got it here. It was inside of my Bible, that's why I didn't see it. If you wanted I'll sent it to you. Now that is all I can say, so with best love, dear Sister, I remain your loving naught [sic] child.

Equally representative of pupil work was an essay "About Music" by twelve-year-old Emma:

> God made everything, and He gave power to the birds to have music, and to the brook, and to the wind too. If you stand near the telegraph wires when the wind is blowing you will hear lovely music. Some birds have hardly any music. The pretty birds cannot have a nice music,

because they have something pretty already; and the birds that are plain have a lovely music in their throats, because they have only dull feathers to cover them—they are not pretty outside....

There is music in everything. Someone told me there was music too when everything was quite still, you could not *hear* that kind of music, but you could feel it in your heart.[37]

Talent was also encouraged in other areas. The bishop's mother-in-law reported with some astonishment in 1895 "that of the teachers standing before their classes, *two* were Indian girls, being in fact the more advanced pupils" who have become "efficient teachers, and are occupied in tuition five hours for five days each week." She received a note inviting her to an evening party organized by the Indian girls "quite by themselves...the writing inside (one now lies open before me) such as no English maiden need be ashamed to own." To her pleasure, "Among the attractions were a piano-forte duo, a piano solo (a well-known Mazurka, I have forgotten by whom). The execution of this last was a marvel to me; no mistakes were made, and the quick running passages given with light, easy fingering." A year later Rosie passed the Royal Academy of Music examinations alongside eight White pupils.[38]

Achievement did not necessarily come at the cost of complete alienation from traditional Indian culture. While pupils went home only during the summer holidays, contact did not disappear. Because the sisters also ministered to local Indians, including many pupils' families, they were regularly invited to Christmas festivities and to the spring Prize Day. Moreover, "whenever there is a service for the Indian adult congregation in the school chapel, and this happens about twelve times a year, the children are allowed to attend, and are taught to take their part in the portion of the service sung in the Indian language."[39] When girls did go home for the summer, many like Mary wrote freely to the sisters about their adventures, their letters suggesting a lack of strictures on behaviour.[40]

On the other hand, there is no question but that pupils had to reconcile the two cultures in their minds. Indicative of the dilemma is a long letter written to the sisters in 1900 by Mali, a pupil at the school from 1885 to 1897. She had just attended a potlatch, even though they had been forbidden by law since 1884. The letter is significant because Mali could accept both traditional Indian culture and Christianity, because she felt free to share her views with the sisters, and because they then considered it suitable to publish the letter in the school magazine. Mali began by detailing how

after an absence of many years, I went back to live among my people for few months, and I saw again some of their customs which must appear to white people as very strange, and sometimes very wrong—but I think it is because they do not understand.

She went on to explain how the potlatch is "our way of praying for the burial of our dead....I think you would call it etiquette, and the Indians are very particular about it." A lengthy analysis of the ceremony followed, and Mali summed up:

> Potlatch is an old custom, and I do not think the Indians will ever give it up....I think if some of our friends, I mean our *real* white friends like the Sisters and Miss Moody [a longtime teacher] would come, they would see for themselves; you cannot understand unless you see, and the Indians would be so glad, and there would be a chance to teach them more to be good Indians and Christians too, and not what they often feel, that to be Christians they must leave off being Indians and try to be like white people, giving up even what is harmless in their old customs.

Although no evidence exists that any of the sisters or Miss Moody ever took up Mali's invitation, it is clear from her letter that they were not unreceptive to discussion of differences between the two cultures.[41]

Thus, while Indian pupils at All Hallows rapidly became physically separate and unequal in work duties, they were recognized through the turn of the century as possessing comparable intellectual capacity. Individual advance depended on individual ability and initiative, and many achieved much. As a knowledgeable observer of the national scene reported to the Department of Indian Affairs in 1904: "It is beyond doubt that Indian children have the capacity to learn and that the reason of nonsuccess in education is not to be found in want of intelligence."[42]

EDUCATIONAL INEQUALITY

Despite demonstrated intellectual capacity, the paths of Indian children diverged from those of young Whites both at All Hallows and across Canada after the turn of the century. The explanation for the growing inequality must be sought in large part at the federal level. Disenchantment with the goal of assimilation coincided with the assumption of ministerial responsibility for Indian affairs by Clifford Sifton in 1896. As his biographer has concluded, Sifton demonstrated during his ten-year tenure "an unvaryingly parsimonious attitude toward the Indian."[43] Up to that date it was generally accepted that while residential education was expensive, it must be regarded, "when viewed with relationship to the future interests of the country, as an excellent investment." Just a year into Sifton's tenure came the assertion in the department's annual report that "only the certainty of some practical results can justify the large expense entailed upon the country by the maintenance of these schools." The report went on: "to educate children above the possibilities of their station, and to create a distaste for what is certain to be their environment in life would be not only a waste of time but doing them an injury instead of conferring a benefit upon them."[44] The die was cast. In retrospect it seems clear that the move away from assimilation would have less to do with the lifestyles of ex-pupils than with the inability of Sifton and, more generally, White Canadian society to accept Indians even at the bottom rung of the dominant socioeconomic order, much less as equal human beings. Indeed, Sifton's eventual successor stated as early as 1897, "We are educating these Indians to compete industrially with our own people, which seems to me a very undesirable use of public money."[45]

Supposed Indian "inability to mingle freely with white communities" became the pretext for a change in policy which was probably already inevitable.[46] Sifton himself led the way: "I have no hesitation in saying—we may as well be frank— that the Indian cannot go out from school, making his own way and compete with the white man....He has not the physical, mental or moral get-up to enable him to compete. He cannot do it."[47] The focus soon became "the danger...of inculcating habits, tastes and ideas calculated to produce unfitness for and discontent with a subsequent environment from which the prospect of escape is most remote." And: "great caution has to be observed to avoid the danger of unfitting the pupil for the surroundings to which their destiny confines them."[48]

A decade and more of discontent with assimilation culminated in 1910 in a revised, more frugal policy intended "to fit the Indian for civilized life in his own environment....To this end the curriculum in residential schools has been simplified, and the practical instruction given is such as may be immediately of use to the pupil when he returns to the reserve after leaving school....Local Indian agents should carefully select the most favourable location for ex-pupils" with "most careful thought given to the future of female pupils" in order that they be "protected as far as possible from temptations to which they are often exposed." Since such temptations were perceived as emanating primarily from contact with White men of "the lowest type," this meant in effect young Indian women's exclusion from any independent role in White society. "If we can keep them on their reserves, in their homes, they will not be in the way of temptation." The problem with boarding schools' curriculums as they had previously existed was quite simply that "the girls are made too smart for the Indian villages."[49]

While raising the per-pupil subsidy, the new policy effectively restricted enrolment in existing residential schools through health regulations requiring more space per child and physical improvements whose cost had to be borne principally by the religious group operating a school. In the provision of new facilities, emphasis was on fairly simple day schools offering a little education to more children at far less cost to the federal government; the goal was less alienation from the culture to which pupils must now return. Any threat of the young Indian successfully entering White society was thus effectively removed.

The changing federal attitude soon rebounded on All Hallows. The school's mother superior had early opposed any change in federal policy, writing to authorities as early as 1901:

> Many people urge a shorter period of education and training as being more profitable both to the church and to the state by enabling greater numbers to pass through the school; but seventeen years experience has proven the great unwisdom of this advice.[50]

Yet the school gradually accepted the federal shift away from academic achievement, perhaps in part because a new mother superior arrived from England in 1907 less familiar with the school's traditional objectives. A White pupil has even suggested that she was "second-rate," lacking her predecessor's "knowledge of *human* nature, not so good to judge character."[51]

Up to that time, both the school magazine and the annual report submitted to the Department of Indian Affairs had stressed Indian pupils' intellectual growth and academic progress. Thereafter neither did. The school magazine turned its attention to the activities of White pupils, whose social events alone merited four pages in 1908 compared with under a page for those of Indian girls. White pupils studied in increasing numbers for McGill matriculation examinations and external music and drawing examinations, and in 1908 one pupil received the first gold medal awarded in Canada by the Royal Academy of Music.[52] The greater academic accomplishments of White pupils merely reflected more general shifts occurring in British Columbia. Expectations concerning mean length of schooling were rising, as evidenced by an increase in the number of public secondary schools across the province, from four in 1900 to thirty-one a decade later and forty-nine by the First World War.[53] Thus, even as federal authorities were moving to curtail educational opportunities for young Indians, White Canadians were raising academic standards for their own offspring.

The annual reports submitted by All Hallows to the Department of Indian Affairs similarly turned their attention away from Indian girls' academic accomplishments. In 1904 the report had stressed how the Natives "compare very favourably with white children of the same age; in fact, in several examinations where they have had the same papers, the Indian girls have gained the higher marks of the two."[54] Through the first decade of the century, virtually all Indian pupils at All Hallows completed the allowable six grades, as evidenced by a total during these years of 31 per cent enrolled in grades 1-2, 35 per cent in grades 3-4, and 34 per cent in grades 5-6.[55] From 1907, however, the emphasis in reports to federal authorities shifted to the girls' acquisition of practical skills suitable for life on the reserve. The 1908 report highlighted, for instance, the introduction of traditional cedar basket-making as "some practical handicraft which will stand them in good stead when returning to their homes."[56] No further mention was made either of classroom achievement or of Indian pupils' preparation for external music or drawing examinations.

Thus All Hallows accepted changing federal priorities and, publicly at least, the notion of almost inherent inequality between Indians and Whites inside as well as outside of the classroom. Not surprisingly, in the years between 1910 and the closure of the "Indian school" in 1918, the proportion of Indian pupils reaching the two upper grades fell sharply to just 18 per cent, compared with 49 per cent enrolled in grades 1-2.[57] No longer was academic achievement a priority.

The federal policy shift not only destroyed All Hallows's original vision for its Indian pupils but also doomed the school itself. More stringent health regulations meant that, in order to receive full funding and so become financially viable, All Hallows had to raise at least $10,000 on its own to construct a new dormitory. Just half that sum had been acquired by 1917. At that time, an English mission society which had recently established a boys' school at nearby Lytton offered to take over All Hallows' pupils. The sisters, emotionally exhausted from a third of a century of financial hardship in conditions of extreme physical isolation, gratefully accepted the proposal. Their Indian school was closed, followed by its White counterpart two years later in 1920. The sisters returned home to England.[58]

THE LIFE STYLES OF FORMER PUPILS

Based on the number of Indian pupils annually admitted into grade 1, about 250 girls passed through All Hallows, remaining on average about three years. At a cost of considerable alienation from traditional Indian culture, pupils were indoctrinated into Christianity, made conversant in the English language, given at least basic literacy, and familiarized with European methods of housekeeping and cleanliness. As well, in the words of one young pupil, "we were taught very nicely too [sic] behave ourselves, learn our manners and taught how to behave ourselves when we leave here and go out into the world."[59]

To prepare girls to "go out into the world" was a prime function of the school. From its earliest years, the sisters were committed to pupils becoming, if they so chose, "a very useful, permanent element of the working community of the Province."[60] Their practical training in household duties was intended to permit them to obtain the bottom rung of the White socioeconomic order, while their academic achievement gave some girls the possibility of rising further. For young White women of similarly modest background, few employment opportunities existed in the late nineteenth century. The work viewed as most viable for Indian girls was domestic service, which also allowed acquisition of additional familiarity with the dominant culture in semi-sheltered conditions.

As early as 1886, a pupil was sent out "into service" in Victoria, the report two years later indicating that not only was she performing her job but that she had also been persuaded to teach Sunday school at the Anglican cathedral. Soon additional girls were placed into service, "giving satisfaction." In the autumn of 1899, an older pupil recorded being taken by Miss Moody to the provincial exhibition and having the opportunity to visit with Mali and Rosie, both nursemaids in Vancouver. Her one disappointment was not having time to accompany Mali to see the monkeys in Stanley Park, the incident suggesting that Mali, who had left the school two years before, had already achieved some familiarity with the city. It is clear from the varying bits of evidence which survive that numerous pupils went into domestic service, some of them becoming nursemaids or governesses, and at least one a nurse.[61]

On the other hand, the sisters were always quite content that their pupils should marry and thus "carry the leaven of Christian training into their Indian homes." As early as 1900, the local Indian agent was commenting that girls "who have been educated and who have taken up housekeeping show a marked improvement in their homes as compared with those of their less fortunate neighbours who have never received any education." Other girls married after several years in domestic service or some other occupation, not necessarily to fellow Indians. "Some have married respectable Englishmen and are comfortable settlers." Soon former pupils were sending "their little daughters to be brought up and educated in the old school which sheltered the childhood and girlhood of these young mothers."[62]

Other pupils directly returned home, sometimes to care for motherless siblings or invalid parents. Experience as a pupil-teacher was often put to good use, the mother superior noting in 1901 that "from more than one quarter pleasing testimony has been afforded as to the success of former pupils in carrying on this work after they have returned to their own people." Exemplary was Christina, an early pupil whose mother had died while she was at school. The cleric at Lillooet reported in 1900 that she was "going heart and soul into the teaching of the younger family."

> I spent Tuesday there and examined her pupils during the evening.... She has a regular system of marks, and gives conduct marks also, for the time out of school hours. You may well feel encouraged at finding your seed sown in the past, thus bearing fruit.[63]

For lack of information, it is impossible to be more than suggestive concerning the lifestyles chosen by All Hallows's pupils during these early years, when federal policy favoured assimilation. Their choices were not easy, nor did they necessarily reach their goal. As Althea Moody, a longtime teacher at All Hallows, wrote in 1900:

> It is very probable that the results, of the first efforts in this direction, may not meet with marked success, but "Rome was not built in a day," and no work that is worth doing in this world succeeds all at once....Still it is obvious that a thing has no chance of success until it is at least *begun!*[64]

What is clear is that pupils from All Hallows, as well as from other schools, did for a time retain the option to choose their destiny. The reports of Indian agents in British Columbia reveal that many educated young women entered domestic service, while others became teachers in mission day schools about the province. In 1903 came the assessment that "among the younger Indians English is freely spoken, and their ambition to a greater extent inspires them with a desire to attain that condition which will put them on a level with the white man." The report a year later from the agent in the Lytton area was similar: "They dress well and live more like their white neighbours than was formerly the case. These improvements are more noticeable among those who have attended school." British Columbia's Indian agents agreed with Miss Moody in seeing pupils as a transitional generation:

> The ex-pupils find their education so convenient in their ever-increasing intercourse with the whites that there is no doubt that they will be anxious to see their children in turn acquire an education, and from these children better results may be expected.

> It is considered by many that the ultimate destiny of the Indian will be to lose his identity as an Indian, so that he will take his place fairly and evenly beside his white brother. It is only by systematically building from one generation to another that this will be accomplished. The ex-pupils

merely form the second link in a chain between barbarism and civilization. Some of them are married and have children attending the schools, but they will only be the third link.[65]

However, that third link was not to be.

All Hallows's acquiescence to the federal shift away from assimilation paralleled its de-emphasis on academic achievement. In 1907 concern was expressed for the first time over "the dangers and temptations to which the Indian girl is specially exposed in our great cities." Increasingly, pupils' aspirations were directed homeward rather than toward the larger society. Not only was basket-making introduced; pupils were now taught when doing laundry not how to use appliances available if going into domestic service but rather "to make use of such simple, homely contrivances as they would be likely to have to use in after-life, as, for instance, boiling their clothes in coal-oil tins to which wooden handles have been attached." In 1912 came a verbal sigh of relief that "very few, as a rule," were choosing to go into domestic service. A year later, the admission was voiced that only those "who had no homes, have lately been placed out in service," for we "prefer, when possible, to send them home."[66] Pupils from All Hallows, like young Indians across Canada, had lost their freedom of action.

With the closing of All Hallows came another blow affecting many lives. For some girls, the school had been the only home they ever knew, for most of them it remained a centre of permanence to which they would periodically return and be refreshed. As a visiting English cleric observed, All Hallows "has produced amongst the pupils a deep spirit of loyalty, equally towards their teachers and their Alma Mater."[67] Numerous girls visited each Christmas and Prize Day, and many were regular correspondents. While the latter exchange continued, in some cases for decades after the school's closure, the living link disappeared. Not only was direct physical contact made impossible, but educational aspirations for many daughters were quashed.

CONCLUSION

During the third of a century that All Hallows was in existence, from 1884 to 1918, separation and inequality became the norm for young Indians not only at that school but across Canada. The Anglican church, under whose auspices All Hallows was founded, had believed in Indians' equal potential given educational opportunities. The school's concern that pupils utilize their intellectual capacity as well as obtain work skills coincided with the policy of assimilation advocated by the Department of Indian Affairs during the late nineteenth century.

Despite a difficult transition to school life, many Indian pupils achieved much within a short time, and some at least were able to reconcile differences between Indian and White cultures within their own minds. A number ventured out into the dominant society, and while only scattered evidence survives, it seems fairly clear that a few at least chose to remain there either through career or marriage. Certainly, All Hallows influenced lifestyles, as is evident by the many who maintained contact and by those who sent daughters back to the school. Most importantly, through the turn of the century the schooling provided at All Hallows maximized the opportunity for educated young Indians to choose their destiny rather than having it imposed upon them.

Federal parsimony together with White refusal to accept educated young Indians into the dominant socioeconomic order reordered All Hallows' priorities. The school's original difficulty in securing federal funding makes clear that the Department of Indian Affairs was never overly generous with its support. If assistance had come earlier, no "Canadian School" would have existed. Even with federal support, All Hallows was still expected to obtain additional funding to cover part of its expenses. In short, no federal expectation had ever existed that the conditions of Indian education ought as a matter of course to be made maximally conducive to achieving its goal of immediate assimilation. For that reason alone, assimilation was never given a fair chance of success.

Much more importantly, the possible success of assimilation very rapidly became of itself an undesirable outcome. White Canadians did not want young Indians entering their socioeconomic order, even at the bottom rung. That such a threat was perceived is perhaps the best evidence that the assimilation policy was having an effect. To what extent Indians would have been successful in White society, if the federal policy in favour of assimilation had been allowed to continue, is of course impossible to know. Contemporaries in British Columbia familiar with conditions among that province's Indians believed that not only was change occurring, but also that its effect would be cumulative with each successive generation. The principal opposition to assimilation did not come from Indians but rather from the dominant society. First came the demand for physical separation in the classroom, then more general unwillingness to allow educated young Indians into the work force.

What is certain is that the federal reversal of policy in 1910 removed even young Indians' option to enter the larger society with all its discrimination and prejudice. Their potential to mitigate some of that prejudice through the examples of their own lives was taken away. Young Indians were forced back onto the reserve, and the dominant society was for a generation and more left comforted in believing that Indians were, after all, inferior. As one White pupil at All Hallows observed, only at a school reunion in the late 1950's did she finally meet any of the school's Indian girls and discover that "the rules of the old days were rather silly."

NOTES TO CHAPTER SIX

1. The Sisters of All Hallows at Ditchingham, Norfolk, and especially Sister Violet, have generously provided both hospitality and access to the order's archives. I am also grateful to Garth Walker of the Anglican Archives, Diocese of New Westminster, for assistance in locating materials, and to Jean Friesen, Verna Kirkness and J.R. Miller for their comments on an earlier version of this essay presented to the B.C. Studies Conference in February 1984.

2. Department of Indian Affairs [DIA], *Annual Report* [*AR*], 1900, 132-33, and 1910, 273; and Duncan R. Scott, "Indian Affairs, 1867-1912," in *Canada and Its Provinces*, ed. Adam Shortt (Toronto: Edinburgh University Press, 1914), 616.

3. DIA, *AR*, 1872, 12.

4. The history of the diocese is recounted in Lyndon Grove, *Pacific Pilgrims* (Vancouver: Fforbez Publications, 1979).

5. Herbert H. Gowen, *Church Work in British Columbia* (London: Longmans, Green, and Co., 1899), 113-17.

6. Gowen, *Church Work*, 85-89, 122-24, 137-45; also *New Westminster Quarterly Paper* [*NWQP*], no. 6, November 1885, 7-13.

7. *NWQP*, no. 2, October 1884, 9, 19; and Sister Violet, *All Hallows, Ditchingham: The Story of an East Anglian Community* (Oxford: Becket Publications, 1983), 37. Also see *Historic Yale* (Vancouver: Vancouver Section, British Columbia Historical Association, 1954).

8. *Churchman's Gazette* [*CG*], March 1884, 331 and 335; Gown, *Church Work*, 132-34; and *NWQP*, no. 2, October 1884, 9, 18, and no. 4, April 1885, 23-27.

9. See Jean Barman, *Growing Up British in British Columbia: Boys in Private School, 1900-1950* (Vancouver: University of British Columbia Press, 1984), 7, 8.

10. See *CG*, February 1891, 794-801; August 1888, 540; February 1889 Supplement, 580; February 1890, 5; *NWQP*, no. 7, June 1886, 11-13, no. 9; November 1888, 33; and no. 67, March 1896, last page; and *All Hallows in the West* [school magazine, *AHW*] 2, no. 3, Christmas 1900, 63-64.

11. DIA, *AR*, 1885, 123; *NWQP*, no. 10, November 1888, 25; and *East and West* [the order's magazine, published in England], All Saints 1888, 34-35.

12. *NWQP*, no. 11, March 1889, 27-28; *CG*, August 1888, 539; Diocese of New Westminster, *Monthly Record*, no. 4, December 1889, 5; and DIA, *AR*, 1896, xxxvii. On federal Indian education policy and practice, see H.J. Vallery, "A History of Indian Education in Canada" (Master's thesis, Queen's University, 1942), 122-23; John Webster Grant, *Moon of Wintertime: Missionaries and the Indians of Canada in Encounter since 1534* (Toronto: University of Toronto Press, 1984), 176-77; Scott, "Indian Affairs," 612-24; and DIA, *AR*, esp. 1889, xi. The department distinguished between "industrial" schools intended for older pupils and semi-industrial "boarding" schools for their younger counterparts. The latter, located closer to reserves, were supported at about half the rate of the former and were of far less interest to federal officals. See DIA, School Branch Letterbooks, 1893-96, and School Files, vol. 6001, 1879-1941, Public Archives of Canada [PAC] (microfilm copies in Provincial Archives of British Columbia [PABC]). The distinction disappeared after about 1910. All Hallows was a boarding school.

13. *NWQP*, no. 11, March 1889, 28; no. 65, May 1895, 7; *CG*, August 1888, 540; February 1889 supplement, 580; February 1890, 5; July 1890, 725; August 1890, 730; and February 1891, 794 and 801; Diocese of New Westminster, *Monthly Record*, no. 12, (August 1890), 6; *Over the Rockies*, April 1897, 15, and July 1900, 24; and *Work for the Far West* [hereafter *WFFW*], 1909, 18.

14. *NWQP*, no. 65, May 1895, 8.

15. Interview by Imbert Orchard with Mrs. Clara Clare, Yale, 1964, accession no. 400, Aural History Division, PABC.

16. *East and West*, All Saints 1897, 516, and All Saints 1898, 564-65; and WFFW, 1901, 15.

17. DIA, *AR*, 1900, 254; 1903, 271; 1904, 236; and 1911, 381.

18. Interview with Mrs. Lavinia Brown, Lytton, 4 October 1983; and Clare interview. For the role of local clerics, see also *AHW* 1, no. 2, Michelmas 1899, 23.

19. *AHW* 2, no. 1, Ascension 1900, 18-20; 3, no. 1, Ascension 1901, 4 and 19-20; Indian number, no. 1, Easter 1911, 8; 8, no. 11, Whitsun 1908, 78; and 1, no. 3, Christmas 1899, 36; *East and West*, Winter 1893, 240-41; and *NWQP*, no. 4, April 1885, 25-27. Until All Hallows's last years, Indian pupils were generally distinguished only by a Christian first name, given at baptism. See *East and West*, Winter 1893, 237-40.

20. "Record of Indian Girls [at All Hallows and St. George's Schools], 1910 to 1922," in possession of Rev. A.W. Harding, Lytton Hospital, Lytton. James Redford has determined that at two other British Columbia residential schools, Methodist Coqualeetza and Catholic Kuyper Island, both coeducational, fully 45 and 50 per cent of pupils during these years had lost one or both parents. See his "Attendance at Indian Residential Schools in British Columbia, 1890-1920," *BC Studies* 44 (Winter 1979/80): 48.

21. DIA, *AR*, 1895, xxiii; 1900, 256, 290; 1903, 317; 1907, 259; 1908, 270; 1910, 334, 340; 1911, 378; 1912, 395; 1913, 407; and "Record of Indian Girls," entries 157 and 166.

22. *CG*, April 1888, 502; August 1890, 729; Diocese of New Westminster, *Monthly Record*, no. 11, July 1890, 6; and "Yale's Mission School," *Vancouver Daily World*, 5 July 1890.

23. *CG*, Feb. 1891, 794-95, and August 1891, 842.

24. *NWQP*, no. 67, March 1896, 19; *East and West*, Winter 1895, 375; *WFFW*, 1897, 14; and *AHW* 2, no. 3, Christmas 1900, 63, and 3, no. 3, Christmas 1901, 72.

25. Interviews with Mrs. Lily Rogers, Vancouver, 7 March 1980; Mrs. Mary Hickman, Chilliwack, 17 December 1983; Mrs. Doris Lazenby, North Vancouver, 4 February 1980; Mrs. Lorraine Pindermoss, Vancouver, 12 February 1980, and Clare interview.

26. Brown interview; *AHW* 6, no. 8, Ascension 1906, 544-46, and Indian number, no. 1, Easter 1911, 25; and DIA, *AR*, 1896, 593-94; 1911, 390; and 1913, 404, 409.

27. *East and West*, 1886-1919; Sister Violet, *All Hallows*, 25.

28. Victoria Orphans Home, *AR*, 1886, quoted in Patricia T. Rooke and R.L. Schnell, *Discarding the Asylum: From Child Rescue to the Welfare State in English-Canada* (New York: University Press of America, 1983), 165.

29. DIA, *AR*, 1896, 394.

30. *CG*, Aug. 1890, 729; Diocese of New Westminster, *Monthly Record*, no. 14, October 1890, 3; *NWQP*, no. 65, May 1895, 7; *WFFW*, 1897, 15; *AHW* 2, no. 3, Christmas 1900, 64; and DIA, *AR*, 1909, 409; 1910, 516; and 1913, 532.

31. Hickman interview.

32. *AHW* 3, no. 3, Christmas 1901, 71-73; 6, no. 8, Ascension 1906, 518 and 539; 8, no. 12, All Saints 1908, 91; and Indian number, no. 1, Easter 1911, 18-19.

33. DIA, *AR*, 1895, xxii; 1891, xii; and 1892, xiii-xiv. Also 1896, xxxvii.

34. *CG*, August 1887, 433; and April 1888, 502.

35. DIA, *AR*, 1894-97. Only schools in existence long enough for pupils to have reached the upper grades were included in the calculations.

36. *WFFW*, 1897, 14.

37. Diocese of New Westminster, *Monthly Record*, no. 13, September 1890, last page; and *WFFW*, 1901, 14. Letters were not edited for publication, and many girls did have trouble with English grammar; see *AHW* 1, no. 2, Michelmas 1899, 27-28. Pride in Indian pupils' academic accomplishments is also evident in "All Hallows School," *Vancouver Daily World*, 3 August 1899.

38. *NWQP*, no. 65, May 1895, 7-8; *WFFW*, 1896, 13; *East and West*, Winter 1894, 308; and *AHW* 1, no. 2, Michelmas 1899, 25, and 2, no. 3, Christmas 1900, 64.

39. DIA, *AR*, 1906, 442-44. See also *AHW* 1, no. 2, Michelmas 1899, 30; 2, no. 1, Ascension 1900, 17-20; 3, no. 1, Ascension 1901, 20-21; Indian number, no. 1, Easter 1911, 22; *East and West*, Winter 1894, 307 and 310; and *Sh'Atjinkujin: Parts of the Communion Service of the Church of England, Privately Printed for the Use of the Lower Fraser Indians in the All Hallows' Mission Chapel, Yale, B.C.* (London: Darling & Son, 1894), copies of which are in PABC.

40. See, for example, *AHW* 1, no. 2, Michelmas 1899, 21-22; 1, no. 3, Christmas 1899, 41; 2, no. 2, Michelmas 1900, 33-34; and Indian number, no. 1, Easter 1911, 17 and 25.

41. *AHW* 2, no. 3, Christmas 1900, 66-67; and DIA, *AR*, 1884, 104. For other, less introspective letters, see *AHW* 1, no. 2, Michelmas 1899, 23-24, and 2, no. 2, Michelmas 1900, 35-36. On

the significance of the potlatch, see Forrest E. LaViolette, *The Struggle for Survival: Indian Culture and the Protestant Ethic in British Columbia* (Toronto: University of Toronto Press, 1973).

42. Inspector of Indian Agencies to Deputy Superintendent General, 4 June 1904, in DIA, School Files, vol. 6001.

43. D.J. Hall, "Clifford Sifton and Canadian Indian Administration, 1896-1905," *Prairie Forum* 2 (1977), 128. See also his *Clifford Sifton,* vol. 1: *The Young Napoleon, 1861-1900* (Vancouver: University of British Columbia Press, 1981), 127-28 and 269-71. Sifton was also minister of the interior; its budget nearly quintupled during his tenure, while that of Indian affairs rose less than 30 per cent. The national budget doubled. On the policy shift, see also Grant, *Moon of Wintertime*, 191-97, and E. Brian Titley, "Duncan Campbell Scott and Indian Education Policy," in *An Imperfect Past: Education and Society in Canadian History,* ed. J.D. Wilson (Vancouver: CSCI, University of British Columbia, 1984), 141-53.

44. DIA, *AR,* 1894, xxi; 1897, xxvii; and 1898, xxvii. For evidence that the shift came directly from Sifton, see Hall, "Clifford Sifton," 133 n 32.

45. Canada, House of Commons, *Debates,* 1897, col. 4076, 14 June 1897, quoted in Hall, "Clifford Sifton," 134. Widespread fear of economic competition is suggested by the assurance contained in a 1901 brief to the Department of Indian Affairs offering to assist young Indians' assimilation into White society: "Nothing that we propose doing for the Indian is going to injure the prospects of the white labourer." See Katherine Hughes on behalf of Association for Befriending Indian School Graduates to DIA, 15 September 1901, in DIA, School Files, vol. 6001.

46. See DIA, *AR,* 1911, 388; 1900, xxxiii; 1901, xxviii-xxix: and 1904, xxvii and xxix. No evidence exists in the school correspondence files of the Department of Indian Affairs that Indians themselves were ever consulted about the proposed change in direction.

47. *Debates,* 1904, cols. 6946-56, 18 July 1904, quoted in Hall, "Clifford Sifton," 134.

48. DIA, *AR,* 1903, xxvii; and 1905, xxxiii.

49. Scott, "Indian Affairs," 616; and DIA, *AR,* 1909, xxxiv; 1910, 273-75; and 1911, 337.

50. DIA, *AR,* 1901, 415.

51. "Notes of reaction-elaborated" in the Rev. Heber Greene papers, Anglican Archives, Diocese of New Westminster.

52. *AHW* 8, no. 12, All Saints 1908, 96.

53. British Columbia, Department of Education, *Annual Report,* 1915, 20; and F. Henry Johnson, *A History of Public Education in British Columbia* (Vancouver: University of British Columbia, 1964), 61. Totals include both high schools and superior schools offering instruction through grade 10.

54. DIA, *AR,* 1904, 402. See also 1905.

55. By comparison across British Columbia just over a fifth of all young Indians enrolled in a residential school reached the two upper grades.

56. DIA, *AR,* 1908, 416.

57. A similar decline to 18 per cent occurred at residential schools across the province. Even then the proportion was somewhat higher than at residential schools throughout Canada. In the years 1910-18, 53 per cent across Canada were enrolled in grades 1-2, just 14 per cent in grades 5-6.

58. *East and West,* All Saints 1911, 2033; Winter 1912, 30; Winter 1913, 76; Winter 1914, 19; and All Saints 1917, 26-27.

59. *AHR* 1, no. 2, Michelmas 1899, 27.

60. *East and West,* All Saints 1890, 33; Diocese of New Westminster, *Monthly Record,* no. 14, October 1890, 3; and DIA, *AR,* 1898, 390, and 1900, 421.

61. *East and West,* All Saints 1888, 36; Easter 1889, 31; All Saints 1889, 31; All Saints 1896, 466; All Saints 1897, 515-16; *CG,* August 1888, 539; August 1891, 843; *NWQP,* no. 9, March 1888, 15; and *AHW* 1, no. 3, Christmas 1899, 47-48.

62. *NWQP.* no. 65, March 1895, 8; *East and West,* Winter 1895, 380, and Winter 1903, 800; and DIA, *AR,* 1896, xxxviii; 1903, 423; 1900, 255; 1908, 448; 1905, 367; and 1910, 517.

63. DIA, *AR,* 1901, 413; *East and West,* Winter 1899, 600; and *AHW* 1, no. 1, Ascension 1900, 13.

64. *AHW* 2, no. 2, Michelmas 1900, 41-42.
65. DIA, *AR*, 1908, 270; 1903, 317; 1904, 236; 1911, 374; and 1913, 400. Rolf Knight argues that "the pinnacle of Indian labour and entrepreneurship within the broader economy [of British Columbia] was reached during the period 1890 to WWI." See his *Indians at Work: An Informal History of Native Indian Labour in British Columbia, 1858-1930* (Vancouver: New Star Books, 1978), 185.
66. DIA, *AR*, 1907, 407; 1910, 516; 1912, 501; and 1913, 532. A contemporary has suggested that the change came much earlier, writing in 1901 that schools "seem to have withdrawn their encouragement for the outward movement" of female pupils into domestic service. See Hughes brief.
67. DHA, *AR*, 1903, 424; 1906, 443; 1912, 583; 1913, 532; *AHW*, Indian number, no. 1, Easter 1911, 28-29; and Clare interview.

7

A Very Imperfect Means of Education:
Indian Day Schools in the Yukon Territory, 1890-1955

Ken Coates

The people and government of Canada have always been slow to recognize the opportunities of the country's northern districts and to accept the responsibility that goes with sovereignty over this vast land. The administration of the Yukon Territory, and in particular the limited attention given to the Native people, provides solid evidence of decades of conscious neglect. The Indian day school programme established in the Yukon in the twentieth century illustrates the impact of this disregard for the north and also offers insights into the marginal position assigned to the national day school system by the Department of Indian Affairs.

Until the Klondike Gold Rush, which began in 1896, Canadians found little use for the far northwest, leaving the area to Natives, fur traders, and a few American miners. Following the discovery of gold, the government increased the size of the regional North-West Mounted Police contingent, dispatched a small field force to help preserve the peace, and installed a modest administration. A new era had begun in the North, one in which the federal government accepted its responsibilities and awakened to the potential of the region.[1]

Federal authorities, however, balked at the suggestion that extensive measures were required, claiming that the gold fields would soon be mined out. Instead, they began to dismantle regional services as soon as political conditions allowed. The North would not be integrated into the national administrative system, nor would there be a northern equivalent of the National Policy to draw the region into the mainstream of the Canadian economy. Instead, efforts were made to reduce official activities in the area, and until the Second World War, the federal government paid little attention to its northern colonies. The handling of Native affairs, particularly Native day schools, illustrates both the evolution and impact of this northern policy.[2]

On the southern plains, immigration, economic development, and a dream of empire forced a major change in government-Indian relations. To prepare the West for settlement, the federal government negotiated treaties with the Natives, assigned them to reserves and, as the cornerstone of an explicit policy of assimilation, offered a variety of educational programmes. Initial experiments focused on residential schools, but when that system floundered, the government turned to the less expensive day school option. Native advocates in the Yukon, particularly Anglican missionaries, expected that this national programme would be extended to the territory.[3] The government disagreed and challenged the missionaries' claims that even a modest educational system was necessary for the Natives of the North.

There were two reasons for the negative federal response. One was specific to the Yukon; the other was national in scope. The government's general reluctance rested on a belief that the territory could not sustain permanent development. Convinced that the people would leave as the gold ran out, the government passed regulations that almost guaranteed the exodus. As well, the Yukon was unlike the southern plains; its cold, long winters and scanty resources precluded sustained growth. As a consequence, the measures taken in the South to encourage permanent Euro-Canadian settlement, including treaties, reserves, and schools for the Natives, were not readily forthcoming in the North. Because White settlement was not increasing, and because the Natives could continue their harvesting activities, the federal government saw no benefit in educating or relocating the Native population. On a national scale, the Yukon Territory had been assigned a very low priority; what few resources the government was prepared to expend nationwide on Native affairs would be first allocated elsewhere.

The Yukon experience also illustrates the federal government's marginal commitment to the Indian day school programme across the country. The modest day school system that developed in the territory represented an attempt to evade educational responsibility for the Natives. There was little concern with the quality of instruction or the impact of the teaching. Until the 1950's, when a national commitment to Indian education finally emerged, the government seemed to view day schools as a politically expedient means of evading its declared intention to educate the Indian children of Canada.

FEDERAL EDUCATION POLICY

By the time that the question of a suitable education programme for the Yukon Indians arose early in the twentieth century, the federal government was re-evaluating its earlier attempts to assimilate Natives through the school system. After the department assumed responsibility for Natives in the Canadian West and North, following the acquisition of Ruperts Land in 1870, priority had been given to industrial schools. Most officials believed that Indian children receiving a "useful" education (manual and industrial skills, basic literacy and teaching in hygiene, manners and Christian morality) would abandon the nomadic, harvesting pattern of their parents for contemporary industrial opportunities. Such a programme was seen as particularly effective if students were separated from their parents and placed in a boarding facility. Day schools existed across the country, but educators placed little value on their offerings. They were "a very imperfect means of education," according to the Department of Indian Affairs. Consequently, they were accorded a marginal role in Native schooling. Still, two hundred day schools and thirty residential schools operated under the guidance of the Department of Indian Affairs, with the agency relying very heavily on missionaries to implement programmes.[4]

The emphasis on residential schools and the consequent deprecation of day schools did not last long. As graduates of the industrial and boarding schools left their institutions and attempted to find their way in an unfamiliar world, officials began to question the utility of their education. School administrators throughout Canada found that most graduates returned to their homes where, lacking occupational alternatives, they attempted to re-enter a community they had been taught to disdain. Given the high cost of their schooling, the inability of graduates to meet official expectations proved a rather damning indictment. While the missionaries continually defended their institutions, money-conscious government officials viewed such schools with an increasingly critical eye. For political reasons, residential schools in operation could not be shut down, and others would later be opened. Even though many questioned whether useful education could be imparted to Native children still under their parents' sway, the government began to shift its emphasis toward the less expensive day school programme.

The issue remained largely unresolved in the North, however. In remote settings, where the nomadic lifestyle remained the norm, the general improvements adopted to ensure better attendance at day schools, including midday meals, transportation, and better facilities, were of limited benefit. The Department of Indian Affairs *Annual Report* for 1907-1908 commented that "with regard to outlying districts, the boarding school system overcomes the otherwise insuperable difficulty of securing any regular attendance of children among tribes of roving habits." On the other hand, though nomadism negated the efficacy of day or seasonal schools, the government remained hesitant to turn too aggressively to the residential format. Because economic realities demanded a continuation of harvesting in nonagricultural, northern regions, it was generally agreed that "great caution has to be observed to avoid the danger of unfitting the pupils for the surroundings to which their destiny confines them."[5] Native mobility, limited occupational diversity, scattered settlement, and only marginal Department of Indian Affairs commitment demanded that national objectives for Native education be adapted to suit northern conditions.

THE ROLE OF THE ANGLICAN CHURCH

To the turn of the century, the larger debate about Native education scarcely affected the schooling of Indian children in the Yukon. The Anglican church dominated Native missionary and educational work in the Yukon, keeping the territory as a denominational preserve until challenged by the Roman Catholic Church in the 1930's. The first bishop, William Carpenter Bompas, repeatedly argued during the early 1890's that "schooling is the most hopeful branch of mission work," but he found few people willing to provide money for his planned programme.[6] His sponsor, the Church Missionary Society, and the Canadian government both turned down his appeals, the former because Bompas insisted on teaching mixed blood children, the latter because it felt no obligation for such northern work. Bompas proceeded on his own initiative and instructed other missionaries under his direction to do the same. The irregular system which evolved, highlighted by Bompas's tiny boarding school at Buxton Mission, was acknowledged by church and government officials to be of marginal utility. After the Klondike Gold Rush, the Department of Indian Affairs did provide a small block grant to the Selkirk Diocese of the Anglican Church to cover educational expenses. The meagre funds allowed for only limited expansion, however, and did not represent a significant attempt to formalize Native education in the Yukon.[7]

Anglican demands for assistance continued. When Bompas died in 1906, the new bishop, Isaac O. Stringer, picked up his predecessor's favourite cause. Aware of federal reservations about church-run schools, and reflecting a nationwide effort by missionary organizations to rethink the goals of

Native education, the Synod of the Yukon undertook a survey of the requirements of the Yukon Indians. The process culminated with a 1908 petition requesting greater educational assistance, especially a boarding school, and other forms of aid for the Natives. The government responded to the Anglican submission with its customary reticence. Politicians and officials argued that little could or needed to be done for the Natives of the Yukon. Because harvesting patterns remained economically and socially intact, and because federal authorities saw little prospect for economic development after the demise of the Klondike gold fields, further educational initiatives were deemed unnecessary.[8]

Supported by his officials, Frank Oliver, the minister of the interior, defended his government's decision: "I will not undertake in a general way to educate the Indians of the Yukon. In my judgement they can, if left as Indians, earn a better living." The government's reluctance reflected contemporary ambivalence over Native education. Indeed, the national debate on the efficacy of boarding versus day schooling had seriously undermined the federal commitment. By the 1900's, a new consensus had emerged. Instead of developing a national programme, reproduced from region to region with consistent occupational and instructional objectives, organizers sought, in the words of Department of Indian Affairs official Frank Pedley, "to devise a better system of Indian education, applying to each locality methods which would best achieve the desired result." A special committee of the Missionary Society of the Church of England in Canada agreed that schooling should "fit the child to take his place in the locality in which he is to live."[9]

This new policy, suggesting a more flexible approach both to format (boarding, industrial, day and seasonal schools) and to curriculum, emerged at a crucial juncture for northern Native education. Frank Oliver demonstrated the extent to which the government's position was conditioned by the new concerns when he responded to the Yukon Synod's request for assistance:

> My belief is that the attempt to elevate the Indian by separating the child from his parents and educating him as a white man has turned out to be a deplorable failure....The mutual love between parent and child is the strongest influence for the betterment of the world, and when that influence is absolutely cut apart or is deliberately intended to be cut apart as in the education of Indian children in industrial schools the means taken defeats itself.... To teach an Indian child that his parents are degraded beyond measure and that whatever they did or thought was wrong could only result in the child becoming, as the ex-pupils of the industrial schools have become, admittedly and unquestionably a very much less desirable element of society than their parents who never saw the schools.[10]

The Yukon system that emerged after 1908 represented a balance between Oliver's outright rejection of the boarding school, the Anglican clergy's incessant requests for such an institution, and the realities of education in the sparsely populated Canadian North.

DEVELOPMENT OF EDUCATIONAL PROGRAMMES

The Anglican church, as a major national religious institution, enjoyed considerable political influence. Since the Yukon was one of its few areas of ecclesiastical hegemony over a Native population, the church particularly wished to extend its regional control through an extensive education system. The 1908 request for a boarding school and improvements in government programmes for the Yukon Indians represented a thinly veiled appeal by the church for official support of its broader missionary programme. Though unconvinced of the utility of education for northern Natives, Minister of the Interior Oliver eventually succumbed to their entreaties. A decision was postponed temporarily as the department despatched school inspector A.E. Green and British Columbia Superintendent of Indian Affairs A.W. Vowell to investigate the need for schools. Their report, issued in August 1908, indicated a need for a small boarding school and a series of day schools.[11]

The federal government finally authorized the construction of a boarding school in 1910, and by the next year the modest institution established by Bompas had been moved to new quarters. It was soon apparent, however, that the Carcross Residential School would not live up to the promoters' expectations. Missionaries had difficulty convincing parents to part with their children, and the church found it hard to keep staff in the isolated northern location. Most devastating, however, were the problems of adjustment the students faced upon graduation. The clergy hoped that the graduates would be the vanguard of a new Native-Canadian Christian society in the North. Instead, taught to disdain Native customs and living standards, and poorly trained for the few economic opportunities open to them, the children floundered "betwixt and between" a White society that did not welcome them and a Native way of life they no longer accepted.[12]

The Carcross Residential School continued to stand as the cornerstone of Native education in the Yukon. However, its high profile obscured the fact that changing national priorities and regional conditions had resulted in a major expansion of the territory's Native day school programme. Educating children closer to home assumed greater importance, as did changes in curriculum which emphasized teaching adapted to suit local conditions. The continued federal commitment was further demonstrated a decade later when, in 1920, amendments to the Indian Act were passed which "removed from the Indian parent the responsibility for the care and education of his child."[13]

Before 1910, day schools were held only in conjunction with permanent Anglican missions and received limited government assistance. Under such contraints, little could be offered beyond irregular schools at Moosehide, Carcross and Selkirk. The increased funding after 1910 allowed the church to open new schools at Champagne, Teslin and Whitehorse. The number of day schools in operation varied on a yearly basis; schools closed and opened according to the availability of funds and suitable teachers. The system expanded to as many as nine schools in 1916-17 and shrank to as few as two in 1941-42, when wartime financial exigencies brought a withdrawal of federal funds. In addition, most schools operated on a seasonal basis, closing whenever the Natives moved away to hunt or trap. Classes were generally maintained at Moosehide and Selkirk, but schools at Champagne, Teslin, Little Salmon, Old Crow, Rampart House, Ross River and Whitehorse seldom operated for more than a few months each summer.[14]

THE SEARCH FOR TEACHERS

Believing that any education was better than none, Anglican clergy repeatedly opened schools under far from favourable conditions. Having decided in 1916 to establish classes at Ross River and Rampart House, the bishop hired recent graduates of the Carcross Residential School as teachers. The Department of Indian Affairs balked at the appointments on the grounds of academic incompetency. Bishop Stringer came to the defence of Rampart House's instructor Jacob Njootli, writing, "He is perhaps not as well qualified to teach as most of our teachers, but he was the best man available. Again, at this place the Indians have to go off for weeks and months to hunt and fish, so that school can be held only when they come to the post for a few weeks." Thus, though educated Euro-Canadian teachers were preferred, logistical problems dictated a reliance on Natives for some areas. The government reluctantly accepted Stringer's appeal, although it paid the Native teachers less than their White counterparts.[15]

The problems with Native instructors highlighted the Anglican Church's ongoing inability to attract suitable teachers for its Yukon schools. Elsewhere in Canada, and in more comfortable settings than the Yukon, the Department of Indian Affairs experienced difficulty recruiting competent instructors. Given a low pay scale and often unattractive working conditions, few teachers without a missionary zeal for Native education opted for the job opportunities. National problems, though, paled in comparison to those in the Yukon. With an excessively transient non-Native population, and with the day schools centred in remote, seasonal Indian villages, there was no obvious complement of teachers available. The system utilized up to the 1920's was to rely on resident clergy. Usually educated, often with notable commitment, the Anglican clergy provided a seemingly excellent solution. But here too problems emerged. Owing in large measure to the unattractiveness of a longterm northern posting, the church encountered difficulties in its attempts to call missionaries north. Those who came faced major problems with Native languages, a difficulty compounded by the clerical mobility within the Anglican church system. Though, as Anglican clergyman Cecil Swanson later commented, "short-term missionaries are useless," shifting requirements, frequent resignations, and limited funds forced the church to move its staff about regularly.[16]

These missionary-teachers were of several types. Most, like Cecil Swanson, passed through several postings in the Yukon in the midst of a swift climb through the Anglican hierarchy. A few, like Benjamin Totty, whose effectiveness as an instructor was undermined by a serious hearing problem, remained in the region for many years but were of dubious benefit. A third group, consisting of such notables as Bompas, T.H. Canham, Isaac Stringer, and John Hawksley, maintained their commitment and, generally through their language studies, prepared the groundwork for future religious and secular instruction. The teaching load between 1900 and 1920, however, fell predominantly on members of the first two groups. With the exception of Totty, at Moosehide for twenty-eight years, C.C. Brett, seventeen years at Teslin and Champagne, and Kathleen Martin, who as a lay teacher worked a total of eight years at Selkirk, teachers seldom remained in the same area for more than a few summers.

In an attempt to ensure a regular supply of instructors for its summer day schools, the Yukon Diocese established an arrangement in the 1920's with the Anglican Theological College in Vancouver, British Columbia. Under the agreement, the school sent students north, where under the direction of the bishop they provided both religious and educational services to the Natives. The federal government subsidized what was, in effect, an extended training programme by paying the regular day school stipend so long as the theological students maintained a school. Communities like Little Salmon, Teslin, Champagne, and others that had been seldom or irregularly served by clergy now received at least seasonal guidance. While these students brought boundless enthusiasm and unquestioned commitment—clearly evident in the glowing reports of their summers' work—their naive idealism, lack of experience with Natives, and short stint in the North compromised their educational offerings. Students seldom returned to an area for more than two successive summers, compounding existing instructional irregularities.

THE SEARCH FOR PUPILS

Given the day schools' financial and personnel problems, it is not surprising that Native parents failed to respond enthusiastically. Initially, the schools had evoked considerable curiosity. In the 1890's, Bompas claimed a large attendance at his Buxton mission school, although, much to his chagrin, the majority of his students were adults. Similarly, when J. Bythell opened his school at Teslin in 1909, the average age of students was twenty years, and only six of thirty-seven were of school age (six to sixteen years). Such Native enthusiasm was not unusual and was even encouraged by teachers who hoped parental interest would ensure regular attendance by the children. The experience at other centres, notably Champagne, suggests that schools functioned primarily as babysitting centres, with children attending solely at their parents' whim. Schools at the permanent Native villages remained open much of the year, but they too were plagued by inconsistent attendance. At Moosehide, located near Dawson City, the appointment of a truant officer in 1927 had a salutary impact, "improving" daily attendance from nine of twenty-four in 1926-27 to ten of seventeen the following year. While the Department of Indian Affairs could, by 1920, compel students to attend class, nothing could as yet be done about the more general problem caused by Native mobility and parental indifference.[17]

The nomadic nature of the northern Indian population before the 1950's proved an all but insuperable difficulty. With few opportunities in the post gold rush mining industry and only seasonal openings in transportation, most Yukon Natives continued to hunt and trap. Most Natives gathered at central meeting places—Teslin, Champagne, Old Crow, and others—during the summer months but spread out widely for the fall and winter hunts. With the exception of the more settled bands at Moosehide and Carcross, the Indians were away from the influence of the clergy for up to two-thirds of every year. Consequently, establishing regular, reserve-style day schools was impractical. In an attempt to attract students, the church instead offered seasonal schools, opening and closing classes in concert with patterns of group mobility.

Even given these concessions to the Native life style, which obviously affected the quality of education, the Anglican church still found little Native interest in its schools. For all its efforts, before 1945 the church could seldom claim to have contacted more than half the eligible students. Even then, the figures reported to the Department of Indian Affairs were inflated by a consistently low enumeration of Native population and were skewed by the seasonal nature of day school operations. Since average attendance in operating schools was typically in the 40 to 60 per cent range, and because schools usually opened only during the summer, total coverage was lower than the statistics suggest. Though teacher J. Bythell enthusiastically described the many benefits of his Teslin Lake school, records indicate that only seven of the thiry-seven students on his roll attended more than half the classes; sixteen showed up for fewer than ten of the thirty-three sessions.[18] Unfortunately for the Anglican clergy, Bythell's experience typified Native response to day schools.

FACILITIES

Enrolment problems were compounded by variable teaching conditions. Most often, classes were held in missionaries' quarters, though in several places separate buildings were provided. While most classrooms passed the government's informal standards for ventilation, lighting, and cleanliness, the schools lacked most amenities. Teachers encountered regular difficulties securing supplies, a problem compounded by the reluctance of the Department of Indian Affairs to commit itself to ongoing funding for new schools. Indian agents repeatedly challenged church efforts to open new establishments and even tried to withdraw funding from three seasonal schools in 1933. In the 1940's, when Catholic missionaries began work with the Natives in the southern Yukon, they attempted to secure government assistance for their educational offerings. A 1944 request for day school funding for Burwash was received unfavourably. "These [school supplies] could, of course, be provided," wrote the official in charge of Welfare and Training, "but our experience is that once this is done we receive a request shortly afterward for teacher's salary, and rent of buildings, furnishings, etc." This tightfistedness, evident from 1910 to the end of the Second World War, forced the clergy to operate their schools on an extremely small budget.[19]

CONSEQUENCES

The results of teaching under such conditions were predictable. Instructors began anew each year with students who had long since forgotten the previous year's lessons. Several teachers, notably J.R. Bythell at Teslin, tried to overcome the problem of transiency by sending school work with the children. Removed from their teachers, and in conditions scarcely conducive to scholastic pursuits, most children quickly set aside their books. In general, academic impact was minimal. Recognizing the limits under which they worked, some teachers attempted little more than lessons on hygiene, morality, and literacy, all interspersed with a heavy dose of Christian ethics. Others, particularly in the early years, tried much more, incorporating history, geography, and arithmetic into their plans. Such diversity only added to the children's confusion, likely heightened their boredom, and further undermined the already meagre accomplishments of the day schools.[20]

Each day or seasonal school instructor submitted enrolment returns and reports of academic progress on a quarterly basis, and the forms determined the federal grant provided for each class. Standards varied widely, and some teachers apparently elevated students above their level of accomplishment, fearing that poor performance would reflect badly on their instructional skills. But in spite of these facts, the uniform stagnation in educational performance is striking. Few students passed beyond the third grade, even though their names may have appeared on school rolls in seven or eight consecutive years. In 1925, for example, 137 of 138 registered students were in Standards (grades) 1 and 2. Only a handful advanced further. In 1915, 2 out of 168 attained Standard 4, and in 1935 there were 16 children out of a total of 149 enrolled in Standards 4 and 5. As a means of imparting Canadian education or even providing elementary academic skills, the schools performed poorly.

The educational problems did not pass unnoticed. Territorial superintendent of education, T.G. Bragg, wrote in 1907 that "the ordinary day schools are practically useless, and the energy and money expended in maintaining them are comparatively barren of results."[21] The use of summer theological students, and Anglican attempts to expand the day school network, were both similarly discounted by government officials. John Hawksley, an Indian agent and former Anglican missionary, echoed Bragg's sentiments. Writing in 1926, he commented, "whether such intermittent teaching is of any real value is open to question, very little progress is possible under such conditions, it leads me to doubt whether the expenditure is justified."[22] The federal government was clearly prepared to leave the Natives unschooled, ignoring the provisions in the Indian Act which gave it authority to compel attendance. There was little federal commitment to day school education, and the level of interest fell as the programme unfolded. The subsidies continued, but more as thinly veiled support for church missions than as a sign of commitment to Native education.

Anglican clergy, not surprisingly, viewed the schools in a different light. Bishop Sovereign lauded his church's efforts:

> In an intensive training, these teachers [summer students] have given to the Indian a knowledge of the written and spoken English, a training in

simple Arithmetic, a knowledge of the rules of health and sanitation, a love of their country and their Empire and a true loyalty to their Empire's King. Moreover, they are taught the Ten Commandments and a knowledge of God, so that they might grow up as law-abiding citizens. Surely such a training is beyond estimation.[23]

Others were more realistic in their appraisals. Bishop Geddes defended an admittedly flawed education system, claiming that "as Citizens of a Christian country we have a duty or a responsibility to the Native people of Canada" that could only be discharged through schooling. Judging the benefits of day schools, Geddes later wrote, "We may not have been able to take them very far on the Educational Highway but they were learning to read and write, a little arithmetic, and perhaps even more important, the elements of Hygiene, Sanitation and Health habits." He optimistically alleged that "no expenditure that your Branch made in Yukon brought better returns for the small cash outlay involved than the Seasonal Day Schools."[24]

Most clergy recognized the limited success of the day schools. Isaac O. Stringer perceived the situation in its proper context. The apparent church goal of regular school attendance, he argued, contradicted the more general longstanding effort to keep Natives away from trading posts and urban centres. Realistically, Stringer suggested, the church should aim only to impart the seeds of learning, which would be nurtured by the children themselves. In the short term, more limited accomplishments would suffice. Stringer noted that "due to the start they received in schools quite a number of Indians in different parts of the Territory are able to write a letter and read a letter, and also work out arithmetic problems such as are necessary for trading."[25] Though limited, such skills were sufficient preparation for Natives still reliant on harvesting.

The church had two other goals which, if they did not totally overcome the disappointment surrounding the day schools, provided extra justification for their maintenance. The clergy's educational hopes rested with the Carcross Residential School; the day schools were primarily a means of identifying those children likely to benefit from the boarding programme.[26] In a much broader sense, the day schools were, however, also part of the church's larger mission to the Yukon Natives. Since the clergy's aspirations went beyond the religious transformation of their Native charges, the day schools provided a useful means of influencing Indian children. As Bishop Stringer wrote to a new recruit, "it is important that the regular day school should be held whenever possible; not only does it benefit the Indians educationally, but also it is a means of getting an influence over them and doing them good."[27] While clergy agreed that the benefits and terms of regular scholastic pursuits were, at best, minimal, they saw the schools as an excellent, government financed, means of assisting more general "improvements" in the Native lifestyle.

THE IMPETUS FOR CHANGE

The federal government retained its negative view of territorial day schools to the 1940's. The withdrawal of Department of Indian Affairs funding during the Second World War capped several decades of indifference to the clergy's educational activities with of the Yukon Indians. Wartime problems prevented a quick resumption of federal aid, but shortly after war's end, a new approach was in evidence, as witnessed by the gradual emergence of the Canadian welfare state and a new found interest in Canada's economically disadvantaged peoples, including Natives. In the Yukon, the postwar period brought a burst of new initiatives for Natives in health, housing, employment, and financial assistance. Equally, a renewed commitment to Native education emerged. It was soon to have major ramifications for the territorial day school network.[28]

Debate on Native education in the Yukon in the postwar period focused on the need for an enlarged boarding school.[29] Though federal funding for day schools was reinstated, there was little agreement on the future role of the admittedly weak programme. The issue also caused concern at the national level. Native education across Canada came under the purview of a Special Joint Committee of the Senate and House of Commons delegated to conduct an intensive investigation of the Indian Act. In a marked departure from previous segregationist policies, the committee recommended in 1949 that "in order to prepare Indian children to take their place as citizens ....Wherever and whenever possible Indian children should be educated in association with other children."[30] In calling for integrated education, the committee was indirectly encouraging the abolition of reserve-based schools.

In many parts of Canada, including much of the Yukon, such a programme could not be readily implemented. The government continued to rely on residential and day schools to serve children in isolated areas. Changing conditions in the North, however, caused a shift in Native settlement patterns which co-ordinated nicely with the expanded federal commitment to the education of Natives. A dramatic collapse of the fur market in the late 1940's forced many Natives into more permanent settlements, where they sought alternative employment or government aid. The marked expansion in federal assistance programmes meshed, coincidently, with the Natives' financial needs, making them far more receptive than before to government suggestions that they alter their nomadic habits.[31]

The move toward more regular, integrated education began slowly, commencing with a joint Native and White school at Teslin in 1947. Segregationist pressures among the non-Native community proved difficult to break, particularly in Whitehorse, forcing the government to continue a dual system for a time. Whereas in 1945 some 130 Native children attended Indian day schools, by 1954 over 250 were enrolled, while another twenty-five had been admitted to territorial public schools. The pattern then shifted in a new direction. Native day school enrolment fell steadily while the number attending integrated public schools climbed. By 1954, the Department of Indian Affairs could claim with only slight exaggeration that "only a score of school-age Indian children in the entire Yukon Territory were not enrolled in school."[32]

The dramatic increase in enrolments and attendance after 1945 was far from spontaneous. After years of neglecting the education of Native children, the federal government finally committed the necessary human and monetary resources to the programme. More importantly, the government possessed an impressive new lever of power. Under the Family Allowance Act of 1944, mothers across Canada received monthly subsidies from the federal government to assist with the cost of raising children. To qualify for the programme, children had to be under the age of sixteen and had to be attending school. Until 1950, the government ignored the latter provision for Natives in the sparsely settled areas because schools were not available for all children. Once the day school and territorial school systems expanded, the government enforced the rules much more rigidly. If mothers wished to receive the subsidy, their children had to be in regular attendance at an appropriate school. The programme forced difficult choices between Native mobility and the sedentary lifestyle necessary to collect the sizable monthly payments. However, it did ensure a larger student population and more regular attendance.

With expanded funding and better teachers, the quality of education improved significantly. In both the public schools and the remaining Native day schools, Indian children now studied the standard territorial curriculum. After decades of denying the Anglican church the resources to conduct a full education programme, the federal government of the 1950's was taking measures deemed necessary to bring the northern Natives fully into the mainstream of the Canadian educational system.

CONCLUSION

The contemporary experience from 1955 to the present has its own history and has generated its own set of debates. Emphasis on non-Native topics, charges of irrelevant school curriculum and teaching methods, and the questionable utility of southern standards and values in a northern setting have all generated criticism—and occasionally anger— toward the territorial schools. Until changes took place in the 1950's, including legislative initiatives, increased funding, and changes in Native mobility, the day school programme operated by the Anglican Church under the auspices of the Department of Indian Affairs had been but a skeletal affair. Even its greatest supporters, the Anglican clergy, acknowledged its deficiencies. Indifferently funded by the federal government, viewed by many as a simple subsidy for Anglican and later for Catholic missions, the day schools met only the most modest expectations. The Natives of the Yukon questioned the utility of such educational offerings and, through their continued mobility and limited interest, ensured that irregular attendance would undermine the meagre offerings.

Though the Yukon situation was not characteristic of the national experience, it had a great deal in common with other northern and isolated regions where Native mobility continued. On reserves, in more densely settled areas, and wherever Natives had largely ceased their seasonal movements, day schools enjoyed better attendance and greater financial backing, attracted better teachers, and adhered more closely to a standard curriculum. To most government and church school promoters, day schools still represented a poor alternative to the more inclusive residential school. But at least they were inexpensive and allowed teachers to contact large numbers of students. They were a second rate alternative primarily because students did not progress satisfactorily through the scholastic system. Academic achievement in day schools across Canada was only marginally better than in the Yukon. As late as 1950, almost 40 per cent of all students in Indian day schools were in Standard (grade) 1; the figure for the Yukon in 1950 was 45 per cent. Teachers typically ascribed the poor performance to the continuing influence of parents and community, but regardless of the rationale, the day schools simply were not working. The system had not provided a viable national alternative to the flawed residential programme, nor had day schools secured the critical support of Native parents and children. Like the Yukon network, however, the national day school system changed rapidly in the 1950's, giving way where possible to integrated education. With the coercive authority of the Indian Act, the financial power provided by Family Allowance, and much more money for Native education, the government had the tools to implement a much broader, more aggressive system. Most importantly, in the period after 1950, the government finally possessed the will to proceed.

Day schools were not as personally damaging or culturally disruptive as residential schools, nor did education promoters place much stock in their very modest accomplishments. It is important to remember, however, that more Indian children in Canada passed through seasonal or regular day schools than through the portals of the more impressive boarding facilities. That the government proceeded with such an obviously flawed system indicates their marginal commitment to Native education. Day schools provided a politically palatable solution to missionary demands for greater assistance; that the schools had little impact on the students was, until the 1950's, of little consequence.

The particular network that developed in the Yukon Territory also illustrates the especially low priority ascribed to the education of Indians outside the southern agricultural belt. The Yukon, like much of the North, did not face imminent settlement, and the government saw little need to prepare the Native children for a social order they might never face. Deemed to be marginal people living in a marginal part of the country, the Yukon Natives did not request support, or receive a workable education system. Instead, they got a day school network and a residential school designed to placate the Anglican missionaries. Both were fraught with instructional irregularities and administrative problems, and neither contributed much to the education of the children of the North.

NOTES TO CHAPTER SEVEN

1. David Hall, *Clifford Sifton*: vol. 1, *The Young Napoleon* (Vancouver: University of British Columbia Press, 1982), examines the federal response to the gold strike. See also W.R. Morrison, "The Mounted Police on Canada's Northern Frontier" (Ph.D. thesis, University of Western Ontario, 1977).
2. Ken Coates, "Best Left as Indians: The Federal Government and the Natives of the Yukon Territory, 1890-1950," *Canadian Journal of Native Studies* (forthcoming).
3. On residential schools, see Ken Coates, "Betwixt and Between. The Anglican Church and the Children of the Carcross (Chouttla) Residential School, 1910-1959," *BC Studies* 64 (Winter 1985); and J. Gresko, "White 'Rites' and Indian 'Rites': Indian Education and Native Responses in the West, 1870-1910," in *Western Canada: Past and Present*, ed. A.W. Rasporich, (Calgary: McClelland and Stewart, 1975), 163-82. Many leaders of the later Native rights movement emerged out of the residential school environment. See Paul Tennant, "Native Organization in British Columbia, 1900-1969: A Response to Internal Colonialism," *BC Studies* 55 (Autumn 1982): 3-49.
4. Department of Indian Affairs [DIA], *Annual Report [AR]*, 1892, xi, provides a particularly good example of this enthusiasm; DIA, *AR*, 1893, and 1894, xviii. See also 1895, xxii, and 1898, xxvi.
5. DIA, *AR*, 1908, xxxiii; 1906, xxxiii.
6. Bompas to C.M.S., 3 January 1894, Public Archives of Canada [PAC] MG17 B2, Church Missionary Society [CMS].
7. Duncan Scott, Memorandum to Deputy Superintendent General, 2 January 1908, DIA, vol. 3906, file 3078; Bompas to Hon. J.H. Ross, 7 March 1903, DIA, vol. 3962, file 147, 654-1, pt. 2.
8. Missionary Society of the Church of England, Memorandum on Indian Mission Schools by R. Mackay, c. 1906, General Synod Archives [GSA], M75-103, Series 2-14.
9. F. Pedley to F. Oliver, 23 January 1908, GSA, M74-3, 1-A2. Scott memorandum to Deputy Superintendent General, 21 January 1908, DIA, vol. 3906, file 105, 378; Notes of Interview, 26 February 1909, Yukon Territorial Archives [YTA], Anglican Church [AC], New Series, file 2; F. F. Pedley, Deputy Superintendent General of Indian Affairs to Rev. L. Norman Tucker, 21 March 1906, GSA, M75-103, Series 2-14, MSCC. GSA, *Memorandum on Indian Missions and Indian Schools,* submitted on behalf of the Special Indian Committee of the MSCC, 14 March 1906. The concurrence of Anglicans, Presbyterians and Methodists (the Roman Catholics refused to participate in an interdenominational conference) with Pedley's comment (see above) is Pound, "Memorandum of a Conference," 24-27 March 1908, GSA, M75-103, MSCVC.
10. Frank Oliver to A.C.C., 28 January 1908, GSA, M75-103, Series 2-14, MSCC.
11. Report of Messrs. Vowell and Green, 14 August 1908, YTA, AC, New Series, file 2.
12. Ken Coates, "Betwixt and Between."
13. DIA, *AR*, 1920, 13.
14. Geddes to Dr. H.W. McGill, 11 November 1942, on wartime funding cuts, DIA, vol. 6479, file 940-1. pt. 2. Until 1945, annual grants for day schools ranged from $2,100 to $4,800. After the war, allotments rose dramatically, reaching a yearly expenditure of almost $37,000 in 1950-54. The Carcross Residential School and a smaller facility for mixed-blood children in Dawson received much more, with grants, for example, of $16,000 in 1926-29, when day schools received $3,000.
15. D.D. McLean to John Hawksley, 30 August 1916, DIA, vol. 3962, file 147, 654-1, pt. 2; Hawksley to McLean, 1 August 1916, ibid.; Stringer to Hawksley, 24 October 1916, ibid.
16. Cecil Swanson, *Days of My Sojourning.*
17. Bompas to deputy minister of the interior, 15 June 1905, DIA, vol. 3962, file 147, 654-1, pt. 2; CMS, Bompas to CMS, 20 January 1893, CMS; Report of Teslin Lake Mission School, 5 July to 19 August 1909, DIA, vol. 6478, file 930-1, pt. 1; J. Unsworth, "One Month and One Day at Champagne," AC, Unsworth file; W.D. Young to Bishop, 14 October 1927, AC, Young file.
18. Report of Teslin Lake Mission School, 5 July to 19 August 1909, AC, Bythell file.

19. J. Hawksley, "Report of Mayo Band of Indians," 20 August 1917, DIA, vol. 4081, file 478, 700; John Ross to DIA, 2 April 1906, DIA, vol. 3962, file 147, 654-1, pt. 2; O'Meara to Secretary, DIA, 8 December 1909, DIA, vol. 6478, file. 930-1, pt. 1; J. Hawksley, "Report of Forty Mile Band of Indians," 29 March 1917, DIA, vol. 4081, file 478, 698; J. Unsworth, "One Month and One Day at Champagne," AC, Unsworth file; R.A. Hoey to J.E. Gibben, 4 August 1944, DIA, vol. 6478, file 934-1; J.L. Coudert to Philip Phelan, 17 March 1945, ibid.
20. O'Meara to Secretary, DIA, 8 December 1909, DIA, vol. 6478, file 930-1, pt. 1.
21. T.G. Bragg to Alexander Henderson, 14 December 1907, DIA, vol. 6479, file 940-1.
22. Hawksley to J.D. McLean, 20 November 1926, PAC, RG 91, Yukon Government Records, [YG], vol. 74; see also Russell Fernier, Superintendent of Indian Education to J. Hawksley, 27 October 1925, ibid.
23. Rt. Rev. A.H. Sovereign to Secretary, DIA, 21 August 1933, Indian Affairs file.
24. W.A. Geddes to Secretary, DIA, 23 January 1934, DIA, vol. 6477, file 925-1, pt. 1; Geddes to H.W. McGill, 11 November 1942, DIA, vol. 6479, file 940-1, pt. 2.
25. Stringer to Hawksley, 9 February 1925, DIA, vol. 6478, file 931-3, pt. 1; Stringer to Hawksley, 31 January 1925, ibid; Stringer to T. Hipp, 14 February 1930, AC, Hipp file.
26. Most Carcross students had at least some day school experience. See Coates, "Betwixt and Between."
27. Stringer to Middleton, 25 April 1917, AC, Middleton file.
28. Dennis Guest, *The Emergence of Social Welfare in Canada*, rev. ed. (Vancouver: University of British Columbia Press, 1985). For the Yukon Natives, see Coates, "Best Left as Indians."
29. There are many files on this debate. See AC, Carcross Property file. See also Walter "Yukon" to R.A. Hoey, 16 June 1948, DIA, vol. 8762, file 906/25-1-001.
30. Canada, Special Joint Committee on the Indian Act, *Report* (1949).
31. See Ken Coates, "The Alaska Highway and the Indians of the Southern Yukon, 1942-1950: A Study of Native Adaptation to Northern Development," and Julie Cruikshank, "The Gravel Magnet: Some Social Impacts of the Alaska Highway on Yukon Indians," in *The Alaska Highway: Papers of the 40th Anniversary Alaska Highway Symposium*, ed. Ken Coates (Vancouver: University of British Columbia Press, 1985).
32. DIA, *AR*, 1954, 78.

8

The Changing Experience of Indian Residential Schooling: Blue Quills, 1931-1970

Diane Persson

The first direct confrontation in Canada over Indians' control of education occurred in northeastern Alberta in 1970. Local Indians occupied Blue Quills Indian Residential School, resulting in the establishment of the first Native-administered school in Canada. To understand this transformation, it is necessary to look back not only at the changing Indian consciousness of the late 1960's but also at the school's history during the previous four decades. By so doing, it becomes obvious that Indian resistance to educational imposition by church and state, as occurred at Blue Quills, was no sudden phenomenon but rather a persistent theme in Indian education in Canada. This is particularly true when the past is examined not only from the official record but also from the perspective of the participants themselves through the technique of oral history.[1]

Three principal phases make up the history of Blue Quills. The first period, from 1931 to 1945, was characterized by the harmony of goals between the Catholic church, which operated the school, and the state. Both believed that Indians were best civilized by isolation, first in the residential school and then on the reserve. The second phase, from 1945 to 1960, saw a growing separation of goals between church and state. The state sought the education of Indian and non-Indian children together, whereas the church believed that Catholic Indian students should continue to attend separate schools. The third phase, from 1960 to 1970, was characterized by declining church influence, increased government control, and growing Indian involvement in education. At the end of this phase, church and state were in agreement that Blue Quill's utility had ended and the school should be closed. By then, however, the one group which had remained unconsulted through Blue Quill's history, the Indians themselves, were sufficiently self-confident to assert their claim to the school.

FIRST PHASE, 1931-1945

Blue Quills Residential School had its roots in the missionary work of the Order of Oblates of Mary Immaculate, better known as the Oblate Fathers.[2] As early as the mid-nineteenth century, the Oblates began a mission boarding school in northeastern Alberta. In 1898, they built the Sacred Heart Mission on the Saddle Lake Reserve and received permission from Chief Blue Quill's band to move their school to his part of the reserve. Three decades later, following the 1920 amendments to the Indian Act prescribing compulsory school attendance for Indian children, the Department of Indian Affairs undertook to construct a large school central to several reserves. The school was to be administered by the Oblates on a per-capita grant basis, with the teaching staff provided by the Grey Nuns. Pupils from the Saddle Lake school were transferred to the new school on its completion in 1931.

Blue Quills, built to house up to two hundred children, conformed to government specifications for Indian residential schools. The basement contained a laundry room, kitchen, bakery, children's dining room, priests' dining room, and nuns' dining room. The first floor included the chapel, two parlour rooms (one for Indian visitors and the other for non-Indian visitors), classrooms, washrooms, and the priest's offices. The second floor held the nuns' dormitory and community room. The third floor contained the students' rooms. The boys' dormitory, entrance, and play areas outside and inside were on the east side of the building while the girls' areas were on the west side. In addition to the main residential building, a barn was also constructed on the school grounds.

The government's philosophy of Indian education was to provide students with practical skills as well as basic literacy through grade 8. The church was responsible for accomplishing these goals, with limited finances. Thus, Blue Quills had a programme where the students studied in the classroom half the day and performed school jobs for the other half. The girls worked in the kitchen, laundry room, and sewing room, while the boys worked on the school farm with the crops and animals. Apart from the farm employees who supervised the boys' work on the farm, the teachers were all Grey Nuns. They followed the Alberta curriculum for half the day, placing special emphasis on English, reading, domestic science, manual training, and agriculture.

Blue Quills can be described as a total institution, or a place of living and working where a large number of people in a similar situation are cut off from the wider society and live in an enclosed, formally administered setting.[3] The two worlds of a total institution—the residents and the staff—are characterized by differences in power and in mechanisms by which conflict is regulated. When pupils entered residential school, they underwent admission procedures designed to dispossess them of their previous roles and isolate them from the reserve world. Children were either brought to the school by their family or, more often, were "rounded up" by a priest and transported to the school. Upon entering the residence, the child's clothes were removed. After being bathed and deloused, he or she was issued a set of school clothing. After acquiring a uniform which was the same as that worn by others of the same sex and size, the child was given a number. All clothing, towels and eating utensils were marked with the number. Role dispossession continued through such processes as staff insistence that pupils hold their body in a particular attitude, sit at their desks not looking at each other, line up to eat, and so forth. When students were being reprimanded, they were not to look directly at the disapproving staff member. Deference was also required in verbal behaviour. Students were to address the church staff by title, such as "Sister," "Father," or "Sir."

Students were segregated by sex, both in order to maintain control and because of staff concern over student morality. The Catholic church traditionally viewed coeducation as harmful to a Christian education, and during the 1930's segregation was total. Students were separate in the classroom, the dormitory, the playground, and the chapel. In the 1940's, students began to attend classes together, although they sat on different sides of the room. Concern over morality and modesty pervaded every aspect of school life. As recalled by one women: "When we had a bath we had to wear a 'bathing suit', they called it. It was a grey flannelette gown. That's what you had to wear right in the tub, you couldn't even take it off." Another student described the practices which resulted from such concerns:

> When we were 12 and over, our bust started to grow. They used to make us wear this real tight binder, like the kind you wear after you have a baby. They were so tight so they'd be no bulges on the apron, because that was a sin. You know most of those girls now all have flat breasts. They made us feel ashamed of our bodies to keep the virtue and modesty. We were girls and we had to be modest.

Learning to accept regulations was an integral part of the school experience. The students' daily routine was strictly scheduled, from the 6:00 A.M. rising and morning prayers to the 7:30 P.M. bedtime. All activity was subject to the timetable and to staff regulation, including rules calling for silence when eating, the making of beds a certain way, the manner clothes were to be worn, and the form in which requests for toilet paper were made.

The organization of Blue Quills Indian Residential School not only generated and regulated conflict for the students, who as inmates were in a subordinate position, but provided means for those in the dominant position, the staff, to regulate conflict through social control. Four different mechanisms of social control were used: isolation, sanction, persuasion, and conflict absorption. Isolation from the outside community was built into the physical plant. The school was five kilometres from the town of St. Paul and twenty-six kilometres from the closest reserve, Saddle Lake. This distance was far enough to discourage the children from leaving the school on foot and to limit the number of visits parents could make by horse and wagon. "We didn't have any chance to interact with other people. It was an institution with a big wire fence around it, literally."

The use of rewards and punishments were the sanctions most evident in school life. House rules formulated and implemented by the staff specified the main requirements for student behaviour. Extra or special food, religious medals, and preferred jobs were some of the rewards students could anticipate for complying with the privilege system. Punishments, which were the consequence of breaking the house rules, included beatings, denial of food, additional work in the residence and classroom, and withholding of recreational privileges. The employment of rewards by the church as a mechanism of social control is demonstrated by religious activities. Students were encouraged to join groups such as the Missionary Association of Mary Immaculate. As one member said, "We were the elite of Blue Quills since not everyone could go. If your marks were high enough, and if you were a good girl, then you became a member of one of those groups." Rewards attached to religious membership were medallions and pictures and the privilege to attend special bingo parties and picnics. Thus group membership served to reward academic success and then was itself rewarded.

Punishments existed for every offense, minor or major. For instance, "If you smiled at a boy in the dining room, you'd be told to take your plate and walk up and down between the tables, and everyone would laugh at you." Silence during meals was the rule, and "if you were caught whispering or talking, they would put you in the middle of the dining room, and you're shamed." Punishments for running away or "deserting" were particularly severe. As described by one woman:

I was about 12 or 13 when I ran away. We got to our place about 11:30 at night and my mother couldn't believe it. So they took us back the very next morning. The three of us were taken back and that night got a licking. I had welts all over. They had a big strap with little fringes and to top it off all the girls were in their rightful places praying for me. I said, "I'm going to run away again." When I got home my mother really felt bad and they brought me to the agency and showed my marks to the Indian agent. He said he'd look into it.

Another former pupil said, "I never did try to run away because I was told when I went that if I ever did something wrong that I'd get it back at home. So I was afraid on both sides." Although the punishments were often the child's reason for "deserting" in the first place, further punishment was meted out by the staff when the student returned. In addition to being strapped, "if the boys ran away, their heads were shaved right till they were bald. Some of them had to go barefooted for fear they'd run away again."

Persuasion as a form of social control centered on attempts to alter individual attitudes. Religious activities exemplify this. Many students from the 1930's remember the pictorial catechism used at Blue Quills: "They had two roads going up, the one going up to heaven had all white people and the one going up to hell had all Indian people." For one student, the catechism left the message that "if you stay Indian you'll end up in hell." Students were also encouraged to try to change their parents' religious attitudes, to have, for example, Catholic papers in their homes on the reserve although they were not at home themselves. A grade 3 boy "wrote" in the school newspaper:

> I will listen when Sister reads to us in school, so that I can tell my parents when I go home for holidays. We should never go to sun dances, and we should try to stop it if we can by telling our parents it is forbidden by God. We should try to give good example to the children who do not come to school yet. I will never go to a sun dance.[4]

Conflict absorption, or cooptation, refers to the mechanism of social control by which conflict was neither suppressed nor allowed to bring about any substantive change. This was in effect with Indian language use in the school. Two language groups were represented at Blue Quills: the Cree and the Chipewyan. At the school, the Cree speakers always outnumbered the Chipewyans, and relations between them were often unfriendly. A Cree-speaking woman from Saddle Lake described these attitudes: "There was a segregation part in the school. Of course these Chip kids you can see they are Chips. Like the Cree will be really humble. But a Chip will just take and won't say please or anything. But us Crees are different. We say 'please' and 'may

I.' " Many of the Chipewyan-speaking students learned to speak Cree, but the reverse was less common. A Chipewyan-speaking woman from Cold Lake recalled: "Sometimes it was a battle. The Cree would speak their own language and we'd speak ours. You got to know their language faster than they could understand us. They couldn't even talk our language. And we could even say our prayers in Cree."

Conflict was absorbed by encouraging the division between Chipewyan and Cree students. It was also absorbed by teaching the students their catechism in either Cree or Chipewyan. Although students learned to read and write their Native languages, their use was restricted to religious settings. English was the language of instruction, but use of a Native language outside the classroom was tolerated by the staff, and students were seldom punished for speaking in their Native tongue. Some students were grateful to the priests for teaching them to read, write, and pray in Cree and Chipewyan. Other students have maintained resentments, which were compounded by the priests and sisters having frequently spoken their French language among themselves and in front of the children.

> I think trying to kill off our language and culture was the worst thing they could do. They wouldn't even give us their language. I don't think I would feel this way if they'd taught us French. The only thing I know in French is, "Sacré maudit sauvage" [God-damned savage]. Every time the nun got mad, "Sacré maudit sauvage."

Most students got what they could out of a difficult situation and acquiesced to the inevitable. The work component of the school programme allowed for such acquiesence. For the girls, learning to cook and sew were skills they might use after leaving the school, whether to return to the reserve or to seek outside employment. One woman described the advantages of the work programme:

> It used to be a place where you would learn things like sewing and different courses. You learned everything. It was kind of hard for me to decide what to do. I wanted to be a seamstress and I wanted to be a cook. I had everything in my head which I could do and make a living with. It was hard but you made something out of yourself.

Since the school farm was designed to support Blue Quills, it was a mixed farming operation where boys learned how to look after and butcher animals, plant crops and gardens, and care for machinery. One man who attended the school during the 1930's said of his experience:

We weren't getting an education like they are today. It was just get the savage out of the Indian. But it done some good. We learned a lot of agriculture mostly. I think one good thing is that it trained them for agriculture and some are really successfull farmers.

Some students perceived the work experience of the residential school as beneficial in preparing them for adult life.

Come to think of it I have no regrets that I did what I was taught, forced to learn how to make clothes. If I hadn't of learned that my kids would have suffered. And the sense of responsibility. They were very strict there....If I hadn't of learned that strict life of obedience, there would have been times when I'd of made my family suffer.

Acquiescence does not imply an absence of resistance. Acquiescence and resistance are two sides of the same coin, and as such were both present simultaneously. The most common form of resistance was running away from the school. During 1932, the first year of operation of the new school, "desertions" were such a problem that the principal petitioned the government to enforce compulsory school attendance, arguing that the aim of the department "is to civilize Indians, and the only way of civilizing them is boarding schools....The Department of Indian Affairs have made very big expenses for building a new school...and this must not be for nothing."[5] The Indian agent visited the school and spoke to the children about the importance of learning from their classes and manual work lessons and admonished them not to "desert." He reminded them of the state of poverty in which their parents were living, telling them that every day some of their parents came to the agency to ask for food and clothing. Such incidents clearly continued. In 1943, the Indian agent reported, "six boys did run away last night during 15 below weather and arrived on the Saddle Lake Reserve, two with badly frozen feet and one with slightly frozen feet, it was lucky that two did not freeze to death."[6]

During these early years, parental involvement with the school was limited. Parents were permitted to visit their children on weekends in a separate Indian parlour room; they could camp in two guest houses, or shacks, moved from Saddle Lake Reserve. Because of the distance, most children saw their parents only once or twice a year in addition to the summer vacation. For example: "If I was lucky once a year I woud see my mother but my father came several times. To come to St. Paul you had to come with a team [of horses], and it takes a whole day if you lived in Saddle Lake. Half a day to come and half a day back." The second principal reserve from which children came, Cold Lake, was even further away. From the late 1930's, parents could, with the principal's permission, take children into St. Paul for the day.

The reality of the residential school was accepted by some parents. A number had come to the conclusion that the old ways of making a living were disappearing. Partly out of self-interest and self-protection, they saw the necessity of educating their children. On the other hand, the school was characterized by continuously poor enrolment, which may suggest that even though there was very little latitude for parental involvement or much respect for parents by the school, families made their position known. This is evidenced by an entry in the school chronicle in 1932: "The Indians having received an injunction to bring their children to school, otherwise the police will do it, several parents obeyed the order today, but there are still those who turn a deaf ear."[7] At the same time, the Deputy Superintendant General of Indian Affairs wrote to Father Langlois of the Oblate Provincial House that the school's principal "has lost the confidence of a great number of Indians in the vicinity."[8] A main reason was that Indian parents were being denied the right to raise or even know their own children, which was, of course, a major reason for the attempts to establish residential schools by the churches. A Blue Quills student from the 1930's said, "That way of education takes the responsibility away from the parents because they don't see their kids. I don't know how to say it but when you lose some of the responsibility as a parent maybe you're not a whole human being." In 1945 the government made the receipt of Family Allowance dependent upon school attendance. A student has summed up the longterm consequences of such an attitude: "I think residential schools caused a lot of mental anguish between parents and children. It developed to the state where there was a breakdown in the relationship. Education was a colonization of Indian people."

SECOND PHASE, 1945-1960

The effectiveness of the protectionist and isolationist policy of Indian education began to be questioned by the federal government in the years after the Second World War. A Special Joint Committee of the Senate and House of Commons on the Indian Act sat between 1946 and 1948 and was repeatedly urged to abolish separate Indian schools. In 1951, a new Indian Act formalized the general aim of the federal government as the integration of Indians into Canadian society. The placement of Indian children in provincial schools was the principal means of achieving this goal. Existing federal schools also came under closer scrutiny.

The Catholic Church resisted the growing encroachment on its traditional authority over the lives of Catholic Indian children. In the late 1940's, visits from government school inspectors became more frequent.[9] The customary congratulatory comments recorded by the principal in the Blue Quill's school diary changed dramatically:

> This inspector does not appear well disposed in our favour, and even gives the impression of being fanatical, asking trifling questions about religion and its instruction in the school. He held an examination of grade 5 pupils in spelling and arithmetic, and refused to record the beautiful work being done in sewing and needlework. He cannot, however, prevent note being taken of the neatness and contentment of the children.[10]

Theoretically, under the new act, religious rights of pupils were to be protected by insuring that no child could be admitted to a church-run school without written parental consent. But in practice, if parents were reluctant to sign the admission forms for their children, the school principal would sign for them. A priest at Blue Quills said, "Many times in those days the 'X' [on the admission form] came from my own left hand."

Growing tension between state and church resulted in Blue Quills becoming less of a total institution, with new mechanisms put in place to regulate conflict. Contact grew with the outside world. In 1948, for the first time, pupils were allowed to spend Christmas holidays with their parents rather than remaining at the school. One student wrote in the school newspaper, "we could find nothing else to talk about but that. One day in school, the teacher asked a question of an absent minded pupil who naturally could not answer. 'Where were you?' she said. 'At home,' the child replied."[11] By the mid 1950's, students were also going home for Easter holidays.

Education Week, established in 1951, was specifically intended to increase communication with the town of St. Paul. An open house was held, which according to the local newspaper, "attracted many St. Paul residents who toured the school and saw many attractive displays, examples and proof of the versatility of the Indian and what he can accomplish." As well, students visited local industries in St. Paul, including the stockyards, newspaper office, post office, and bank. The last day of Education Week was set aside as an open house for the children's parents, chiefs and councillors from their reserves, and missionaries. A banquet was prepared for them, and a concert was given which included "ancestral war dances" and band selections.[12]

The attitude of the staff toward Native languages changed. As reported by one former student, "You weren't punished if you spoke Cree, although they told you to speak English." Students from the Enoch Reserve near Edmonton came to Blue Quills speaking only English and learned Cree at the school. For children who arrived speaking only Cree, some teachers tried to accommodate them. One teacher said of her experience in the early 1950's:

I had the beginners, perhaps 30 of them. At first I tried to teach them their numbers, and they didn't understand at all. So when I saw I couldn't get through to them that night I took a Cree dictionary and I learned the numbers up to five—peyak, neeso, nisto, newo, neyanan. And I came the next morning and said "peyak," and right away they brightened up and understood what I meant. After that it was easy for me to teach. Each evening I would learn something in Cree, and come the next day and then they'd have to learn it in English. I would put a lot of pictures on cards. They would tell me what it was in Cree, and I would tell them in English. We understood each other this way, and they learned very, very quickly.

Native language use was also facilitated by teaching catechism in Cree and by special programmes through which priests came to learn Cree at the school. Whereas the use of Cree or Chipewyan in religious activities had always been sanctioned, some teachers were now trying to incorporate it into their classrooms.

School life at Blue Quills became more like integrated public schools. The half day work-study programme ended in the early 1950's, which meant that as much time was spent in the classroom at Blue Quills as in provincial schools. The number of secular teachers increased as fewer women entered religious orders, so that by 1960 just two of the eight teachers were Grey Nuns. Secular teachers often initiated new programmes including more social activities. Movies were shown at the school every few weeks; as a teacher explained, "they were good films that I would order from different companies, and I remember when I started giving films there they had been used to seeing only cowboys shows." The school acquired a television set in 1956, and two years later there were four in the school. A student wrote in the school paper:

Father Principal has organized a program which permits us to see the T.V. by groups of about 15. We, the grades 7 and 8, have our turn on Fridays. We see the Plouffe Family and The Last of the Mohicans. On Saturday mornings, the boys see the sports program. In the afternoon, the girls enjoy watching Alice in Wonderland and Wild Bill Hickock.

High school students began to experience integration. At first Blue Quills offered only the elementary grades. Then, in the late 1940's, a few students stayed at the school and studied high school subjects by correspondence. By the early 1950's, students began to be bused to attend grades 9 to 12 in the Catholic integrated high school in St. Paul. In 1952 eight high school students were boarding at Blue Quills and attending classes in town; by 1965 this number had increased to twenty-seven.

High school students were given additional privileges. For example, the girls organized a High School Girls' Club which met Friday evenings to plan socials and discuss problems. Their room, Lourdes Hall, had a kitchenette, and they could take their meals on trays to eat there. "The administrators weren't stupid. The high school students were treated almost royally. They got privileges just to give the feeling, 'I want to be a high school student,' " said a former student.

Blue Quills personnel were less enthusiastic than the students about integration. A teacher wrote that each night "they'd come back and say, 'Sister, we're quitting going to that school. The kids are so noisy we can't study and they answer back.' "[13] However, a student remembered the situation differently:

> In the first group there were about 15 of us who went into St. Paul to school. The kids really didn't give us a hard time. Somehow what we lacked in one thing we made up for in another. So we made friends easily....I kind of felt now you're in with the rest of the world. You've come out of your own little world to get into another world. Kid, you've got to make it.

Through the decade, the Catholic church resisted further change, firmly believing the Indian community to be "a culturally distinct human community with an educational problem and process of its own."[14] Public schools could not provide the benefits of an Indian residential school, such as religious training, teachers knowledgeable in instruction of Indians, and training in Indian leadership.

As well, many aspects of student life at Blue Quills remained as regimented and controlled as they had ever been. Each student was still assigned a number at the beginning of the school year:

> Every utensil was marked with your number—your cup, your tin plate; the number was down on your underwear, and slip, and dresses, and maybe your shoes....We'd be called by our number sometimes too. Like if they wanted your attention, sort of like the army. You used to be tagged with that number all year.

While high school students could have their own soap and toothpaste, younger students would have to share the soap and line up for toothpaste dispensed by a nun. Everything was subject to scrutiny by the school staff. The boys had lockers without locks; the girls carried their comb and hankie in their slip pocket, and these pockets had to be emptied on staff request. The student's mail, coming or going, was read by the principal. When a student asked why this was done, he was told it was read "not for mere curiosity, but to check the content, and in so doing, avoid trouble that may arise from certain letters to certain persons."[15] Boys and girls remained segregated for most purposes. In class they still sat on different sides of the room, and in the playground they were kept apart.

But as Blue Quills became less of a total institution, students began to question the degree of regimentation and doctrination in the residential school system: "The longer I went there the more I began to see that it was a lot of propaganda." Assignment of numbers, dispossession of private property, and segregation by sex alienated students from the staff and from each other.

Students also resented the differences they perceived between the religious principles taught them and their treatment by staff. The religious life of the school was central to the church's efforts to convert and assimilate young Indians while emphasizing the church's essential role in their schooling and in their future. In spite of, or perhaps because of, the religious emphasis of the school, most former students had limited involvement in the Catholic church after leaving school. One man said,

> So much of the religion was drilled in that hardly anyone from my era has practised it in a meaningful way, the R.C. faith. And even today I see some that probably aren't using any kind of religion. Our religion was more or less cast aside, and there was no way to practise it. They said it was a pagan religion and therefore should not be followed.

The academic quality at Blue Quills came into question not only from government school inspectors but from the students themselves. A former pupil assessed the school's programme:

> In social studies we would study about dukes and duchesses. But that was so far removed from what my life was. What did I care about that baloney? So I filled my notebooks with pictures and doodles of my ideas of what history was about.
>
> Most of the big boys had their turn at working in the barn, working with animals...although no one was knowledgeable in that field. No one would tell really what is the best for cattle, how to care for them, things like that to be more or less scientific. No one taught us anything in that regard.

As a consequence, some students came away knowing they were unprepared for adult life.

In terms of dealing with inter-personal problems, for example dealing with stress or pressures, or alcoholism, or any social problems, there was totally no preparation. So therefore you were totally green if you stepped out from the reserve. Certainly many have succumbed and went under because they're unable to cope. Generally one was not prepared to face life.

Another student said, "Going to Blue Quills was like going into a room and not being let out."

The parents' role was ambivalent during this second period. Options such as reserve day schools and public schools meant that they could remove their children from Blue Quills if they so desired. On the other hand, there was still no parental control over the school situation. Despite more contact with their children, little communication took place with school staff. A nun who was a cook at the school said, "I would never have much to do with parents of the children because they're real beggars. If they needed something they could go see the Father, but not at the kitchen door." A teaching nun felt her reluctance to know the parents was beneficial in teaching their children:

> I didn't want to become acquainted with the parents because I was freer then to speak to the children. You see, if I had been acquainted with some parents, with some woman who was getting beaten by her husband I couldn't have talked about it in the classroom. But since I didn't know anybody, I could talk about these things in the classroom and I could tell the children that a man who beats his wife doesn't deserve to live and should be put behind bars.

The one way Indian parents could become involved with their children's education was through the Catholic Indian League. Founded in 1954 by bishops, missionaries and Indians, the league replaced diminishing federal assistance for church-controlled education with Indian support. If the church could no longer rely on government assistance to support its primary role in Indian schooling, then it had to turn to its own religious authority over Catholic Indian people. Members of the league were to be practicing Catholic Indians over eighteen years of age. The aims of the organization were to protect the religious and social rights of the Indian population by uniting into local Indian action groups. Education was a primary concern of the league, and resolutions passed at meetings reflected the church's efforts to establish Indian support for Catholic education. When the league had its regional meeting at Saddle Lake in 1958, it recommended that a semi-boarding school be built on the Saddle Lake Reserve: only nine people out of 117 participating were in favour of busing children to the public school in St. Paul. Most felt that a semi-residential boarding school, where children could go home for the weekends, was preferable to day schools, because of poor home conditions on the reserve, long bus rides, and discrimination against Indian pupils in the school. The tenor of the meeting was expressed by one participant who said, "We are with poor home conditions and far from being ready to integrate with the white population."[16]

THIRD PHASE, 1960-1970

While the Catholic Church remained committed to Indian residential schooling, its control over Blue Quills was increasingly undermined during the 1960's by changing federal policy, by the declining support of the Grey Nuns, and by growing Indian consciousness. Government intervention diminished religious input into school life. The agency superintendent, district school superintendent and federal dieticians each came at least once a year. The agency reported on the general operation of the school, while the school superintendent inspected classrooms and made recommendations to the offices in Edmonton and Ottawa. In April 1969, the non-teaching staff at the school became members of the Public Service Alliance, which formalized their job descriptions, working conditions, and relations with the church. Since the principal was included in this group, his role in hiring staff and setting salary ended. The non-teaching staff had their work week reduced and were given pay rates comparable to others doing a similar job. Thus local leadership was marginalized and the school was reduced to a bureaucratic appendage of the federal government.

With fewer people entering religious orders, the Oblates were unable to rely upon the Grey Nuns to staff the school. Too few of the sisters had acceptable qualifications as teachers. The increasing age and decreasing numbers of nuns also made it necessary to employ more secular staff. After 1964, only one sister taught at the school, and she was the senior teacher who taught the highest grades.

As a consequence, students were increasingly provided with school and social experiences similar to those found in non-Indian schools. The students held a ceremony to honour the new Canadian flag in 1965; they changed the school newspaper "Moccasin Telegram" to a school year book; and they were occasionally taken Hallowe'ening in St. Paul. Blue Quills students developed contacts with students in other Indian schools through sports. In 1961, the first Indian School Track and Field Meet was held at the school, and interschool competitions between schools of the Saddle Lake Agency continued for the next seven years. School life became somewhat less harsh and regimented. Corporal punishment was, except for very severe offences, replaced by a demerit system. When ten points were accumulated for such offences as an untidy locker or untied shoelaces, the student was forbidden to watch the monthly movie. "Or sometimes they'd take you to the movie but make you sit on the other way so you'd just hear what was going on." Although the sexes were separated in the school building and grounds and occasionally in the classroom, the staff began to organize and encourage some mixed social life. For example, social dances were held at the school, although close waltzes were forbidden, and in the winter mixed ice skating was allowed on Sunday afternoons. The students used various means to keep in touch with the opposite sex: "I remember one time we used walkies talkies to socialize with the girls but we were found out because of the wiring system or the pipes. Somehow it got connected with the television and we got caught because our voices came on the television."

All the same, both the students at Blue Quills itself and those being bused to high school in St. Paul remained isolated. One pupil remembered: "I recall we didn't have many prejudices, we never called people 'Chinks' or 'Niggers.' But our world was so small. We were really protected in a way from the outside world." Unlike students of the 1950's, who looked back favourably at their high-school experience, students of the 1960's were often less than enthusiastic. Few friendships were formed with non-Indians, owing in part to discrimination but also to church authorities discouraging contact beyond the classroom and sports field. One student recalled:

> We were not prepared for it at all. We were so used to being with our Native peers that we were not used to be around white people. Just the nuns and priests were the only white contacts we ever had, and maybe the lay people around. And all of a sudden you're thrown in with a bunch of white kids that laugh at you because everybody is wearing coveralls. We were very vulnerable to insults from the white kids. You see the town kids were very different from what we were; they had a hell of a lot more freedom.

During the same decade, other developments undermined the Indian support which the church had been attempting to build over the postwar years. In 1961, the federal government began to sponsor leadership development courses and workshops on the Saddle Lake Reserve which encouraged contact with the non-Indian community. Alberta treaty Indians acquired new rights, including the provincial franchise in 1967. Five years later, a community assessment study funded by the provincial government concluded that "the present situation on the Saddle Lake Reserve seems to be almost totally destructive for any chance of progress by the people."[17] The study charged that the poor administration at Blue Quills School was a major reason for the high dropout rate of Catholic students from the reserve.

By the late 1960's, the church retained little support for its involvement in Indian education either from Indian groups or from the government. School committees established in mid-decade in part out of the earlier Catholic Indian League and supported by federal authorities, were becoming secular vehicles for direct Indian involvement in Indian education. In September 1969, the Saddle Lake School Committee began to pressure the Department of Indian Affairs and the Blue Quills principal to hire more Indian people at the school. A few were hired, making Indians 14 per cent of the non-teaching staff. The school committee, however, still viewed the situation as inequitable, and continued to seek greater participation in Blue Quills, which was increasingly perceived as belonging to Indian people.

In the meantime, in June 1969, the federal White Paper on Indian policy had been introduced in parliament. The White Paper stated that "the separate legal status of Indians and the policies which have flowed from it have kept the Indian people apart from and behind other Canadians." The White Paper's implications almost immediately rebounded on Blue Quills. It proposed that all services to Indian people, including education, be provided by the same agencies and governments as serviced other Canadians. One month after the Saddle Lake School Committee had presented its gievance about employment, and in the midst of discussions of the White Paper, the school committee was told that, when the regional high school opened the following year in St. Paul, the Department of Indian Affairs planned to phase out the classrooms at Blue Quills. Its useful life to federal authorities and to the Catholic church had come to an end.

Once the outside world made clear its intention to close Blue Quills, local Indian commitment to the school formalized. At a meeting held at Saddle Lake in December 1969, the school committee requested that the Department of Indian Affairs turn the operation of the school over to the local reserve communities and that the Natives receive assistance in replacing the existing non-teaching staff with Indian people. The department did not respond to this request and on 14 July 1970, a sit-in began at Blue Quills to get control of the school. As one man explained, "The reason we had that sit-in was so we could take over the school ourselves and run it the way we want. It was our school."

The Saddle Lake School Committee had previously obtained the administrator's permission to use the gym for meetings. This setting became the occupation site. Because no students were in the school's dormitories at the time, people at the sit-in used the residence facilities. The occupation began with approximately sixty people, mostly from reserves in the Saddle Lake Agency, and peaked at about three hundred. At its height there were also Native people from other provinces as well as non-Indian supporters. A former student described the atmosphere:

> There was all sort of things going on at the sit-in, like entertainment, singing, dancing, and we'd stay awake all night telling jokes, especially the old men. I think they brought in all the old men in the area into the big gym. We had blankets spread out and all sorts of Indian entertainment, jokes and dancing, and their own way of praying. Most of the time nobody gave a bad time to anybody and the odd time there'd be big shots coming around flashing cameras. We weren't hurting anybody, just sitting there saying what we wanted and what's been lacking.

The sit-in resulted in meetings in Ottawa between a committee representing seven reserves which supported the sit-in and representatives from the Department of Indian Affairs, The outcome was a ministerial agreement to transfer the operation of the residence and classrooms to the Blue Quills Native Education Council. The school's administration was to be supported financially by the department. The minister viewed this transfer as a unique project — more of a special case than a change in department policy — and he gave the committee six months to make a go of the school. A newspaper in Edmonton pointed out, however, that "what could be learned from an Indian school controlled by the Indian people themselves would be valuable in helping to determine what future policy should be."[18] The St. Paul *Journal* reprinted an editorial published in the Indian newspaper *Native People*, which said that the Blue Quills sit-in had shown Indians were capable of handling their own affairs. "The Federal government has wasted and misspent thousands of dollars on boarding schools....With misspending like that who needs Indian Affairs controlling Indian education? The control of education must lie in the hands of the people."[19]

On 1 September 1970, Blue Quills became the first school in Canada to be officially administered by Indians. Those attending the ceremonies were told by Native speakers that "only now can Indians say that they are equal in the eyes of everyone." The "truth about Indian culture as well as the political and social way of life that the white man leads" would finally be taught.[20] Cree was to be part of the curriculum, and about half of the total staff was Indian, including the administrator and one teacher. An agreement was signed between the department and the Saddle Lake parish of the Roman Catholic church providing chaplaincy services to residential students and staff at Blue Quills. By the terms of that agreement, the administrator would make arrangements for scheduling the priest's visits, which were "not to conflict with the requirements of the school or the residence."[21]

CONCLUSION

Blue Quills's half century as an Indian residential school provides a prism through which to view the more general course of Indian education in Canada. What at first seemed a radical action, the school's physical takeover in 1970, was in reality the logical and almost inevitable consequence of decades of imposition of a policy of assimilation on Indian students, individuals who had since become adults in the locality. As the attempts by church and state to create a total institution faltered, Indian people became more confident of their right to regain control over the education of their children. The most significant aspect of the takeover of Blue Quills is that it marked the end of a passiveness to the imposition of external values; it turned the tide towards Indian self-determination, at Blue Quills and across Canada. A new era in Indian education had begun.

NOTES TO CHAPTER EIGHT

1. During the summer of 1978, fifty-one interviews were conducted with former students, staff, and other individuals resident on the reserves from which Blue Quills drew its students. While the interviews were relatively unstructured, similar questions were covered concerning each individual's personal background, school years attended, reasons for attendance, and perception of school life. Also used were materials available in the Public Archives of Canada, for the Department of Indian Affairs at various levels, in the Provincial Archives of Alberta, the Grey Nuns Archives in Edmonton, the Archives Deschatelets in Ottawa, and the Edmonton *Journal* and St. Paul *Journal* newspapers. For more detail, see Persson, "Blue Quills: A Case Study of Indian Residential Schooling" (Ph.D. diss., Departments of Anthropology and Educational Foundations, University of Alberta, 1980), esp. 14-18.
2. On all aspects of the history of Blue Quills, see Persson, "Blue Quills."
3. See Irving Goffman, *Asylums: Essays on the Social Situation of Mental Patients and Other Inmates* (Chicago: Aldine Publishing Company, 1961).
4. *Moccasin Telegram,* April 1939, in Grey Nun Archives.
5. Oblate Accession 71.220, fol. 57, 8-VIII-340, 9 February 1932, Provincial Archives of Alberta.
6. R.G. 10, vol. 6347, file 751-10, pt. 10, 2 March 1943, Public Archives of Canada [PAC].
7. "Chroniques de Blue Quills Residential School," 1 May 1932, Grey Nun Archives. The original is in French.
8. Oblate Accession 71.220, 26 May and 14 April 1932.
9. In 1945 and 1946 there were three visits a year, in 1947 six and in 1948 eleven.
10. Oblate Accession 71.220, Box 7, Tome II, 10 June 1948. Original in French.
11. *Moccasin Telegram,* April-June 1957.
12. St.Paul *Journal,* 18 May 1951.
13. *Moccasin Telegram,* December 1948-January 1949.
14. André Renaud, *Indian Education Today* (Ottawa: Indian and Eskimo Welfare Commission, 1958), 31.
15. *Moccasin Telegram,* October-December 1955.
16. Oblate-Indian Commission, Saddle Lake, Box 1, file 17, 4 September 1958, Archives Deschatelets.
17. Morton Newman, *Appendix F, Indians of the Saddle Lake Reserve: Community Opportunity Assessment* (Edmonton: Human Resources Research and Development Council, Government of Alberta, 1967), 102.
18. *Journal,* Edmonton, 4 August 1970.
19. *Journal,* St. Paul, 5 August 1970, reprinting editorial published earlier in *Native People* by Alberta Native Communications Society, Edmonton.
20. Ibid., 9 September 1970.
21. "School Establishment, Blue Quills," vol. 1, file 779/1-13-009, December 1970, Department of Indian Affairs and Northern Development, PAC.

Notes on Contributors

Jean Barman is co-investigator in the Canadian Childhood History Project and teaches courses in the Departments of History, and Social and Educational Studies at the University of British Columbia. She is the author of *Growing Up British in British Columbia: Boys in Private School.*

Marie Battiste is Education Coordinator and Principal of Mi'kmawey Elementary School, located on her native Chapel Island Reserve at St. Peters, Nova Scotia. She is co-author of *Issues in Bilingual Bicultural Education Among Native Americans, Indo Europeans and Asian and Pacific Language Groups.*

Ken Coates is assistant professor of History at Brandon University and has published extensively on Native-White relations in the Yukon Territory.

Jacqueline Gresko teaches history at Douglas College in New Westminster, British Columbia and has published on Oblate missionary activity in Western Canada.

Yvonne Hébert is assistant professor of Education at the University of Calgary. She has planned or evaluated several Native language programmes and has published widely on the subject.

Cornelius Jaenen is professor of History at the University of Ottawa. His many publications include the prize-winning *Friend and Foe* and, most recently, *The French Relationship with the Native Peoples in New France.*

Don McCaskill is professor and chairman of the Department of Native Studies at Trent University. Among his recent publications is *Patterns of Criminality and Correction among Native Offenders in Manitoba: A Longitudinal Analysis.*

Diane Persson is Executive Director, Christian Community Service Center, Houston, Texas. She is an anthropologist by profession.

J. Donald Wilson is professor of Social and Educational Studies at the University of British Columbia. He has edited or co-edited seven books on Canadian education and educational history, most recently *Schools in the West: Essays in Canadian Educational History.*

Index